INSTITUTIONAL PROVISIONS AND CARE FOR THE AGED

Anthem South Asian Studies

INSTITUTIONAL PROVISIONS AND CARE FOR THE AGED

Perspectives from Asia and Europe

Edited by
S Irudaya Rajan
Carla Risseeuw
Myrtle Perera

ANTHEM PRESS
LONDON · NEW YORK · DELHI

Anthem Press India
An imprint of Wimbledon Publishing Company India Private Limited (WPCIPL)
WPCIPL is a subsidiary of Wimbledon Publishing Company Limited

This edition first published in India 2011
by ANTHEM PRESS INDIA
www.anthempress.co.in

Distributed by ANTHEM PRESS
www.anthempress.com

Library of Congress Cataloging-in-Publication Data
Institutional provisions and care for the aged : perspectives from Asia and Europe
/ edited by S Irudaya Rajan, Carla Risseeuw, Myrtle Perera.
p. cm. – (Anthem South Asian studies)
Includes bibliographical references.
ISBN 978-9380601090 (pbk. : alk. paper)
1. Older people–Services for–India. 2. Older people–Services for–Sri Lanka.
3. Older people–Services for–Netherlands. 4. Older people–India–Social conditions.
5. Older people–Sri Lanka–Social conditions. 6. Older people–Netherlands–Social
conditions. 7. Older people–Care–India. 8. Older people–Care–Sri Lanka.
9. Older people–Care–Netherlands. I. Irudaya Rajan, S. (Sebastian), 1959- II.
Risseeuw, Carla. III. Perera, Myrtle.
HV1484.I42I57 2011
362.61–dc23
2011020390

ISBN-13: 978 93 80601 09 0 (Pbk)
ISBN-10: 93 80601 09 3 (Pbk)

This title is also available as an eBook.

CONTENTS

ACRONYMS AND ABBREVIATIONS

ACRONYM	EXPANSION
ADB	Asian Development Bank
ADL	Activities of Daily Living
AOW	Algemene Ouderdom Wet or General Old-Age Pension Act
CBS	Central Bureau of Statistics
CENWOR	Centre for Women's Research
CF	Consumer Finances
CSO	Central Statistical Organization
CSPS	Civil Service Pension Scheme
DCC	Day Care Centres
EPF	Employees Provident Fund
EPFO	Employees Provident Fund Organization
EPS	Employee Pension Scheme
ESCAP	United Nations Economic and Social Commission for Asia and the Pacific
ETF	Employees Trust Fund
EU	European Union
FPS	Family Pension Scheme
GDP	Gross Domestic Product
GHQ	General Health Enquiry
GIA	Grant-In-Aid Institutions
GNP	Gross National Product
HIES	Household and Income Expenditure Survey
IADL	Instrumental Activities of Daily Living
IGPF	Integrated General Provident Fund
ILO	International Labour Organization
KAS	Kerala Ageing Survey
KIAS	Kerala Institutional Ageing Survey
KMHS	Kerala Mental Health Survey
LIC	Life Insurance Corporation
MOH	Ministry of Health
NBEPA	Netherlands Bureau for Economic Policy Analysis
NCD	Non-Communicable Diseases
NDC	Non-Financial Defined Contribution
NFBS	National Family Benefit Scheme
NMBS	National Maternal Benefit Scheme
NFHS	National Family Health Survey

NIDI	Netherlands Interdisciplinary Demographic Institute
NIZW	Nederlands Instituut Voor Zorg en Welzijn
NMBS	National Maternal Benefits Scheme
NOAPS	National Old Age Pension Scheme
NSAS	National Social Assistance Scheme
NSS	National Sample Survey
NSSO	National Sample Survey Organization
OECD	Organization for Economic Co-operation and Development
PASL	Population Association of Sri Lanka
PAYG	Pay As You Go
SAA	Social Assistance Act
SES	Socio-Economic Survey
SCP	Social and Cultural Planning Office
SOR	States' Own Revenue
SUBI	Subjective Well-Being Inventory
UN	United Nations
UNDP	United Nations Development Programme
UNFPA	United Nations Population Fund
UNP	United National Party
W/A	Widowed/Aged
WPRs	Worker Population Ratios

LIST OF CONTRIBUTORS

Carla Risseeuw is Professor of Intercultural Gender Studies, Department of Anthropology and Development Sociology, Faculty of Social Sciences, University of Leiden, Netherlands.

E T Mathew is Honorary Professor at the Centre for Development Studies, Thiruvananthapuram, Kerala. He was Head, Department of Economics, University of Kerala.

Godfrey Gunatilleke is the Chairman and a founder member of the Marga Institute, Centre for Development Studies, Sri Lanka.

Myrtle Perera is Vice Chairperson, Marga Institute, Colombo, Sri Lanka. She has been associated with Marga in various capacities such as Member, Governing Council, Executive Director and Senior Research Fellow over the last three decades.

Praveena Kodoth is Associate Professor at Centre for Development Studies, Thiruvananthapuram, Kerala. She was a Fellow at Asia Research Centre of the London School of Economics and Political Science.

Retnakumar is Doctoral Fellow at the International Institute for Population Sciences, Mumbai.

S Irudaya Rajan is Chair Professor, Research Unit on International Migration at the Centre for Development Studies, Thiruvananthapuram, Kerala. He is the coordinator of the Kerala State Development Report prepared for the Indian Planning Commission, Government of India.

Sabu Aliyar is a Post Doctoral Research Fellow in the School of Nutrition at Acadia University, Nova Scotia, Canada, of the Canada-HOPE scholarship.

Sreerupa is a Indian Council for Social Science Research doctoral fellow of Jawaharlal Nehru University at the Centre for Development of Studies, Thiruvananthapuram, Kerala.

Syam Prasad is Indian Council for Social Science Research Doctoral Fellow of Jawaharlal Nehru University at the Centre for Development of Studies, Thiruvananthapuram, Kerala.

LIST OF TABLES

Chapter 5

LIST OF FIGURES

स्वास्थ्य एवं परिवार कल्याण मंत्री
भारत सरकार
निर्माण भवन, नई दिल्ली - 110011

Minister for Health & Family Welfare
Government of India
Nirman Bhavan, New Delhi - 110011

2 0 JUN 2008.

डॉ. अन्बुमणि रामदास
Dr. ANBUMANI RAMADOSS

Foreword

The world is passing through a phase of rapidly changing demographic conditions, predominantly, developing countries like India. The resulting slowdown in the growth of the number of children per couple along with the steady increase in the number of elderly persons per household has a direct bearing on both intergenerational and intra-generational equity and solidarity, which constitutes the basic foundation of human society. Population ageing results mainly from reduction of fertility, a phenomenon that has become virtually universal.

I congratulate the editors, Anthem South Asian Studies, New Delhi, for having brought out this timely publication , 'Institutional Provisions and Care for the Aged'. This book provides interesting insights into the health care arrangements for the elderly, a topic of increasing importance globally, and it should attract the attention of all interested in the health care of the aged.

Population projections made in the book indicate that the number of the elderly would increase from the current level of 90 million to 298 million in 2051 and to 504 million in 2101. The growth rate of the elderly is much higher than the growth of the general population.

Recognizing the health care needs of the elderly, the Ministry of Health, Government of India, has decided to devote large sums of money to provide holistic care through the establishment of the National Institute of Aging.

(Dr. Anbumani Ramadoss)

PREFACE AND ACKNOWLEDGEMENTS

As I write this, the Indo-Dutch Programme on Alternatives in Development (IDPAD), jointly implemented by the Indian Council of Social Science Research (ICSSR) in New Delhi and The Netherlands Foundation for the Advancement of Tropical Research (WOTRO) in The Hague, comes to an end after 25 years of successful research collaboration between researchers in India and The Netherlands. The findings reported in this book come from a large project titled, 'Care of the Aged: gender, institutional provisions and social security in India, The Netherlands and Sri Lanka' carried out with the financial support of the IDPAD.

Since 1981, IDPAD had five phases of research competition to which both Indian and Dutch scholars were invited to submit proposals on different themes of development issues and selected the best 20 to 25 proposals at each phase for funding. In the first phase (1981–4), IDPAD funded 17 proposals on the five research themes: Small-scale industrialization, Export-oriented industrialization, Multinational Corporations, Dairy Development and Women's Studies. The Centre for Development Studies (CDS) and IDPAD have worked together since its inception, however, from the second phase to the fifth phase, CDS faculty members always held research projects with IDPAD.

In its second phase (1985–9), IDPAD funded 19 proposals on research themes such as New International Economic Order, Comparative Perspectives of Asian Rural Transformation and Recent Trends in European Society. The CDS received IDPAD funding for two proposals: *The impact of micro electronics on the worldwide restructuring of the electronics coir industry: A case study of the transfer of technology* (T M Thomas Issac and K Narayanan Nair) and *Diffusion of micro electronics technology* (K K Subrahmanian). In its third phase (1990–6), IDPAD funded 24 proposals on ecology and development, rural transformation in Asia, state and society and international economic order and the CDS received funding for its proposal on non-farm employment in *Kerala: A study of Rural Transformation* (Mridul Eapen).

The IDPAD's fifth phase (1997–2002) funded 28 research proposals on themes such as environment and development, rural transformation, state and society and international economic and institutional order. The CDS received funding for its two proposals: *Collective care arrangements among workers and non-workers in the informal sector* (K P Kannan) and *Emigration from Kerala State in India: social, economic and demographic consequences* (K C Zachariah, E T Mathew and S Irudaya Rajan). The CDS also received additional grants to conduct the follow-up of study on *Return Emigrants in Kerala* (K C Zachariah, P R Gopinathan

Nair and S Irudaya Rajan). The collaborative project the CDS had on international migration with IDPAD funding in 1997 brought wide research attention to the CDS as a major player in the area of international migration. The research grant of the IDPAD in its fourth phase has finally led to the creation of a Research Unit on International Migration in 2006 in the CDS funded by the Ministry of Overseas Indian Affairs, Government of India, currently headed by S Irudaya Rajan.

In the fifth and last phase of IDPAD, 30 research proposals were funded and the CDS received funding for two proposals: *Care of the aged: gender, institutional provisions and social security in India, The Netherlands and Sri Lanka* (S Irudaya Rajan, Carla Risseeuw, and Myrtle Perera) and *Health Status in Kerala: a life course perspective* (K Navaneetham and M Kabir). For me and Carla Risseeuw, this is the second project funded by the IDPAD. In addition, out of the six themes proposed in the fifth phase, both the projects funded for the CDS belong to the theme on population and health, again extending the scope of the CDS as a truly interdisciplinary institution working beyond the confines of applied economic issues but working on every issue, which affects development. Over the past 25 years, the IDPAD has never worked with a research partner outside India and the Netherlands. In its history, our project has been the first of its kind which worked in collaboration with Marga Institute, Colombo, Sri Lanka. This volume is thus an outcome of the joint effort of the CDS (Kerala, India), Leiden University (The Netherlands) and the Marga Institute (Colombo, Sri Lanka). As of now, IDPAD research has led to the publication of 65 books. As we understand, in order to strengthen the research collaboration between India and the Netherlands, the Division of Social Sciences (MaGW) and Science for Global Development (WOTRO) have signed an MOU with the ICSSR on 24 November 2006. We wish the new initiative every success.

The editors are grateful to the respective collaborating institutions for their help in implementing the project. We also thank the IDPAD coordinator in India, Dr Sanchitta Dutta, ICSSR and the IDPAD coordinator in the Netherlands, Dr Cora Govers, WOTRO. As the principal coordinator of the project, I have enjoyed working with Carla Risseeuw (The Netherlands) and Myrtle Perera (Sri Lanka) and I hope to work with them again.

At Anthem Press, I am grateful to Abhijit Mazumder, director and Sridevi Ranganathan, editor, for their hard work and patience throughout this publication process.

S Irudaya Rajan
Principal Coordinator
March 2008

Chapter 1

CARE OF THE AGED IN ASIA AND EUROPE

S Irudaya Rajan
Carla Risseeuw
Myrtle Perera

Introduction

The ageing of population is an outcome of successful demographic transition. One of the unprecedented achievements in the medical history of the twentieth century is the prolongation of the lifespan of human beings. Globally, the life expectancy at birth had been around 47 years in the 1950s. This increased tremendously to 67 years in 2008 – 20 added years in a lifespan of about 50 years. Between the more developed regions and the less developed regions, the gain was impressive among the less developed regions with 24 years against a mere 10 years among the more developed regions (United Nations (UN), 2007). However, the problems associated with an ageing population could be located in a developmental context through institutions that have been shaped by this experience. Institutional factors included on the one hand, the norm of a restricted definition of work as market-related productive activity and the association of ageing with 'non-work' and dependency, and on the other hand, state and market failures to internalize the interests of heterogeneous groups of the aged population. An important aspect here is the feminization of ageing, including the vulnerability of widows, alongside the greater emphasis on women as caregivers.

The recent emphasis in ageing research in the developing world is attributed to the growing number of elderly persons and the institutional failures to render adequate care for them. Population ageing is generally attributed to continuous decrease in fertility levels and constant increase in life expectancy. However, institutional failures to care for the aged could be associated with changing intergenerational contracts witnessed in the erosion of community networks generated in the context of rapid urbanization, modernization, internal and international migration and globalization. The uncertainties in the market, which are in the forefront of the process of globalization in the developing world, have implications for the aged population in terms of increasing vulnerability to poverty, particularly in the absence of adequate social security to protect against any eventuality in old age (Rajan, 2008). In other words, while developed countries have become 'elderly' populations with prosperity, developing countries experience a similar scenario, but with high levels of poverty. This book endeavours to assesses and examine the care for the elderly in both Asian and European contexts. Asia is represented by two countries: India and Sri Lanka, and Europe is represented by the Netherlands. In the history of the Indo-Dutch Programme on Alternatives in Development of over three decades, this is the first and only study supported by a collaboration of Indian and Dutch scholars indicating the emergence of ageing as a 'global' issue rather than an issue of any individual nation.

Moreover, demographically, India is the second largest country with aged persons (defined as persons above 60 years) – about 95 million in 2007 – much higher than the total population of several countries in the world. Sri Lanka is one of the fastest ageing societies in South Asia with a growth rate of the elderly at about 3 per cent (higher than Netherlands too) compared to general population growth rate of 0.8 per cent. On the other hand, everyone living in the Netherlands aged 65 years and above is entitled for a social minimum pension under the General Old Age Pension Act or Algemene Ouderdom Wet (AOW) and Social Assistance Act (SAA) introduced from 1 January 1957 (European Commission, 2001). Let us quickly review the ageing indicators of the three countries under study in this book (Table 1). The growth rate of the elderly, aged 80 years and above, is the highest among all population segments in all the three countries. Similarly, elderly males on an average are expected to live between 17 years in India to 20 years in the Netherlands, whereas females are expected to live about 24 years in the Netherlands (one-fourth of the century). Old age dependency ratio (number of old persons to 100 persons in the working ages) is just nine in India as against 22 in the Netherlands. However, the overall dependency ratio is almost equal for Sri Lanka and the Netherlands. The median age which divides population into two equal parts is 24 for India, 30 for Sri Lanka and 39 for the Netherlands. The index of ageing (defined as the ratio of 60+ to that of underage −15) is just 26 in India as against 113 in the Netherlands. This means that for every 113 elderly persons there are only 100 children in the Netherlands.

Potential support ratio (the number of persons in the working age per person to aged 65+) is about 12 for India and just five for the Netherlands. In Netherlands, every five working persons have to financially support

Table 1: Ageing scenario in India, Sri Lanka and the Netherlands, 2007

Indicators	India	Sri Lanka	The Netherlands
Elderly population 60+ (in millions)	95	2.4	3.3
Percentage of 60+ in the total population	8.1	11.2	20.1
Sex ratio among 60+ (m/f*1000)	91	89	80
Elderly population 65+ (in millions)	65	1.6	2.4
Percentage of 65+ in the total population	5.4	7.6	14.4
Sex ratio among 65+ (m/f*1000)	88	82	73
Elderly population 80+ (in millions)	12	0.3	0.6
Percentage of 80+ in the total population	0.8	1.3	3.7
Sex ratio among 80+ (m/f*1000)	81	72	47
Growth rate of 60+ (%)	2.8	3.2	2.8
Growth rate of 65+ (%)	2.8	3.0	1.8
Growth rate of 80+ (%)	4.3	5.5	1.8
Total fertility rate (per woman)	2.8	1.9	1.7
Life expectancy at birth for males (in years)	63	73	76
Life expectancy at age 60 for males (in years)	17	18	20
Life expectancy at age 65 for males (in years)	14	14	16
Life expectancy at age 80 for males (in years)	7	6	7
Life expectancy at birth for female (in years)	67	78	82
Life expectancy at age 60 for females (in years)	19	21	24
Life expectancy at age 65 for females (in years)	15	17	20
Life expectancy at age 80 for females (in years)	7	8	9
Young dependency ratio	49	34	26
Old dependency ratio	9	11	22
Total dependency ratio	58	45	48
Index of ageing	26	48	113
Median age	24	30	39
Potential support ratio	12	9	5
Parent support ratio	3	3	8
Labor force participate rate among elderly males (%)	50	23	6
Labor force participate rate among elderly females (%)	12	5	3
Percentage married among elderly females	44	41	48
Percentage married among elderly males	81	81	77
Percentage of elderly living alone among males	2	1.4	17
Percentage of elderly living alone among females	5	5	47
Percentage illiterates among male elderly aged 65+	48	n.a	n.a
Percentage of illiterates among female elderly 65+	80	n.a	n.a
Statutory pensionable age for male (in years)	58	55	65
Statutory pensionable age for female (in years)	58	50	65

Source: United Nations (UN), 2007.

one elderly person. The parent support ratio (the number of aged persons above 85 divided by the number of aged 50–4 per 100 persons) is only three in India and Sri Lanka as against eight in the Netherlands. Care of the elderly in the Netherlands is of crucial importance even today as compared to the situation in the other two countries, but these two latter countries are underway to a similar situation which they would reach in the immediate future.

In both Sri Lanka and India, the elderly continue to work beyond 60 years of age as reflected in the data presented in Table 1. Owing to the extensive social security system, work participation rates among elderly males and females are very low. Most often, it is the spouse who provides critical care in old age. Close to 80 per cent of the elderly males currently live with their spouses in all the three countries as against only 40 per cent among elderly females. Women who care for everyone are left to fend for themselves in extreme old ages, a plight which indicates a higher proportion of women living alone: 5 per cent in India and Sri Lanka and 47 per cent in the Netherlands.

Based on this understanding, the following sets of researchable issues were addressed in the project funded by the Indo-Dutch Programme on Alternatives in Development. They are:

(a) Assessment of emerging trends, levels and characteristics of the elderly populations in the three countries over a long period of time with special emphasis on gender composition and widowhood, using the existing census data and other survey statistics and the new projections generated by the researchers. This is expected to unravel the implications of the process of ageing for the economy and society. By doing so, this research is proposed to generate the backdrop for the special survey on the elderly both in Sri Lanka and Kerala, one of the demographically most advanced states in India (Zachariah and Rajan, 1997, 2004)

(b) Estimation of the life expectancy at birth among men and women and at later ages along with the production of healthy and disability-free life expectancy. We also assess the disease patterns and handicaps among the elderly and make projections of the costs of health services of the elderly with different kinds of morbidity conditions.

(c) Documentation of the policies and programmes to provide social safety nets for the elderly such as pensions, provident funds, insurance, welfare fund, widow pension and old age allowances at the national and sub-national levels and their financial implications in the future. We also expect to document the pension reforms in India and Sri Lanka.

(d) Study of the living arrangements, economic security (work, care, modes of finance for subsistence, basic minimum needs, poverty) with emphasis on elderly women, widows, female-headed households, elderly living alone and with spouses.

(e) The manner in which states, civil societies and families define and contain the 'fallouts' of the process of ageing of population. How have shifting intergenerational contracts affected the provisions made for the elderly? In the process, how do modern societies constitute, perceive, and seek to support the aged? How are the contributions of the aged perceived?

(f) The experience of the elderly with regard to empowerment. How do we understand the growing failure of institutions like the conjugal neo-local family to internalize the interests of the aged and the provision of residential care arrangements for them (such as old age homes and day-care centres)? We would like to take a closer look at the problems of structural violence towards the aged/widows. Do existing institutional provisions for the elderly correspond to their perceptions of their own interest? Do elderly persons have a 'voice' in the existing institutions? What are the demands for, and the state prescription of 'euthanasia'?

(g) The ways in which gender, marital status and class inscribe the process of ageing differently. What constitutes widowhood in terms of gender, sexuality, age, occupational groups and caste/religion? Keeping in mind the variations in lineage practice, especially changes in the matrilineal contexts of Kerala, India and Sri Lanka, how does marriage, the primacy of the conjugal neo-local family and property rights (inheritance and access to resources) shape and delimit the 'choices' of heterogeneous elderly groups, particularly widows? From a historical perspective, what factors influence cross-cultural and regional variations especially in terms of differences in status or sociocultural responses to the care of the elderly?

We have undertaken research on the above data, using a cross section of methods. The research methodology includes population projections, sample surveys in India and Sri Lanka, group discussions and case studies. Surveys among different groups of the elderly as well as among groups of care providers were done in different cultural contexts. The full research report submitted to the Indo-Dutch Programme on Alternatives in Development formed a voluminous major report (Rajan, Risseeuw and Perera, 2006). Using the above report, we have selected major issues of research, which form the basis for this collection of essays.

Besides this introduction, the book comprises of ten chapters: five chapters on the various facets of ageing and caring issues in India, two chapters on Sri Lanka and one chapter on a comparative perspective on Sri Lanka and the Netherlands. A brief review of each of these chapters is presented before we proceed to discuss in detail the findings of the Kerala Ageing Survey (KAS) and the emerging issues of elderly care in Sri Lanka.

The 2001 Indian census has shown that the elderly population of India, consisting of 28 states and seven Union Territories, was around 77 million. In 1961, the elderly population had been only 24 million; it increased to 43 million in 1981 and to 57 million in 1991. The proportion of elderly persons in India had risen from 5.63 per cent in 1961 to 6.58 per cent in 1991 and to 7.5 per cent in 2001. Currently, one in every 12 persons in India is an elderly person. At the state level, in absolute numbers, Uttar Pradesh has the highest number of elderly persons (11 million) and Kerala had the highest proportion of the elderly (10.5 per cent). One of the reasons for conducting the ageing survey in Kerala is its high proportion of elderly population and it having entered the final stages of demographic transition. One of the major contributions of this chapter is the projection of the elderly population for a period of 100 years. (Rajan and Aliyar, Chapter 2 of this volume) India's elderly population (60 years and above) is expected to reach 300 million in 2051 and 500 million in 2101. In 2051, for the first time in India's history, the number of children below 14 years would be lower than the number of people above 60 years of age.

At present, 33.07 per cent of the elderly in India live without their life partners. Widowers among old men form 14.98 per cent as against 50.06 per cent widows among old women. Among the oldest-old (80 years and above), widowhood is much more common. Almost half of the population in this age group lives without a spouse. A gender-wise analysis shows that 71.11 per cent of women were widows while only 28.89 per cent men were widowers among the oldest-old of 80 years and above. Significantly, nearly 77 per cent of the elderly in India live either with their children without spouse or co-reside with spouse and children. This finding reflects the social convention of co-residence with children as the most preferred living arrangement (theoretically the arrangement to take care) for the elderly. Another 12 per cent of the elderly live with their spouses while only 5.2 per cent of them live alone and 4.4 per cent live with others – relatives or non-relatives. (Rajan and Aliyar, Chapter 2 of this volume) Although only a small percentage of the elderly live alone in India, results indicate that old women are more likely than old men to be living alone (8 per cent vs 3 per cent) and that older men are more likely than older women to live with their spouses (15 per cent vs 8 per cent) or with spouse and other members (61 per cent vs 29 per cent).

Self-assessed current health status is a subjective measure closely associated with the feelings of well-being and quality of life. In the National Sample Survey (NSS) (2004) when asked to rate their health status (as 'excellent', 'very good', 'good / fair' or 'poor'), nearly 70 per cent of the aged reported their health status to be ranging from 'excellent' to 'good/ fair' while more than a quarter of them reported their current health to be poor. Nearly 8 per cent of the elderly in India have severely restricted physical mobility (they cannot move and are confined to bed or home) while a disproportionately higher percentage of women have restricted mobility as compared to men (9.1 per cent vs 6.8 per cent). This is an important care issue which India needs to address in the future. The prevalence of ailment is the highest among the elderly population (60 and above) compared to other age groups, with slightly more than 30 per cent reporting some kind of ailment (Rajan and Sreerupa, Chapter 3 of this volume) The average hospitalization rate in the country per 1,000 aged persons is 76 as compared to 16 in the age group of 0–14 years. Among the elderly, there exists considerable gender difference in the rates of hospitalization, a much greater proportion of men are hospitalized than their female counterparts (87 vs 67 per 1,000). Similarly, serious disadvantage is experienced in the utilization of inpatient care services in rural areas with only 66 rural aged persons being hospitalized as against 107 urban elderly per 1,000 elderly persons. Health care utilization among the elderly needs greater investment both by the respective families and the governments.

Using the concept of usual status (principal and subsidiary) of work from different rounds of the Indian NSSs, we find that the Worker Population Ratios (WPRs) of the entire elderly population increased from 38.45 per cent in 1983 to 39.15 per cent in 1987–8 and to 40.82 per cent in 1993–4, but that it declined to 36.63 per cent in 1999–2000. While the male WPRs increased from 58.79 per cent in 1983 to 60.46 per cent in 1987–8 and to 62.87 per cent in 1993–4, it declined to 56.79 per cent in 1999–2000. On the other hand, female WPRs declined marginally from 17.96 per cent in 1983 to 16.80 per cent in 1982–8 and rose to 18.27 per cent in 1993–4, again falling to 16.32 per cent in 1999–2000. In order to revisit the employment status of the elderly, we have used the raw data of the 55th round. The NSS provides a detailed break-up of different types of employment to capture the work intensity among the elderly. Among the 14 categories of employment, the following categories (own account worker, employer, unpaid family worker, worked as regular salaried, casual labour in public and other works, attending domestic duties and engaged in household work) are added to arrive at work participation rates of the different age groups. The revised rural work participation rates among males and females were 59 and 66 respectively in the 55th round – seven points higher among females compared to males (Mathew and Rajan, Chapter 4 of this volume). The rates were 57 for males and 62 for urban areas. Thus, in India, 63 per cent of males and 58 per cent of females continue to work beyond 60 years of age. As they grow older, work participation rates decline; however, even at 80 years and above, 22 per cent of males and 17 per cent of females continue to work in India. Higher work participation rates in old age in India is due to lack of social safety nets and high levels of poverty (Clark, York and Anker, 1997; Rajan, 2002)

Yet another dimension of social security and care for the elderly is that on the basis of ownership of assets and property. The NSS's 52nd round collected data on the broad questions of ownership and management of property and financial assets. The responses were divided into four categories under property and financial assets – those owning and participating in management, owning but not participating in management, not owning but participating in management and not owning or participating in management (Kodoth and Rajan, Chapter 5 of this volume). The evidence indicates that around 60 per cent of rural and urban females and around 30 per cent of rural and urban males did not own any property or financial assets. Significantly, gender disparity became more obvious from an analysis of the proportion of men and women who both owned and participated in the management of property as against those who owned but may or may not have managed property. An interesting feature that emerges from the analysis is that the proportion of aged persons who do not own either property or financial assets is higher in the southern Indian states than in other regions of India though the proportion of the aged is much higher in them than in the rest of India.

In India, 33.5 per cent of the elderly were economically independent and nearly 52 per cent were fully dependent predominantly on their children for livelihood and economic support. As expected, sex-wise analysis of the situation reveals that a much higher proportion of old women (72 per cent) are fully dependent on their children than older men (32 per cent). Hence it is seen that a considerable proportion of the elderly in India is economically vulnerable and requires state-led social security programmes. In this context, a clear understanding of the current position of pensions and social security in India is an important requirement not only for financial security, but also for care of the elderly. For instance, the 2001 census has shown that there were 631,000 elderly beggars in India. (Rajan and Prasad, Chapter 6 of this volume). As per the authors' assessment, about 13 per cent of the elderly received civil (service) pensions from the respective state and central governments. Kerala leads the states with 19 per cent coverage of its elderly population through pensions, followed by West Bengal and Tamil Nadu with 14 per cent each. Bihar, Uttar Pradesh, Rajasthan and Orissa stand below the national average, states in which the economic misery of the elderly is intensive. About another 30 per cent of the elderly received various types of old-age pensions (national old-age pension, state old-age pension, widow pension, handicapped pension, welfare fund pensions (in Kerala)) from the public exchequer.

The first five chapters of the book cover various facets of ageing in India such as demography of ageing, widowhood, living arrangement, employment, health status, pensions and social security, and inheritance of assets and property and all aspects lined for the care of the elderly. The last five chapters deal with Sri Lanka and the Netherlands and their comparative social setting for public and private care for the elderly.

Sri Lanka is one of the societies in the developing world in which ageing is the fastest. During the intercensal period 1981–2001, the proportion of the population in the age group over 60 years of age has increased from 6.6 per cent to 9.2 per cent. According to the population projection, the elderly will account for approximately 20 per cent of the population in 2026 (Perera, Gunawardena and Gunatilaka, 2008). The process of ageing being witnessed in Sri Lanka is the outcome of policies and programmes, which rapidly reduced mortality over a period of 50 years and increased the average lifespan from 46 years in 1946 to 74 years in 2001. Fertility which had reached the replacement level in the mid 1990s continued to decline further resulting in a corresponding decline in the share of the population under 15 years of age, from 35 per cent in 1981 to 26 per cent in 2001 (Godfrey Gunatilleke, Chapter 7 of this volume). The rapid changes that have taken place are imposing severe constraints on the capacity of the country's economy as well as its social institutions to provide the standards of economic and social security that should accompany demographic changes and the process of ageing. While these problems affect the ageing population as a whole, they become more acute in the case of elderly females. They face greater disadvantages in terms of both economic and social status. Their participation in the workforce is about half of that of males. Their average earned income is also about one-half that of males. Marriage laws, property laws and laws of inheritance are weighed against females in some of the systems of personal law in force. As a result, their condition of dependence in old age, when measured in terms of financial and other assets, tends to be much higher than that of males. This state of dependence has to be placed in the context in which females outlive males by approximately five years. In the prevailing conditions, the care for the aged is borne by the family and networks based on kinship. The institution of the family itself is undergoing far-reaching changes that tend to reduce its capacity to fulfil the traditional role it has played in the care of the aged. Meanwhile, the state has taken several initiatives to respond to the problems of ageing. It has established special institutions to deal with the problems of ageing and the needs of the old population commencing in 1982, following the Vienna World Summit on Ageing. A national policy and a plan of action have been formulated and legislation has been enacted to protect and promote the rights of the elderly.

The varied needs and experiences of the aged were obtained from both culture-based and occupation-based assessment in order to provide guidelines for public policy for social security and health care for the aged in Sri Lanka (Perera, Chapter 8 of this volume). A total of 270 elderly persons in Sri Lanka were surveyed among the Hill Country and the Southern Sinhalese Plantation and Sri Lankan Tamils, Muslims, and different occupational groups such as agriculturists and fisherfolk. The analysis has made an attempt to assess the living arrangements and co-residence patterns, social and supportive networks, institutional arrangements (elderly homes and day-care centres), financial capability, public assistance, inheritance issues, economic activity, disease and disability patterns, and food habits.

The European population is becoming older very fast compared to the populations of the rest of the continents. The Netherlands, one of the leading nations in the European Union (EU) is not an exception to the greying of population. However, the UN estimates indicate that the growth of the elderly in the Netherlands is expected to be slightly lower compared to other European populations as a whole (UN, 2005). For instance, the European elderly over 60 years of age who constituted 12.1 per cent in 1950 reached 20.7 per cent in 2005 and is expected to reach 34.5 per cent by 2050. The Netherlands on the other hand, had 11.5 per cent elderly in 1950, which grew to 19.2 in 2005 and will be increasing to 31.3 per cent in 2050. (Rajan and Retnakumar, Chapter 10 of this volume) Similarly, the European Commission's estimates suggest that at present, the elderly population (65+) constitutes 2.3 million and is likely to arrive at 4.3 million by the year 2050 (Carone et al., 2005). Owing to ageing, the total population of the Netherlands would increase from the current level of 16.3 million to a peak level of 17.9 million by 2040 and record a decline thereafter. The total population of the Netherlands would be about 17.7 million by 2050. The proportion of the elderly staying in the Netherlands too follows the

European pattern. More than a quarter of the elderly (35 per cent) stay alone, with a higher proportion of females (47.4 per cent) than their male counterparts (16.9 per cent) in the Netherlands in 1994.

Owing to the integration it has achieved of public–private participation in providing pensions, the Dutch pension scheme of retirement is regarded as a benchmark for other continental welfare states to emulate (Riel et al., 2002). The pension scheme of the Netherlands may be broadly classified into three categories each constituting a pillar of the pension system. The first component is a state-sponsored retirement pension scheme meant for all the elderly citizens. It is provided under the Dutch National Old Age Pensions Act of 1957, popularly known as AOW. It provides for a compulsory retirement pension for every living citizen in the country aged 65 years and above with a fixed amount of money per month. In order to avail of the pension scheme, the claimant has to be a resident of the Netherlands and between 15 and 65 years of age. It is based on the principle of Pay As You Go (PAYG). The amount an elderly person receives depends upon the domestic situation and the number of years the person has been insured under the AOW scheme. Married or cohabiting retired persons who have built up their full AOW entitlement (after 50 years) receive pensions worth 50 per cent of the net minimum wage. A single pensioner receives 70 per cent of the minimum wage and a single pensioner with a child aged less than 18 years of age, receives 90 per cent of the net minimum wage. The amount of pension to an individual depends on his/her marital status as well as other non-retired earnings of his/her partner, etc. An elderly person of 65 years of age is eligible to apply for a supplementary pension amount provided his/her spouse's age is below 65 years of age and the amount of pension is insufficient for their survival. The AOW scheme is the main source of income for about 1.7 million elderly persons (out of 2.2 million) aged 65 years and above. Only one in five persons between 65 and 75 years receives a supplementary pension over and above the AOW (Social Cultural Planning Office (SCP), 2001). Secondly, there is a work related supplementary pension scheme arranged between workers and employers. The representatives of employers and trade unions manage this scheme. About 90 per cent of workers and about 50 per cent of all pensioners receive pensions under this scheme. Thirdly, individuals do arrange pension schemes for their financial support. This scheme has nothing to do either with the government or the employer. Broadly speaking, the first pillar constitutes about 50 per cent of old-age pensions. The second and the third pillars constitute 30 per cent and 20 per cent respectively. All these point out that the first two pillars have a very strong base in the pension scheme of the Netherlands. In this context, Carla

Risseeuw reviews the social setting and the demand for senior homes in Sri Lanka and the Netherlands (Chapter 9), and the changing public care system for elders in the Netherlands (Chapter 11).

KAS

Sampling Design: KAS

The sample for KAS is based on the second Kerala Migration Survey (2003) conducted by the Centre for Development Studies, Thiruvananthapuram (details, Zachariah and Rajan, 2005). The household was the ultimate sample unit for the Kerala Migration Survey. The survey covered 10,000 households and enumerated 47,830 members. All elderly members in the 10,000 households throughout Kerala were to be for the conduct of the KAS 2004 (more details, see Table 2). To study the similarities and dissimilarities of the elderly living in households as well as in institutions (old age homes), the senior editor extended the survey to cover all old age homes and their inmates in Kerala, in 2005. This survey is called Kerala Institutional Ageing Survey (KIAS). In a nutshell, KAS covered 5,013 elderly persons living in households whereas KIAS covered 4,865 elderly persons living in institutions.

At the time of writing this, the KAS survey is being repeated in Kerala in 2007. One-fourth of the elderly have been already revisited in four districts of Kerala and the results are highly impressive. Out of a total of 1,329 elderly, resurveyed during October–December 2007, 140 could not be located (about 10.5 per cent). Among the 1,189 elderly households visited, the respondents indicated that only 123 elderly persons had died during the past three years, since we met them for the first time in 2004. In other words, 90 per cent of the elderly had survived during the past three years, indicating thereby the added number of years of life in Kerala and the addition to the care dimensions of the elderly population in the state (Rajan, 2008).

The purpose of both KAS and KIAS was to examine the determinants of healthy ageing, social security, property rights and institutional provisions in the context of care for the elderly. Other than the socio-economic characteristics of the elderly, the survey also canvassed aspects such as children and grandchildren, attitudes and beliefs, old age support systems, Subjective Well-Being Inventory (SUBI), General Health Enquiry, labour force participation, pensions, lifestyle and life satisfaction, health problems and health utlization, disabiltiy, Activities of Daily Living (ADL) scale, Instrumental Activities of Daily Living (IADL) scale, falls, behavioural factors, food frequency, eating behaviour and nutritional assesment. The report is under preparation (Rajan, Johnson and Aliyar, 2008); however, we limit our present discussion to health concerns and health care utilization, mental health and other care issues among the elderly in Kerala based on the KAS.

Table 2: KAS and KIAS

Districts	KAS, 2004			KIAS, 2006		
	Male	Female	Total	Male	Female	Total
Thiruvananthapuram	218	266	484	185	230	415
Kollam	178	175	353	62	128	190
Pathanamthitta	142	185	327	37	48	85
Alappuzha	149	168	317	62	103	165
Kottayam	221	263	484	446	516	962
Idukki	52	46	98	111	138	249
Ernakulam	257	317	574	401	829	1230
Thrissur	155	203	358	183	397	580
Palakkad	184	205	389	52	30	82
Malappuram	225	253	478	10	16	26
Kozhikode	237	271	508	92	126	218
Wayanadu	31	48	79	98	90	188
Kannaur	180	250	430	161	276	437
Kasargode	62	72	134	14	24	38
Kerala	2291	2722	5013	1914	2951	4865

Source: Rajan, Johnson and Aliyar, 2008.

Morbidity and Chronic Illness

Our results reveal that joint pains were the most often reported morbidity among the elderly, with women reporting a higher percentage (53 per cent) than men (41 per cent). The next highest morbidity seems to be forgetfulness or loss of memory, with again females (33 per cent) outnumbering males (27 per cent). Other common health problems which more than 10 per cent of the elderly reported include having no energy (27 per cent), sleep problems (21 per cent), chest pain (20 per cent), stomach problems (14 per cent) and chewing or dental problems (13 per cent) (See Table 3). Two more important observations are: firstly, in all the types of morbidity reported in the KAS, women reported higher prevalence rates than men; similarly, as age increases, morbidity levels also increase with the highest prevalence reported from among the oldest-old.

Table 3: Morbidity among the elderly in Kerala, KAS 2004

	60+			60–69		70–79		80+	
	Male	Female	Total	Male	Female	Male	Female	Male	Female
Having no energy	23.6	29.8	26.9	16.3	23.1	28.4	34.9	39.8	44.4
Forgetfulness /Loss of memory	27.0	32.6	30.1	19.8	26.3	30.2	35.3	47.4	51.9
Sleep problems	19.4	22.4	21.0	15.3	19.5	21.2	23.8	30.6	31.3
Chewing/ Dental problems	12.2	13.9	13.1	8.7	10.9	14.6	16.4	19.7	20.3
Chest pain	18.2	21.1	19.7	16.7	20.5	21.5	21.1	15.5	23.0
Joint pains	41.0	53.2	47.6	37.6	51.0	43.4	57.2	48.4	52.4
Immobility	5.4	8.1	6.9	3.2	6.4	6.9	7.7	10.2	15.8
Incontience (no bladder control)	2.7	3.9	3.3	1.3	2.5	2.8	4.1	7.9	8.6
Stomach problems	13.1	14.1	13.6	12.2	12.7	12.6	16.2	17.8	15.2

Note: Special tabulations from the KAS.

Along with information on common morbidity, the KAS also canvassed the prevalence of some common chronic illnesses among the elderly such as: arthritis, asthma, emphysema or bronchitis, Alzheimer's, cancer, diabetics, heart problems, hypertension, blood pressure and osteoporosis (Table 4). Out of the eight chronic diseases, which require continuous treatment, the prevalence rate is seen to be much higher among women than men, in the case of four diseases. High blood pressure/hypertension emerges as the single largest chronic disease among the elderly in Kerala, followed by arthritis, asthma, emphysema or bronchitis and diabetics. Osteoporosis, which is an emerging chronic disease, was reported less often. This was perhaps related to the silent nature of this disease.

Health Care Utilization and Physical Activities

For medical needs, close to 40 per cent of the respondents accessed public hospitals and 57 per cent used private hospitals (Table 5). The reasons for access, private vs public, varied. Most of them accessed public hospitals for the free service provided whereas, those who accessed private hospitals did so for the availability of better services, care and attention.

Table 4: Chronic illnesses among the elderly in Kerala, KAS 2004

	60+			60–69		70–79		80+	
	Male	Female	Total	Male	Female	Male	Female	Male	Female
Arthritis	18.9	24.5	22.0	16.4	23.5	21.8	27.8	21.7	21.1
Asthma, emphysema or bronchitis	14.2	10.4	12.2	12.1	10.0	16.0	11.1	17.8	10.4
Alzheimer's /Dementia	1.4	1.5	1.5	3.2	4.4	4.6	5.7	7.2	5.4
Cancer	1.5	1.3	1.4	1.5	0.9	1.8	2.0	1.0	1.3
Diabetes	18.2	15.8	16.9	17.7	17.6	19.6	15.4	16.1	9.6
Heart problems	10.6	8.4	9.4	8.9	7.6	13.1	9.5	10.5	9.4
Hypertension/ High Blood Pressure	26.2	36.0	31.5	23.6	34.9	30.0	39.3	26.6	33.4
Osteoporosis	2.4	4.2	3.4	2.3	4.5	2.9	4.8	2.0	1.6

Note: Special tabulations from the KAS.

Table 5: Health care utilization among the elderly in Kerala, KAS 2004

	60+			60–69		70–79		80+	
	Male	Female	Total	Male	Female	Male	Female	Male	Female
Government Hospital	38.93	40.85	39.98	39.30	41.74	38.42	40.09	38.82	39.04
Private Hospital	57.66	55.62	56.55	56.62	54.78	59.41	56.15	57.24	57.75

Note: Special tabulations from KAS.

In the study, only about 36 per cent had routine medical check-ups – slightly higher among elderly men than among elderly women. Among them, monthly check-up was done in the case of about 27 per cent indicating that one-fourth of the elderly received proper medical attention and care in the later years of age (Table 6). This may be due to the fact that the elderly are not covered by any health insurance to undertake medical check-ups, except for hospitalization charges. Among the elderly, one in every two took medications on a regular basis. The cost of managing any chronic disease in old age is extremely high. It is high time that we develop policies and programmes for each disease management separately to help the poor elderly to maintain good health in their old age.

Approximately 60 per cent of the elderly participated in physical activities mostly in the form of household activities; the proportion reduced from 66 per cent among the old to 36 per cent among the oldest-old

Table 6: Medical checkup and medication among the elderly in Kerala, KAS 2004

		\multicolumn{3}{c}{60+}			60–69		70–79		80+	
		Male	Female	Total	Male	Female	Male	Female	Male	Female
Routine medical check-up		36.14	35.01	35.53	34.4	34.6	39.8	37	33.6	32.1
Frequently go for medical check-up	Weekly	2.40	2.68	2.55	1.5	2.5	3.6	3.2	3	2.4
	Monthly	27.59	26.78	27.15	26.3	26.2	30.4	28.8	25.3	24.3
	Yearly	3.32	2.31	2.77	3.7	2.1	3.1	2.6	2.3	2.7
Now taking medications		49.37	51.73	50.65	45.4	50.7	55.6	55.1	49	48.1

Note: Special tabulations from the KAS.

Table 7: Physical activities among the elderly in Kerala, KAS 2004

Age Group	Sex	%
60+	Male	59.4
	Female	58.2
	Total	58.8
60–69	Male	65.5
	Female	66.4
70–79	Male	57.1
	Female	55.8
80+	Male	41.1
	Female	31.0

Note: Special tabulations from the KAS.

(Table 7). Physical activiity declines among females as age advances, and it may be due to the high prevalence of joint pains among them. Self reported participation rates in physical activity decreased with advancement in age.

Disability Profile

In the KAS, we enquired about the prevalence of disability as it plays a crucial role in the quality of life of the elderly. Among the three disabilities enquired into, the problem of vision was reported to have very high prevalence, of over 70 per cent. Visual disability increased with age, with close to 80 per cent reported from among the oldest-old, slightly higher among males than among females (Table 8). The second highest disability faced by the elderly in Kerala is disability of walking, with one out of every five elderly persons reporting this handicap. As against the vision handicap, walking disability is highly prevalent among women than among men, with 46 per cent females reporting as handicapped among the oldest-old. In the case of hearing and walking disability at later ages, women overtake men.

Table 8: Disability profile among the elderly in Kerala, KAS 2005

	60+			60–69		70–79		80+	
	Male	Female	Total	Male	Female	Male	Female	Male	Female
Vision problem	71.89	69.76	70.74	67.6	64.8	74.9	74.8	80.9	78.1
Hearing problem	13.57	14.36	14.00	7.1	6.7	16.3	17.2	32.2	38.5
Walking problem	18.64	22.15	20.55	11.7	13.8	21.6	26.1	38.2	46.3

Note: Special tabulations from the KAS.

As disability in seeing and walking might lead to falls among the elderly, we have enquired about falls and injuries sustained. One out of every four elderly persons had fallen down during the previous few years and the proportion was slightly higher among women than among men in all the elderly groups. Among them, 4 per cent had sustained no injuries, 10 per cent had continuous pain, 5 per cent had minor cuts and another 6 per cent had fractures (Table 9). Falls lead to dependency and to a bedridden state for the elderly reducing the quality of life in old age. It is time for countries in Asia and Europe to develop fall prevention strategies to help the elderly. The study also showed that prevalence of falls and fracture rates was high resulting in worsening of disability.

Table 9: Incidence of falls among the elderly in Kerala, KAS 2004

	60+			60–69		70–79		80+	
	Male	Female	Total	Male	Female	Male	Female	Male	Female
Fallen down	20.82	27.88	24.66	20.9	25.3	20	31.4	22.7	30.2
Injuries sustained									
None	3.32	3.93	3.65	3.4	3.5	3.4	4.7	2.6	4
Pain	8.86	11.61	10.35	8.7	11.4	8.3	13	10.9	9.4
Minor (cuts, bruises)	4.19	4.78	4.51	4.2	3.8	3.9	5.6	4.9	6.7
Fracture	4.45	7.57	6.14	4.6	6.6	4.3	8.1	4.3	10.2

Note: Special tabulations from the KAS.

Behavioural Factors and Dietary Patterns

Some of the behaviours during adult ages and continuous usage of certain hazardous substances have serious implications for the state of health at later ages of life. The KAS canvassed three behavioural patterns among the elderly: smoking, drinking and chewing. Gender differences were clearly observed in behavioural practices with men leading in smoking cigarettes and drinking alcoholic beverages and women in chewing betel leaf. One out of every four elderly men was found addicted to smoking and the proportion declined from 32 per cent among persons in the 60–9 years age group to 15.79 per cent among the aged 80 years and above (Table 10). Similarly, one out of every five elderly men was addicted to alcohol and the proportion declined from 22 per cent among the young-old to 13 per cent among the oldest-old.

Dietary patterns showed that 90 per cent among both elderly men and elderly women consumed three meals a day with a greater tendency for the young-old and the oldest-old age groups to skip or miss meals. Our survey indicated that about 14 per cent missed meals among the 60–9 years age group and this increased to 21 per cent among those aged 80 years and above. Among the oldest-old, 21 per cent missed meals, the reasons for which need serious investigation (Table 11). This practice could have been due to stomach problems or non-availability of special meals suggested by doctors or problems of dental health. Interestingly, 80 per

Table 10: Behavioural factors among the elderly in Kerala, KAS 2004

Behavioral	60+			60–69		70–79		80+	
factors	Male	Female	Total	Male	Female	Male	Female	Male	Female
Smoke cigarettes/ beedi	27.54	0.92	13.09	31.6	0.9	25.8	0.9	15.8	0.8
Drink alcohol	19.82	1.10	9.65	22.3	0.7	18.6	1.5	13.2	1.9
Chew betel leaf	13.44	18.99	16.46	12.9	18.1	13.1	19.3	16.4	21.9

Note: Special tabulations from the KAS.

cent of the elderly in Kerala reported to be non-vegetarians and the proportion of vegetarians increased with age, due to problems of digestion and tooth decay. Approximately 30 per cent were on a special diet such as diabetic diet or low salt diet.

Mental Health

Mental health is often not talked about in discussions on general health. As Kerala leads the country with the highest suicide rates (32 per 1 lakh population as against eight for India as a whole), the KAS made an attempt to assess the state of mental health of the elderly using two sets of modules: SUBI and General Health Questionnaire (GHQ).

SUBI was developed by Nagpal and Sell (1985). Its original version consists of a 40-item questionnaire. For each item there are three response options. It yields a total score as well as subscores for the positive (well-

Table 11: Eating behaviour among the elderly in Kerala, KAS 2004

		60+			60–69		70–79		80+	
		Male	Female	Total	Male	Female	Male	Female	Male	Female
Number of meals per day	One Meal (B/L/D)	2.05	2.28	2.17	1.8	1.9	2.4	2.6	2	2.9
	Two meals (B/L/D)	7.90	9.40	8.72	7.7	7.7	7.4	10.6	10.2	13.6
	Three meals	90.05	88.32	89.11	90.5	90.4	90.2	86.9	87.8	83.4
Missing meals		14.01	17.23	15.76	13.7	13.6	13.1	20.8	17.4	23.8
Type of food eaten	Vegetarian	17.77	20.17	19.07	16.9	18.5	17.9	21.9	20.7	23
	Non-Vegetarian	81.80	79.24	80.41	82.6	81.1	81.7	77.4	78.9	76.2
	Eggetarian	0.35	0.33	0.34	0.4	0.3	0.3	0.4	0.3	0.3
	Others	0.09	0.26	0.18	0.1	0.1	0.1	0.4	0	0.5

Note: Special tabulations from the KAS.

being) and negative aspects (ill-being). The results for well-being/ill-being are validated through factor analysis. 11 factors are identified from which a short version consisting of three highly sensitive factors are taken for the purpose of the present study. This short version is an eight-item questionnaire and the factors pertain to general well-being – positive effect, expectation achievement congruence and confidence in coping. Human well-being is measured on the basis of eight questions with three multiple choices and the scores are based on the chosen answer. The lower the score the better is the well-being of the individual and vice versa. In the earlier Kerala Mental Health Survey (KMHS), Keralite men reported comparatively higher levels of well-being than women. The mean score for men (17.35) is significantly lower than that for women (17.9). The difference is statistically significant. Well-being diminishes as age advances in both men and women (Mohamed, et al., 2002).

SUBI is influenced by a host of socio-economic and demographic variables, which explain individual differences. It contains three primary components: people's emotional responses, depressive symptoms and satisfaction in life, and it was able to tap the components of SUBI and found some pair-wise differences between age groups that emerged as significant. The maximum scores are 24 and the minimum eight. Elderly men have comparatively higher levels of well-being than women, except in the oldest age group of 90 years and above. The mean score for men, 15.88 is lower than that of women, 16.91. The difference is statistically significant (Table 12).

Table 12: Index of subjective well-being inventory by age and sex, KAS 2004

Age	Number of elderly		Mean		t value *	Significance
	Male	Female	Male	Female		
60–69	1194	1487	15.41	16.57	–1.934	0.036
70–79	790	839	16.08	17.09	–1.186	0.127
80–89	274	341	16.94	17.70	–1.658	0.059
90+	33	40	19.12	18.93	–0.940	0.181
Total	2291	2707	15.88	16.91	–2.1489*	0.0242

Note: Special tabulations from the KAS.
* t values are highly significant.

Well-being diminishes as age advances in both men and women. However, among men a sudden decline is observed in well-being between the ages of 80–90, indicating widowhood and loss of care by spouses, at extreme old age. A woman's well-being declines marginally after 60 years and the decline continues further to reach 18.93 among women of 90 years of age and above.

Table 13: Negative and positive symptoms among the elderly in Kerala, KAS 2004

Age Groups	At least one Negative Symptom (%)		
	Male	Female	Total
60–69	27.9	33.7	31.1
70–79	27.9	33.7	31.1
80–89	40.5	46.0	43.6
90+	57.6	57.5	57.5
	At least one Positive Symptom (%)		
60–69	38.0	28.7	32.9
70–79	32.2	27.1	29.5
80–89	29.6	23.2	26.0
90+	21.2	22.5	21.9

Note: Special tabulations from the KAS.

Analysis of positive and negative symptoms based on eight questions indicates that about 31 per cent of the elderly reported at least one symptom of being emotional or depressive or dissatisfaction with life, and that it increased to 58 per cent among the elderly above 90 years of age. There is a clear gender difference in the incidence. Similarly, 33 per cent of the elderly in the age group 60–9 years reported one positive symptom and the proportion declined to 22 per cent among the oldest-old. Though there is a clear differential reported between men and women in the young-old, gender differences become negligible once they reach 90 years of age (Table 13).

Developed by Goldberg (1972), GHQ has found application in a variety of psychiatric and non-psychiatric contexts and has been translated, revalidated and used in many countries including India. It has been used in many studies related to analysis of economic situation, occupation and unemployment (Strandh, 2000; Warr et al., 2004; Banks et al., 1980). GHQ is available in several versions of varying lengths. The 12-item GHQ has the advantage of brevity and hence convenience of administration and scoring. It is also as sensitive and valid as the longer versions. It consists of the 12 'best items' of the original 60-item questionnaire; that is, those items that were most discriminating in the determination of the clinical status and were not endorsed by a physically ill control group. In India, the 12-item GHQ has been validated against the Indian Psychiatric Survey Schedule and has been found to demonstrate excellent sensitivity and specificity; that is, it is able to accurately identify the presence of psychological disturbance with few false negatives and false positives (Shamsunder et al., 1986). Each of the 12 items of the questionnaire has four possible response choices. The scoring is simple, the total score being a summation of the scores on each item. In surveys, the GHQ can be used as a dimensional measure of psychological disturbance and can also be used to identify a 'case'. In the former situation, the total score is used to indicate the degree of psychological distress. In the latter situation, a threshold score is used so that persons scoring above the threshold are identified as potential psychiatric cases. Thus, for the 12-item GHQ, the recommended threshold score is two and above. The higher the score, the lower is the mental health. Keralites show significant gender disparity in mental health status. In general, females are lower in scale than men in mental health (Mohamed, et al., 2002). This is found to be true based on the results from KAS also. As age advances, mental health deteriorates both among men and women, with a score of 2.6 which is highly significant (Table 14).

Table 14: Index of General Health Questionnaire, KAS 2004

Age	Mean			t value *	Pearson's R	Significance
	Male	Female	Total			
60–69	2.0	2.1	2.1	−1.000	0.8049	0.16
70–79	2.1	2.3	2.2	−1.430*	0.6124	0.08
80–89	2.2	2.5	2.4	−1.360*	0.4524	0.09
90+	2.6	2.6	2.6	−0.752	0.0628	0.23

Note: Special tabulations from the KAS.
* t values are highly significant.

Several epidemiological studies have reported that the physical, mental, and social well-being of elderly individuals are very closely interrelated. With the rapid increase in the elderly population, the health of elderly individuals and those with mental depression has become a major public health problem in Kerala. In this situation, an extension of lifespan is no longer the goal of the elderly, an improvement in functional independence and the achievement of a better quality of life being more important. It is necessary to improve not only physical functioning but also mental health condition in order to achieve a high quality of life. In Kerala, no previous studies exist on the mutual relationship between physical functioning and mental health status. In this study, we have estimated the correlation between these two functions among the elderly population. The study has clearly observed various mental health problems among the elderly in Kerala. Females have lower mental health problems irrespective of age; this disparity is particularly significant in two broad age groups, 70–9 years and 80–9 years. In the case of other age groups, differences do exist but they are not statistically significant. As age advances mental health declines for both men and women. Even when GHQ is broken into three components, males are found to fare better than females in terms of mental health (Table 15).

Table 15: Anxiety, social dysfunction and severe depression among the elderly, KAS 2004

Age	Anxiety		Social Dysfunction		Severe Depression		No. of Observations	
	Female	Male	Female	Male	Female	Male	Female	Male
60–69	2.04	2.20	2.04	2.18	1.88	2.03	1194	1487
70–79	2.20	2.35	2.17	2.32	2.04	2.15	790	839
80–89	2.31	2.51	2.28	2.50	2.13	2.33	274	341
90+	2.67	2.64	2.62	2.70	2.47	2.54	33	40
Total	2.14	2.29	2.12	2.27	1.97	2.11	2291	2707
Minimum Value=1* Maximum Value= 4*								

Mean Age		Standard Deviation	
Total	69.97	7.45	
Male	70.14	7.75	
Female	69.97	7.62	

Note: Special tabulations from the KAS.

Although this study focuses on the health of the elderly in the state of Kerala, the information gained from the surveys has striking similarities to those in other nations in the Asian and the non-Asian world alike. The determinants of healthy ageing might be similar, if not identical, to those in other areas that have similar social and environmental conditions. As such, the findings and the evidence based recommendations made in this Kerala study have international applicability.

Intergenerational Transfers among Elderly in Sri Lanka

The changing living conditions of the ageing population need to be seen in the context of the emerging trends. At present the population is ageing in a situation in which marriages are relatively stable and divorce rates quite low. Therefore, the average ageing person, male or female, is likely to have enjoyed the living conditions of a stable family. Assuming two old persons per household and making adjustments for the never-married and widowed, the number of households containing old persons over 60 years of age, would be in the range of 1 to 1.2 million or about 25 per cent of the total number of households. From the existing data from the censuses and surveys it is not possible to draw any firm conclusions regarding the intergenerational composition of such a family, if we assume that an average elderly woman of over 60 years of age was married at the age of 23 years and had two children who are married, and in all likelihood have children. Therefore, the majority of old persons and particularly elderly females are likely to be living in three generational households.

The females who are now over 60 years of age would have lived during a period when people generally had three to five children. Therefore, the families of today's old population would be relatively large with three to five children. Consequently, the present generation of old people enjoy a family support base which is substantial. However, with declining fertility, the average female would not have more than two children. Increasingly, in the future, the responsibility for care and maintenance of parents in old age would devolve on this small family. If the family continues to play the primary role of caretaker and provider of the elderly, the sharing of responsibility will take place within the narrow ambit of an average family of two children. This is a situation quite different from what prevailed in the past when intergenerational obligations and responsibilities could be shared within larger families and kinship networks.

During the period 2001–31, the dependency burden would decline to a ratio between 55 and 60, before rising again. The policies and programmes for ageing should take advantage of these lower levels of dependency to build up a capacity that would enable the country to cope with the rapid increase in old age dependency from 2036 onwards. At present, over 30 per cent of the elderly females have outlived their spouses and they have to adjust to conditions of widowhood. These proportions would continue to grow. The majority of males will pre-decease their spouses and would therefore obtain some degree of care and support from their spouses throughout their old age. The higher life expectancy of females would mean that the care of elderly females would require major shares of human and financial resources. Health and other services for the elderly would therefore need to address the special needs of elderly females The 'old-old' and the 'very old' age cohorts would continue to expand. These age cohorts would have children who would have shed some of their parental responsibilities and grandchildren who would have formed their own households. In such situations, the intergenerational sharing of responsibility could lighten the burden of care of the elders. The very old, above 80 years of age, who are the least active and the most dependent physically, would continue to increase and comprise the most vulnerable category, requiring systems of care and support quite different from the ones needed for the young-old and the 'old-old'.

National Policy Framework for the Well-Being and Care for the Elderly in Sri Lanka

The national policy on elders that has evolved in Sri Lanka has drawn both on the traditional value systems that defined the role and status of elders as well as the international initiatives of the UN that focused on the rights of elders. The family is the main resource for the care and maintenance of elders in Sri Lanka. The traditional value systems and religious beliefs have inculcated in the population respect for elders, and instilled a sense of moral obligation to the family and community to protect them. These values play a major role in the intergenerational relationships and the rights and responsibilities within the family. In such an approach to the care of elders, the role of the community and the state becomes residual that deals only with situations in which the family support system fails or is not available. On the other hand, the international initiatives derived from the rights-based approach have found expression in the covenants and treaties relating to human rights. The rights-based approach gives emphasis on the responsibility of the state and social institutions in protecting and promoting the well-being of the elderly. The rights and duties that exist in the relationship between the citizen and the state come to the centre. This approach concerning the elderly population was first elaborated in the international plan of action adopted by the UN World Assembly on Ageing convened in Vienna in 1982. Sri Lanka was a participant in that conference and subscribed to the plan of action and its recommendations.

Along with many other member states of the UN, Sri Lanka was guided by the Vienna Plan of Action which proposed the implementation of national programmes and policies to protect and promote the well-being of the elderly in the following areas: health and nutrition, protection of elderly consumers, housing and environment, family, social welfare, income security and employment. The plan includes 62 specific recommendations covering these five areas.

The Government of Sri Lanka followed up on the Vienna Plan of Action by establishing a National Committee on Ageing in 1982. The National Committee on Ageing functions under the Ministry of Social Welfare as a coordinating and apex body to advise it in policymaking and the formulation of national plans and programmes for the welfare of the elderly people. It comprises senior officials of the Ministry of Social Welfare and the Department of Social Services, professionals in the field of ageing and representatives from other government agencies whose policies have a bearing on the well-being of the elderly and Non Governmental Organizations (NGOs) and Voluntary Organizations who undertake services for the elderly. The National Committee on Ageing coordinates the public and the non-government sector activities for elders. It also serves as a focal point for the country's contacts with agencies such as Economic and Social Commission for Asia and the Pacific (ESCAP), United Nations Development Programme (UNDP), and their international programmes dealing with the elderly.

In 1991, the UN adopted 18 principles regarding the rights of old persons. These were organized in five categories relating to the well-being of the elderly: independence, participation, care, self-fulfilment and dignity. Sri Lanka broadly accepts these principles as the framework for policies and actions relating to the aged population. This framework which is reproduced below provides useful criteria for the purpose of the analysis and assessment of Sri Lanka's national policies on the elderly.

Independence

(a) Old persons should have access to adequate food, water, shelter, clothing and health care through the provision of income, family and community support, and self-help;

(b) Old persons should have the opportunity to work or to have access to income-generating opportunities;

(c) Old persons should be able to participate in determining when and at what pace withdrawal from the labour force takes place;

    (d) Old persons should have access to appropriate educational and training programmes;

    (e) Old persons should be able to live in environments that are safe and adaptable to personal preferences and changing capacities;

    (f) Old persons should be able to reside at home for as long as possible.

Participation

    (a) Old persons should remain integrated in society, participate actively in the formulation and implementation of policies that directly affect their well-being and share their knowledge and skills with younger generations;

    (b) Old persons should be able to seek and develop opportunities for service to the community and to serve as volunteers in positions appropriate to their interests and capabilities;

    (c) Old persons should be able to form movements or associations of old persons.

Care

    (a) Old persons should benefit from family and community care and protection in accordance with each society's system of cultural values;

    (b) Old persons should have access to health care to help them maintain or regain optimum levels of physical, mental and emotional well-being and prevent or delay the onset of illness;

    (c) Old persons should have access to social and legal services to enhance their autonomy, protection and care;

    (d) Old persons should be able to utilize appropriate levels of institutional care providing protection, rehabilitation and social and mental stimulation in a humane and secure environment;

    (e) Old persons should be able to enjoy human rights and fundamental freedoms when residing in any shelter, care or treatment facility, including full respect for their dignity, beliefs, needs and privacy and for the right to make decisions about their care and the quality of their lives.

Self-Fulfilment

    (a) Old persons should be able to pursue opportunities for the full development of their potential;

    (b) Old persons should have access to educational, cultural, spiritual and recreational resources of society;

Dignity
  (a) Old persons should be able to live in dignity and security and be free of exploitation and physical or mental abuse;
  (b) Old persons should be treated fairly regardless of age, gender, racial or ethnic background, disability or other status, and be valued independently of their economic contribution.

Social Development Policy, Well-Being and Care for the Elderly

It is not possible to consider the situation of the old population in Sri Lanka and the policies relating to them independent of the policies that are designed to improve the well-being of the population as a whole. Therefore, in order to assess Sri Lankan national policy on elders in terms of the UN principles, we need to examine the overall level of human development the country has achieved and the extent to which the elderly population has shared in that process. The favourable social indicators in health and education have been achieved mainly as a result of five key national programmes that were implemented consistently through all the changes of government over the entire period from the mid 1940s to the present day. These were: free education from the primary to the tertiary level through state financed educational institutions; free preventive and curative health care through services delivered by the state; food security through a food rationing system which was replaced by a food stamp in 1978 and household allowances under the Samurdhi programme in 1994; and a livelihoods programme for the rural poor through free distribution of state land, provision of irrigation and housing, and free extension services. A national policy on housing promoted the widespread ownership of housing through redistribution of the existing housing stock and state assistance for rural and urban housing. Ceiling on ownership of houses in 1972 led to considerable redistribution of urban lower middle class homes from owners to tenants. The million housing programme, the village expansion schemes, Gamudawa (village reawakening) and the new agricultural settlements increased the housing stock and family ownership of homes through new construction.

The old population of 60 years of age and above, which comprised of 9.2 per cent of the population in 2001 has been able to share the benefits of social development policies and all the processes that produced high social indicators. Their present status and current living conditions are an outcome of these development policies. However, economic indicators have lagged behind social indicators and as a result the growth of per capita incomes and household incomes has been slow. High rates of unemployment prevailed in the 1970s and the 1980s. Nearly 25 per cent of the population is in absolute poverty and malnutrition in terms of being underweight, and anaemia is highly prevalent in all age groups. Although democratic political institutions have functioned with a fair degree of effectiveness empowering all age groups, they have not been able to accommodate the multi-ethnic character of the country, and landed the country in a costly war that has displaced more than 600,000 persons and retarded the growth of the economy. These negative indicators at the national level are reflected in the elderly population as well. The elderly are found among the poor, the malnourished, the refugees and the displaced. In the case of the demographic profile, beneath the national averages there exist sharp regional disparities and gender inequalities.

The old population would also be participating in many of the national initiatives that protect the rights and promote the well-being of various population groups. These include the poverty reduction strategy, Samurdhi, the Women's Charter and the plan of action on women, and the plan of action for the differently abled. The elderly poor will benefit from the poverty reduction strategies and the elderly women from the Women's Charter and the plan of action for women. The destitute among the old receive monthly allowances under a public assistance scheme. However, for these programmes to be fully effective in regard to the needs of the elderly groups that fall within their ambit, it would be necessary to identify the old population that these programmes include and make age-specific adjustments for that purpose. There is no evidence to suggest that such an elder-specific approach has been clearly articulated in these national initiatives. Prior to the initiatives taken after 1982, the problems of ageing had not been even perceived as requiring special attention. The small proportion of the old, for whom the traditional support of the family was not available, was accommodated in institutions which were run by government and voluntary organizations.

At this point, what needs to be stressed is that the current status of the old population is the outcome of the past mix of policies in which a core of equity-oriented social policies had played a major role. From 1977 onwards, Sri Lanka attempted to accelerate growth and introduced sweeping economic reforms taking the country in the direction of a market economy in which the private sector became the main agent of economic growth. While all parties have committed themselves to retaining the core of the social welfare programme, the right represented by the United National Party (UNP) has emphasized rapid growth and cost effectiveness of the state sector with a larger degree of privatization; the Centre and the

Left have called for a better balance between equity and growth in which the social welfare component is kept intact and enhanced.

Government Initiatives on Ageing

Within this mix of social and economic policies which were national in dimension and coverage, the government formulated and implemented policies and programmes that were specifically directed at the old population and the promotion of their well-being. These came mainly as responses to the UN initiatives commencing from the decisions taken in the Vienna World Assembly in 1982 .These are enumerated and described in the government's report to the UN General Assembly in 2000 on the follow-up to the World Social Summit and the government's statement to the Second World Assembly on Ageing in 2002. The government lists the following initiatives:

    (a) Protection of the Elders Act No. 9 of 2000. The Act provides for the
- Establishment of the National Council for Elders;
- Protection of the rights of elders;
- Registration of persons and organizations providing services to elders;
- Establishment of a National Fund for the Welfare of Elders;
- Appointment of Boards to inquire into complaints of elders and determine claims for their maintenance and other miscellaneous matters relating to their problems;
- There is provision in the Act for old persons to take legal action if their rights are not secured.

    (b) Social security schemes such as contributory and non-contributory pension schemes of the state;

    (c) Voluntary pension schemes for farmers and fishermen;

    (d) Financial assistance in the form of allowances for the elderly needy which includes the Public Assistance scheme, Samurdhi;

    (e) Special identity cards for persons over 65 years of age, entitling them to preferential treatment in obtaining services from busy government departments, hospitals and banks;

    (f) Preferential interest rates for senior citizens on their fixed deposits and savings in the banks, mainly the National Development Bank;

    (g) Institutional care for the old, day-care centres for elderly people run by the government, non-governmental and voluntary organizations. These centres look after elders when the members of their family are out of their homes;

(h) Introduction of home nursing services. A scheme for training home nurses has been started with the assistance of Helpage Sri Lanka;

(i) Training and awareness programmes, health camps; and

(j) Services to disabled elders with the assistance of voluntary organizations.

The Act is a landmark piece of legislation by the government to protect the rights of elders. The Act, however, is limited in scope when compared to the initiatives taken with regard to children and women. The Act establishes two institutions. One is an apex body to advise the government on 'promotion of the welfare and rights of elders' in which elders are represented. It therefore enables elders to participate in the process of identifying their needs and formulating policies and programmes that affect their lives. The council can play a role in putting into operation the UN principle of participation but like many such national advisory bodies functioning in other areas, its performance would depend on the leadership that it is able to provide and on the resources, human and financial, that are available to it. The second institution established by the Act deals with the rights of elders. These rights of elders which are the subject of Part 2 of the Act are restricted to maintenance of parents by children. Here the Act reinforces the central role of the family and the right of dependent parents to claim maintenance from their children. It establishes a maintenance board to adjudicate on such claims.

The activities listed from (b) to (g) are designed to address the other needs of elders which are related to independence, care, self-fulfilment and dignity. However, the coverage of all these activities is as yet limited to relatively small proportions of elders and to selected locations, mainly in the urban sector. There has been no comprehensive survey of the needs of elders on a nationally representative scale and therefore it is not possible to make any reliable assessment of the impact of these measures on the well-being of the old population as a whole. The post-1982 government policies on ageing have attempted to incorporate the rights-based approach to what is primarily a family centred support system, as is evident in the Act to protect the rights of elders. These different elements, however, do not yet form a well integrated whole within an internally consistent policy framework.

The assessment indicates that the present generation of elders have been the beneficiaries of three types of policies and programmes. First, they have participated in the social development policies that have benefitted the population in general. They have also been included in the targeted programmes such as Samurdhi and the action plan for women. Finally, they have become the subject of special attention in the post-1982 policies on ageing. The outcome of these policies and their impact on the elderly population could be best observed and assessed by examining the existing socio-economic conditions in which the elders live.

Vulnerability of the Aged and Policy Indications for Care

Our survey findings in Sri Lanka are utilized to identify settings of the aged who are currently experiencing deprivation and of others who are vulnerable. Four different settings of elders in the sample are utilized to examine these issues.

- Elders who live alone;
- Elders who live with children and are dependent on children's support;
- Elders who live with and support their children.

This analysis provides guidelines for policy measures for different categories as relief for the already deprived and measures to prevent the vulnerable from falling into deprivation.

Elders Who Live Alone

In the sample survey, elders who lived alone were all widows: significantly, they belonged to a relatively younger age group among the elderly. They had low incomes some of which were stable and others uncertain. They had children with whom they interacted often. Some owned their houses while others lived as tenants. Although this arrangement was not a traditional one, particularly for females, some adduced reasons that were traditional such as 'not wanting to move out of' their own homes. Being single too could also mark a shift from traditional attitudes. A desire to live apart from adult children who were 'troublesome', such as a son who drank alcohol, indicated family rifts that prompted them to live alone. This arrangement was made possible because they had their own income, however small it was, and also uncertain incomes in some other cases. They all faced problems – security, poor health, disease and health impairment were the key features of deprivation and vulnerability. Those among them who had only a single health problem, minor problems and no chronic diseases were, nonetheless vulnerable to illness when they would be in need of care, as they turned older or became very old. Some females were in a state of deprivation already with up to seven health problems, chronic long-term diseases and minor impairments. These were already needing, but not getting health care. Compounding their deprivation was their stated inability to meet their critical needs of food, medicine and health care. At least one of them whose son was alcoholic, desired to enter an elders' home at the time when she would need intensive health care. But there exists no process to provide such needs of elders and currently institutions discourage admission to elders who are ill. The demand for institutions and the inability to meet it, was evident in the long waiting lists of applications for entry into elder's homes.

To sum up: the situation of those who were described as deprived, stated that they were unhappy in their current situation while others reported that they were moderately happy. High vulnerability arises from the inevitable consequences of untreated, or inadequately treated, chronic diseases of the aged such as diabetes, hypertension and heart disease, owing to financial problems.

Widowed elders were found in the two clusters of the rural hill country; the Sinhalese and the Low Income Urban Cluster. While this situation could be likely within the Low Income Urban Clusters as well, it is highly untypical in the culture-based family traditions of the Hill Country Sinhalese.

Elder Living with Elderly Spouse

The presence of another, though elderly, person would place this category of elders in a slightly better position than those who live alone. Nonetheless, they faced situations of severe deprivation, moderate depression, and different types of vulnerabilities. These elders were males who were totally dependent on elderly females as caregivers.

Two elders in the young-old age group lived in rented temporary houses. Their married children lived separately on their own. The elders were compelled to live alone because their children too were poor and could not support them. They referred to the constant frictions they had to deal with, while living with their married children. They were severely deprived on several counts. Their only income was the government poverty allowance which amounted to Rs 20 a day for both of them together which could not provide them even a cup of tea. The allowance was fixed low because their children were expected to support them. Often they went without meals. They could eat only because the wife, herself a female elder who, despite her poor health, worked as a daily domestic help in a home and brought food for both from the house where she worked. To add to their problems, the male elder had a long-term chronic disease with some organ impairment. They could not afford the medication for these ailments. It is likely that over time these ailments would worsen. Such a situation would place a severe burden of care on the wife. This was a situation which demonstrated the inadequacy of the government social assistance and also the unrealistic bases on which the amount of assistance was determined.

> An increase in the disability of my husband will compel me to stop going to the house for domestic work. We will then lose the small income and the food which comes with my work. At that point we will be without support from the children or from an institution. (Female elder/caregiver)

The others in this group, who lived alone by choice, were dependent on children for their income and expected children's support and care when required. They were currently experiencing minor health problems. They belonged to all income groups. Those elders in the Sri Lankan Tamil Cluster, for example, had financial help from children who had migrated to western countries, on account of the conflict in their settlement in the north. They, however, feared that they could become bereft of care when their health began to deteriorate. The expectations from children were based on a tradition of filial obligation which elders believed would be fulfilled by their children too.

In this category, male elders could stay apart from children because they were dependent on female elders whose vulnerability, when the health condition of their spouses deteriorates would become even greater than that of the male elder. The female elders in these partnerships felt insecure and uncertain of their plight if they happened to need care themselves. They stated they could not expect their spouses to act as caregivers even if they were physically able, since it was a role for which they were not traditionally equipped.

Elders Living with and Supported by Children

This group of elders presents the reality of elders living with and being dependent on children, as different from the expectation of the earlier group. Three categories of elders were found living with and being dependent on children. The first type comprised of elders, mostly widows, and a few others who were separated from their husbands. They had no income of their own and were dependent on their children. Moreover, they were placed in low income households in which the married children and their families were coping with poverty or severe financial constraints. Most of the widows had major impairments, more than one health problem and long-term diseases. Perhaps these conditions left them with no choice but to live with their children. They experienced shortages of food, medicines and health care because the children, who could not afford to spend on them, were too busy with their own work to be able to spare time for health care for elders and found them a burden on the household economy. Elders in these situations, deprived of basic needs, were dissatisfied and unhappy. Nonetheless, they accepted the fact that neither they nor the children had any alternative.

The second type was single males who were widowers. They were equally deprived and vulnerable. The third type was married elders. Although they were dependent on children, the males had small incomes of their own while female elders were dependent on their spouses, their children or both. More females than males experienced shortages of food, medicine and health care, whereas male elders had female elders as caregivers in times of illness.

The fourth type was the unmarried female who was worst off, living with relatives who had no filial obligations to care for the elder. In one example, the sister's children were living with an elderly woman because she owned the house and it would pass on to the sister. She had health problems and long-term diseases but was short of money for medication and special food, and summed up her state as 'very unhappy'.

Married elders supported by children had severe deprivations irrespective of their gender status because of the incapacity of the children to provide for two elders. In such instances, both children and their families were themselves placed in extremely deprived and vulnerable situations.

The majority of elders in this category, who faced this situation of deprivation and vulnerability, were notably in the low and the middle income levels, spread across all groups, but mostly in the plantations of Tamils and Muslims, Southern Sinhalese and Hill Country Sinhalese Clusters. The Agriculture Cluster showed some differences with less number of elders with health problems, and less dependent because they contributed their labour to cultivation. Currently, a situation of interdependence rather than dependence between elders and children provide a reasonably good quality of life for elders in this cluster. This situation, however, could change into one of deprivation and dissatisfaction with the onset of old age diseases and multiple health problems, which among agricultural elders appears to set in only at much later stages than in the rest. Such a situation was present in an unlikely environment of a household in the high income group in which the elder experienced shortages in special food, medicine and health care from children whose demands had priority over the needs of the elder. A feeling of unhappiness was expressed by the elder in this situation of co-residence with children.

A 69-year-old man lives with his wife and unmarried daughter. Their main income of Rs 340 a month is from Samurdhi (government poverty allowance). Their married children live in the same area but they too are poor and not able to help financially. He used to cultivate rice but since he developed hernia he cannot work. They have rented out their field and get a small rent which is quite irregular. Their house is of brick but it needs extensive repairs and their clothes are worn out. They hardly eat even a solid meal each day often making do with a cup of tea at lunch time. He is unable to get treatment for his hernia because of the cost of going to a hospital. 'I can't even afford a new sarong to wear to the hospital, leave alone finding the money for travel for two of us. If you can, please help me to get a place in an elder's home', he reports.

A widow aged 65 years lives alone in a small house while her married daughters live not too far away. Nevertheless, she receives no help from them. Their husbands are alcoholics and there are constant conflicts, even physical assaults, in their homes. She can never even think of living with any one of her children. She has diabetes and hypertension. When she attended a clinic she was asked to purchase drugs for which she did not have money. Her only income is a superannuation benefit from the place of work (Transport Board) of her son who died while in service. She has a problem with her spine and she cannot prepare even a basic meal. Her widowed daughter-in-law comes over to her house and cooks one bare meal – rice and one curry. When the daughter-in-law is unable to come over, she has to manage with a cup of tea for a meal. She is advised to have a special diet but this is not possible for her. Even getting basic food is a serious problem; 'How can I think of a special food?', she asks.

A 65-year-old male elder lives with his elderly wife. Their main income is the government poverty allowance of Rs 340 and a charity allowance of Rs 170. They earn an additional Rs 1,000 or so a month when the wife is called to cook meals in neighbours' houses. At such times she brings home leftover food. Their children are married and they live some distance away. They are too poor to be of any help, even to visit their parents. The elderly eat scrappy meals of yams or boiled jackfruit (a starchy fruit). They have a small house of brick walls and a makeshift roof. The male has asthma but he cannot go for treatment because of the cost involved and the difficulty of travelling to the hospital. He has willed the house to his wife 'so that she will have at least a roof over her head when I am no more', he reports.

Elders Living with and Supporting Children

Elder satisfaction could be expected to be high within a situation in which elders are in a position of strength and mutual support in respect of the different needs of the two categories of household members, the aged and the non-aged. Unhappiness was, nevertheless, expressed by elders who had no ailments but were socially vulnerable or deprived; family friction, lack of independence and the burden of elders having to care for children, brought greater dissatisfaction to them since they were also the providers of children's needs.

An elderly widower 74 years of age, lives with one of his sons and his family. The son cultivates rice and with his small income supports his family. The father is an extra mouth to feed and the wife resents his presence in their house. Because of constant friction with the son's wife he at times goes without food. Sometimes he goes to a neighbour's house for a meal. When he falls ill and needs care he does not get it from the daughter-in-law. He is dependent on his son for all his needs. Even the house belongs to the son. 'My day begins and ends in misery', mumbles the elderly person in Sri Lanka.

Both the elderly man and wife living with and supporting children did not bring forth the care and support that they expected from their children as they suffered from chronic diseases and impairments. Most of the elderly experience deprivation not only in low income households but also in middle and high income households, in the form of shortages of food, medicine and health care.

In this category, widows were supporting children with sources of income they had derived from their spouses. The ownership of the house too had come to them from their spouses. Nevertheless, they experienced shortages in critical personal needs which they denied themselves in order to provide their children's needs. These situations were seen, although unevenly spread, across all clusters, more markedly in Plantation Tamil, Southern Sinhalese and Low Income Urban Clusters.

References

Banks, M H, Clegg, C W, Jackson, P R, Kemp, N J, Stafford, E M and Wall, T D, 'The Use of the GHQ as an Indicator of Mental Health in Occupational Studies', *Journal of Occupational Psychology*, Vol. 53, 1980, pp.187–94.

Carone, Giuseppe, Costello, Declan, Diez Guardia, Nuria, Mourre, Gilles, Przywara, Bartosz and Salomäki, Aino, 'The Economic Impact of Ageing Populations in the EU 25 Member States', Economic Paper No. 236, Directorate General for Economic and Financial Affairs, Brussels, 2005.

Clark, Robert L, York, Elizabeth Anne and Anker, Richard, 'Retirement and Economic Development: An International Analysis' in De Jong, Phillip R and Marmor, Theodore R, ed, *Social Policy and The Labour Market*, Brookfield, Ashgate, 1997, pp.117–46.

European Commission, 'Budgetary Changes Posed by the Ageing Population', Economic Policy Committee, EPC/ECFIN/655/01, Brussels, 2001.

–, 'Pension Schemes and Projection Models in EU 25 Member States', European Economy Occasional Papers No. 35, Economic Policy Committee, Brussels, 2007.

Goldberg, D P, *The Detecting of Psychiatric Illness by Questionnaire: A Technique for the Identification and Assessment of Non-Psychotic Psychiatric Disease*, Oxford University Press, London, 1972.

Mohamed, E, Rajan, S Irudaya, Kumar, K Anil and Mohammed, P M Saidu, 'Gender and Mental Health in Kerala', Report of the KMHS submitted to the Gender Network, Institute of Social Studies Trust, New Delhi, 2002.

Nagpal, R and Sell, H, 'Subjective Well-being', SEARO Regional Health, Paper No. 7, WHO, New Delhi, 1985.

Perera, Myrtle, Gunawardena, Asoka and Gunatilaka, P P M in Rajan, S Irudaya, ed, *Social Security for the Elderly: Experiences from South Asia*, Chapter 5 (Sri Lanka), Routledge, London/New York/New Delhi, 2008, pp.225–77.

NSSO, 'Morbidity, Health Care and the Condition of the Aged', NSS 60th Round, (Jan–June 2004), Report No. 507, Ministry of Statistics and Programme Implementation, Government of India, 2006.

Rajan, S Irudaya, 'Social Security for the Unorganized Sector in South Asia', *International Social Security Review*, Vol. 55, No. 4, 2002, pp.143–56.

–, ed, *Social Security for the Elderly: Experiences from South Asia*, Routledge, London/New York/New Delhi, 2008.

–, *The Second Wave: Kerala Ageing Survey Revisited*, Centre for Development Studies, Kerala, 2008.

Rajan, S Irudaya, Johnson, Shanthi and Aliyar, Sabu, *Ageing Surveys in Kerala: Issues for Policy,* Centre for Development Studies, Thiruvananthapuram, 2008.

Rajan, S Irudaya, Risseeuw, Carla and Perera, Myrtle, 'Care of the Aged: Gender, Institutional Provisions and Social Security in India, Netherlands and Sri Lanka', Indo-Dutch Programme on Alternatives in Development Project Report, Indian Council for Social Science Research, New Delhi, 2006.

Riel, Bart van, Hemerijck, Anton and Visser, Jelle, 'Is There a Dutch Way to Pension Reform?', Working Paper No. 202, Oxford Institute of Ageing, 2002, [http://www.ageing.ox.ac.uk].

SCP, 'What Does the Government Do for the Older People?', Netherlands, 2001.

Shamsunder, C, Sriram, T G, Muraliraj, S G and Shanmughan, V, 'Validity of a Short 5-Items Version of the General Health Questionnaire', *Indian Journal of Psychiatry*, Vol. 28, 1986, pp.217–19.

Strandh, M, 'Different Exit Routes from Unemployment and their Impact on Mental Well-being: the Role of the Economic Situation and the Predictability of the Life Course', *Work, Employment and Society*, Vol. 14, No. 3, 2000, pp.459–79.

UN, 'World Population Prospects: The 2004 Revision Population Data Base', United Nations Population Division, New York, 2005, [http://esa.un.org/unpp].

–, 'World Population Ageing 2007', Department of Economic and Social Affairs, Population Division, New York, 2007.

Warr, P, Butcher, V, Robertson, I and Callinan, M, 'Older People's Well-being as a Function of Employment, Retirement, Environmental Characteristics and Role Preference', *British Journal of Psychology* 95, 2004, pp.297-324.

Zachariah, K C and Rajan, S Irudaya, eds, *Kerala's Demographic Transition: Determinants and Consequences*, Sage Publications, New Delhi/Thousand Oaks/London, 1997.

Zachariah, K C and Rajan, S Irudaya, 'Gulf Revisited: Economic Consequences of Emigration from Kerala – Emigration and Unemployment', Working Paper No. 363, Centre for Development Studies, Thiruvananthapuram, 2004, [www.cds.edu].

Zachariah, K C and Rajan, S Irudaya, 'Unemployment in Kerala at the Turn of the Century: Insights from CDS Gulf Migration Studies', Working Paper No. 374, Centre for Development Studies, Thiruvananthapuram, 2005, [www.cds.edu].

Chapter 2

POPULATION AGEING IN INDIA

S Irudaya Rajan
Sabu Aliyar

Introduction

The world is witnessing a scenario of rapidly changing demographic conditions, predominantly in developing countries. The resulting slowdown in the growth of the number of children per couple along with the steady increase in the number of elderly persons has a direct bearing on both intergenerational and intragenerational equity and solidarity, which constitute the basic foundations of human society. Population ageing results mainly from reduction of fertility, a phenomenon that has become virtually universal. Since 1950, the proportion of old persons in the total population has been rising steadily, from 8 per cent in 1950 to 11 per cent in 2007, and it is estimated to reach 22 per cent in 2050 (United Nations (UN), 2007). Ageing will also have an impact on economic growth, via savings, investment, consumption, labour market behaviour, pensions, taxation and intergenerational transfers. In the social sphere, this phenomenon influences family composition and living arrangements, demand for housing and migration, and the need for health care services. On the political front, population ageing may shape voting patterns and political representation (UN, 2007). The recent emphasis on studies on elderly persons in the developing world is attributed to their increasing numbers and deteriorating living conditions in the later years of life. While increasing numbers are attributed to demographic transition, deteriorating social and economic conditions are a result of the fast eroding traditional family system in the wake of rapid modernization, internal and international migration and urbanization.

India accommodates 77 million elderly persons, a figure second only to the number of elderly in China, according to the 2001 census. Economic, social and health aspects of this fast growing segment of the population pose a great challenge to all socio-economic sectors in India. In this context, this chapter overviews the trends in ageing in the past and projects the emerging scenario for the next 100 years, using the 2001 age structure and the available trends in fertility, mortality and migration rates.

Global Ageing

At the world level, the number of old persons is expected to exceed the number of children for the first time, in 2047 (UN, 2007). In developed regions where population ageing is far advanced, the number of children dropped below that of older persons in 1998. In 2007, the United Nations Commission on Population and Development focused its work on the changing age structures of populations and their implications on development. Table 1 shows the global demography of the aged in 2007.

Table 1: The global demography of the aged, 2007

Major areas/ Region (in millions)	60+			65+			80+		
	Total	Male	Female	Total	Male	Female	Total	Male	Female
World	704.8	317.7	387.1	495.1	216.1	279.1	94.2	33.7	60.4
More developed regions	252.0	106.1	145.9	188.8	76.2	112.6	47.9	15.3	32.6
Less developed regions	452.8	211.6	241.2	306.3	139.9	166.5	46.3	18.5	27.8
Africa	50.1	22.7	27.4	32.5	14.4	18.1	3.8	1.5	2.3
Europe	153.5	62.8	90.7	116.8	45.7	71.1	27.8	8.4	19.4
Latin America and the Caribbean	52.7	23.7	29.0	36.5	16.1	20.4	7.4	2.9	4.5
Northern America	58.3	25.6	32.7	42.2	17.8	24.3	12.2	4.3	8.0
Oceania	4.9	2.3	2.6	3.5	1.6	1.9	0.9	0.3	0.6
Australia/New Zealand	4.4	2.0	2.4	3.2	1.4	1.8	0.9	0.3	0.6

Source: UN, 2007.

The pace of population ageing is more rapid in developing countries than in developed countries. Consequently, developing countries have less time at their disposal to adjust to the consequences of population ageing. Moreover, population ageing in developing countries is taking place at lower levels of socio-economic development than has been the case for developed countries. Currently, there are 704.8 million elderly persons; among them, 70.8 per cent (495.1 million) belong to the age group of 65 and above. Even at the age of 80 years, there are 94.2 million persons, and it is important to note that the global sex ratio at 80+ is just 558 males per 1,000 females. More than 60 per cent (452.8 million) of the elderly live in less developed regions and Asia accounts for 55 per cent of them (Table 1).

The median age for the world population now is around 28 years and it is likely to reach 38 years in 2050. Among those aged 60 years or more, the fastest growing segment is that of the oldest-old of 80 years and above. Their numbers are currently increasing at 3.9 per cent per year. Today, persons aged 80 years or above account for about one in every eight old persons (60 years or more). By 2050, this ratio is expected to increase to approximately two in every ten old persons.

Overview of India's Elderly

The 2001 census has shown that the elderly population of India, consisting of 28 states and seven Union Territories, was around 77 million. In 1961, the elderly population had been only 24 million; it had increased to 43 million in 1981 and to 57 million in 1991. The proportion of elderly persons in India has risen from 5.63 per cent in 1961 to 6.58 per cent in 1991 (Rajan, Mishra and Sarma, 1999) and to 7.5 per cent in 2001 (Rajan, 2007). This trend is true of other old age groups as well. The elderly population, aged 70 years and above, which had been a mere 8 million in 1961 rose to 21 million in 1991 and to 29 million in 2001 (see Table 2). The proportion of the elderly above 70 years of age to total population increased from a mere 2 per cent in 1961 to 2.9 in 2001. In 1961, Indian Census reported 99,000 centenarians. The corresponding number in 2001 was 139,472.

Table 2: Number and proportion of elderly by different age groups, India, 1961–2001

Age	Number (in millions)					Per cent of Elderly to the Total Population				
	1961	1971	1981	1991	2001	1961	1971	1981	1991	2001
60+	25	33	43	57	77	5.6	6.0	6.49	6.76	7.5
70+	9	11	15	21	29	2.0	2.1	2.33	2.51	2.9
80+	2	3	4	6	8	0.6	0.6	0.62	0.76	0.8
90+	0.5	0.7	0.7	1	1.8	0.1	0.1	0.1	0.2	0.2
100+	0.01	0.01	0.01	0.01	0.1	0.02	0.02	0.02	0.02	0.01

Note: Compiled by the authors from the last five censuses.

The growth rate among different groups of the elderly namely 60+, 70+ and 80+, during the decade 1991–2001 was much higher than of the general population growth rate of 2 per cent per annum. The sex ratio among the elderly in India favours males as against the trend prevalent in other parts of the world (see Table 3).

Table 3: Sex ratio and growth rate among the Indian elderly, 1971–2001

Age	Sex Ratio of Elderly (males per 1000 females)				Growth of Elderly (%)		
	1971	1981	1991	2001	1971–81	1981–91	1991–2001
60+	1066	1042	1075	1028	2.78	2.72	3.04
70+	1030	1026	1084	991	3.13	3.08	3.32
80+	950	990	1090	1051	2.54	4.35	2.35
90+	897	892	1019	1131	0.66	5.08	n.a
100+	798	844	896	1782	0.19	0.44	n.a

Note: Estimated by the authors from the last four censuses.

India is one of the few countries in the world in which males outnumber females. This phenomenon among the elderly is of prime importance because female life expectancy at ages 60 and 70 is slightly higher than that of males. However, at any given age, there are more widows than widowers. Reasons for this unusual phenomenon need to be identified in a wider context. Since the beginning of the twentieth century, life expectancy at birth among Indian males had been higher than that among females until the first half of the 1990s. Besides this unusual demographic pattern of excess, female mortality at infant and childhood ages, the analysis gets further complicated by the phenomenon of age exaggeration among the aged. Thus, the above observation of more males in old age does not reveal a true picture of the situation among elderly persons (details, see Mari Bhat, 1992; Rajan, Sarma and Mishra, 2003). In India, the sex ratio of the aged as well as of the old-old favours males. Reasons for more males in old age may consist of under-reporting of females, especially widows, age exaggeration, low female life expectancy at birth, and excess female mortality among infants, children and adults (Sudha and Rajan, 1999, 2003; Mari Bhat, 2002). Notwithstanding the several analytical and statistical problems indicated above, it cannot be disputed that the preponderance of females in extreme old ages needs to be brought to the attention of planners and policymakers.

Available findings on ageing suggest that fertility has played a more predominant role in the ageing process compared to mortality. As far as India is concerned, there has been a substantially greater reduction in mortality than in fertility since 1950. For instance, while the crude birth rate declined from 47.3 during 1951–61 to 22.8 in 1999, the crude death rate fell more steeply from 28.5 to 8.4 during the same period. Logically, therefore, India is expected to undergo a faster decline in fertility in the immediate future compared to decline in mortality because mortality has already reached low levels. The ageing process in India will, therefore, be faster than in other developing countries. Moreover, the transition from high to low fertility is expected to narrow the age pyramid at its base and broaden it at the top. In addition, improvement in life expectancy at all ages will allow more old people to survive, thus intensifying the ageing process. In this context, an examination of the phenomenon of increasing life expectancy indicates that the gain is going to be shared more and more by old people which will make them live increasingly longer lives. Table 4 provides evidence in support of this observation. It may be seen that males are expected to live 16 years beyond the age of 60 and ten years beyond the age of 70, the corresponding years for females being 18 years and 11 years respectively. Urban females are expected to live for an additional two years at age 60 than their rural counterparts.

Table 4: Expectation of life at ages 60 and 70 for India

Period	Male			Female		
	e0	e60	e70	e0	e60	e70
1970–75	50.5	13.4	8.6	49.0	14.3	9.2
1976–80	52.5	14.1	9.6	52.1	15.9	10.9
1981–85	55.4	14.6	9.7	55.7	16.4	11.0
1986–90	57.7	14.7	9.4	58.1	16.1	10.1
1991–95	59.7	15.3	10.0	60.9	17.1	11.0
1995–99	60.8	15.7	10.3	62.5	17.7	11.6
1996–00	61.0	15.8	10.4	62.7	17.8	11.7
1997–01	61.3	16.0	10.6	63.0	18.1	11.9

Note: Compiled from life tables produced by the Registrar General of India for various periods.

State-Wise Analysis

Uttar Pradesh led with the highest number of the elderly (11 million) followed by Maharashtra (8.5 million), West Bengal (5.7 million) and Tamil Nadu (5.5 million). The least number of the elderly are found in the Union Territory of Lakshadweep (Table 5). In terms of the proportion of the elderly in the population, the low fertility state of Kerala ranks number one, with 10.5 per cent of its population, in 2001. Punjab and Himachal Pradesh occupy the second largest position in terms of the percentage of the elderly, followed by the states of Tamil Nadu (8.9) and Maharashtra (8.7). Dadra & Nagar Haveli registered the lowest proportion (4). The percentage of the

Table 5: Elderly in India, 2001 Census

Rank	India/States	60+		70+		80+	
		Population	%	Population	%	Population	%
	INDIA	76826245	7.5	29376651	2.9	8060098	0.8
01	Kerala	3338428	10.5	1402678	4.4	389332	1.2
02	Punjab	2200153	9.0	939859	3.9	299106	1.2
03	Himachal Pradesh	548890	9.0	245121	4.0	81152	1.3
04	Tamil Nadu	5545499	8.9	2097100	3.4	557029	0.9
05	Maharashtra	8464895	8.7	3094957	3.2	780039	0.8
06	Goa	112858	8.4	41928	3.1	10969	0.8
07	Pondicherry	81082	8.3	31939	3.3	8223	0.8
08	Orissa	3044221	8.3	1168791	3.2	293770	0.8
09	Uttaranchal	655726	7.7	258515	3.0	70331	0.8
10	Karnataka	4065985	7.7	1611495	3.0	457643	0.9
11	Andhra Pradesh	5798171	7.6	2082435	2.7	505185	0.7
12	Haryana	1590118	7.5	656182	3.1	184587	0.9
13	Tripura	232896	7.3	106606	3.3	35296	1.1
14	Chhattisgarh	1506393	7.2	534077	2.6	135486	0.7
15	West Bengal	5708014	7.1	2275599	2.8	670812	0.8
16	Madhya Pradesh	4292242	7.1	1609752	2.7	436919	0.7
17	Uttar Pradesh	11701369	7.0	4470314	2.7	1273057	0.8
18	Gujarat	3502295	6.9	1310502	2.6	374579	0.7
19	Rajasthan	3829791	6.8	1473636	2.6	394208	0.7
20	Manipur	145775	6.7	61569	2.8	17211	0.8
21	Jammu & Kashmir	678384	6.7	274603	2.7	82415	0.8
22	Bihar	5513117	6.6	2046843	2.5	566871	0.7
23	Lakshadweep	3732	6.2	1288	2.1	381	0.6
24	Jharkhand	1580601	5.9	553844	2.1	148144	0.5
25	Assam	1562062	5.9	601856	2.3	169824	0.6
26	Mizoram	49066	5.5	20108	2.3	5313	0.6
27	Sikkim	29144	5.4	11018	2.0	2716	0.5
28	Delhi	720743	5.2	269146	1.9	70929	0.5
29	Daman & Diu	8045	5.1	2930	1.9	811	0.5
30	Chandigarh	44977	5.0	18170	2.0	5216	0.6
31	Andaman & Nicobar Islands	17478	4.9	6222	1.7	1676	0.5
32	Meghalaya	105870	4.6	39790	1.7	11258	0.5
33	Arunachal Pradesh	49967	4.6	18063	1.6	5655	0.5
34	Nagaland	90540	4.5	37709	1.9	13644	0.7
35	Dadra & Nagar Haveli	8818	4.0	2618	1.2	611	0.3

Source: Based on the 2001 census.

Table 6: Sex ratio among the elderly, 2001 Census

India/State	Sex Ratio (Females per 000 males)		
	60+	70+	80+
India	1028	991	1051
Andaman & Nicobar Islands	766	827	932
Sikkim	772	734	752
Nagaland	780	786	765
Jammu & Kashmir	846	820	837
Bihar	882	827	811
Uttar Pradesh	886	821	830
Arunachal Pradesh	889	892	900
Chandigarh	891	887	953
Assam	949	876	923
Meghalaya	957	991	1050
Delhi	963	925	996
Punjab	971	865	922
Mizoram	977	1019	1184
Lakshadweep	979	1024	1177
Manipur	986	988	1033
Haryana	991	863	884
Uttaranchal	1002	952	984
Jharkhand	1005	945	891
Tamil Nadu	1013	977	1040
Himachal Pradesh	1021	997	1027
Orissa	1022	958	892
West Bengal	1047	1032	1093
Tripura	1064	1105	1230
Rajasthan	1084	1108	1261
Madhya Pradesh	1084	1112	1240
Andhra Pradesh	1099	1051	1215
Karnataka	1111	1137	1258
Gujarat	1148	1239	1410
Maharashtra	1150	1063	1218
Chhattisgarh	1181	1182	1175
Pondicherry	1222	1239	1249
Daman & Diu	1239	1370	1886
Kerala	1247	1319	1472
Goa	1260	1424	1553
Dadra & Nagar Haveli	1270	1381	1406

Source: Based on the 2001 census.

Table 7: Indices of ageing, 2001 Census

State	Median Age	Index of ageing	Age Dependency ratio
Jammu & Kashmir	21.6	18.7	11.6
Himachal Pradesh	24.5	29.1	15.1
Punjab	24.2	28.8	15.2
Chandigarh	24.6	17.2	7.6
Uttaranchal	21.5	21.2	13.8
Haryana	21.8	20.9	13.3
Delhi	23.5	16.0	8.4
Rajasthan	20.1	16.9	12.8
Uttar Pradesh	19.6	17.2	13.6
Bihar	19.5	15.8	13.0
Sikkim	21.6	15.4	9.0
Arunachal Pradesh	19.8	11.3	8.3
Nagaland	20.0	12.4	7.7
Manipur	23.1	20.6	11.1
Mizoram	21.7	15.6	9.3
Tripura	23.3	21.6	12.3
Meghalaya	18.1	10.8	8.6
Assam	21.6	15.7	10.3
West Bengal	24.1	21.4	11.9
Jharkhand	20.6	14.7	10.8
Orissa	24.1	24.9	14.1
Chattisgarh	22.3	19.6	13.0
Madhya Pradesh	21.1	18.4	13.1
Gujarat	23.6	21.0	11.5
Daman & Diu	23.6	18.7	7.5
Dadra & Nagar Haveli	22.3	11.3	6.6
Maharashtra	24.4	27.2	14.8
Andhra Pradesh	24.4	23.7	12.6
Karnataka	24.3	24.1	12.7
Goa	27.6	33.9	12.5
Lakshadweep	23.0	18.0	10.3
Kerala	27.9	40.2	16.5
Tamil Nadu	27.0	33.0	13.9
Pondicherry	26.5	30.8	12.6
Andaman & Nicobar Islands	24.5	16.7	7.5
All India	22.7	21.1	13.1

Source: Based on the 2001 census.

elderly in the 80 years and above category, is the highest in Himachal Pradesh (1.3 per cent), followed by Kerala (1.2 per cent).

India is one of the few countries in the world in which males outnumber females. However, among the elderly, female life chances are higher. Thus, at any age, there are more widows than widowers. Moreover, according to the 2001 census, the sex ratio among the Indian elderly of 60 years and above is 1028 females for 1000 males. The trend is in favour of males in the age group of 70+ years; but it becomes favourable for females in the population of 80 years and above. Kerala has recorded the highest sex ratio – 1,247 females per 1000 males. The situation improves further to 1,319 among the elderly of 70+ years, and to 1,472 among the elderly of 80 years and above (Table 6).

Table 7 shows various indices of population ageing in India. Kerala has registered the highest median age (27.9 years), indicating its status as a forerunner of demographic transition, followed by Goa (27.6 years), Tamil Nadu (27 years) and Pondicherry (26.5 years). The highest index of ageing in the country is also reported for Kerala (40.2) followed by Goa (33.9), Tamil Nadu (33.0) and Pondicherry (30.8). This is also true for median ageing and dependency ratio of the aged.

Regional Ageing Scenario, 1961–2101

Since 1961, India's elderly population (60+) has grown from 25 million to 77 million in 2001. Our projections indicate that the proportion of the elderly would reach 20 per cent in 2051, 25 per cent in 2071 and 30 per cent in 2101. Similarly, the numbers would increase from the current level of 77 million to 298 million in 2051 and to 504 million in 2101. There were only 9 million persons aged 70 years and over, in India in 1961; it increased to 30 million in 2001 and it is expected to rise to 131 million in 2051 and 273 million in 2101. Similar trends are reported for the age group of 80 and above too (Table 8).

A few comments on the projections are called for. We have used the 2001 census totals and applied them to the age structure projected by the Registrar General of India as the base population (Registrar General of India, 1996, 1999); assumptions on future fertility and mortality trends are based on past trends as revealed by the Sample Registration System and other sources such as the first and second rounds of National Family Health Surveys (Visaria and Rajan, 1999; Guilmoto and Rajan, 2001, 2002, 2005; Rajan, Sarma and Mishra, 2003). The projection period ranges from 2001 to 2101. It is also important to note that the number of projected elderly persons above 60 years of age in 2061 were already born in 2001 and our projections are therefore likely to be valid for the next 60 years.

Table 8: Emerging ageing scenario, 1961–2101

Year	60+		70+		80+	
	Population (millions)	%	Population (millions)	%	Population (millions)	%
1961	25.0	5.6	9.0	2.0	2.0	0.6
1971	33.0	6.0	11.0	2.1	3.0	0.6
1981	43.0	6.5	15.0	2.3	4.0	0.6
1991	57.0	6.8	21.0	2.5	6.0	0.8
2001	76.8	7.5	29.4	2.9	8.1	0.8
2011	96.5	8.1	42.4	3.5	10.9	0.9
2021	133.0	9.9	52.4	3.9	15.8	1.2
2031	184.1	12.7	74.8	5.1	19.7	1.3
2041	233.3	15.3	104.4	6.8	28.8	1.8
2051	298.2	19.1	131.3	8.3	40.5	2.5
2061	346.5	22.4	171.6	11.0	51.6	3.2
2071	377.2	24.5	195.5	12.9	69.8	4.5
2081	422.3	26.9	212.7	14.1	77.6	5.3
2091	463.6	28.7	247.8	16.1	88.8	6.1
2101	504.7	30.1	273.0	17.2	105.5	7.1

Source: Census of India (1961–2001), Aliyar and Rajan, 2007.

Figure 1: Age structural transition, India: 2001–2101

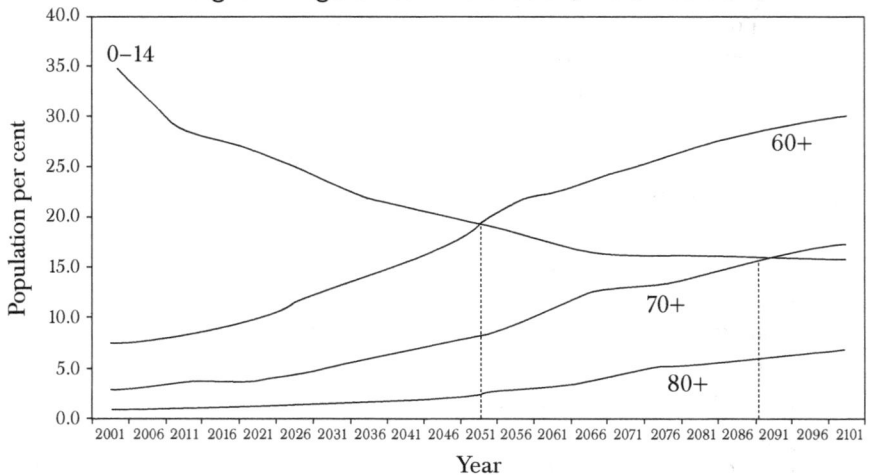

Figure 2: Age pyramids, India: 2001–2101

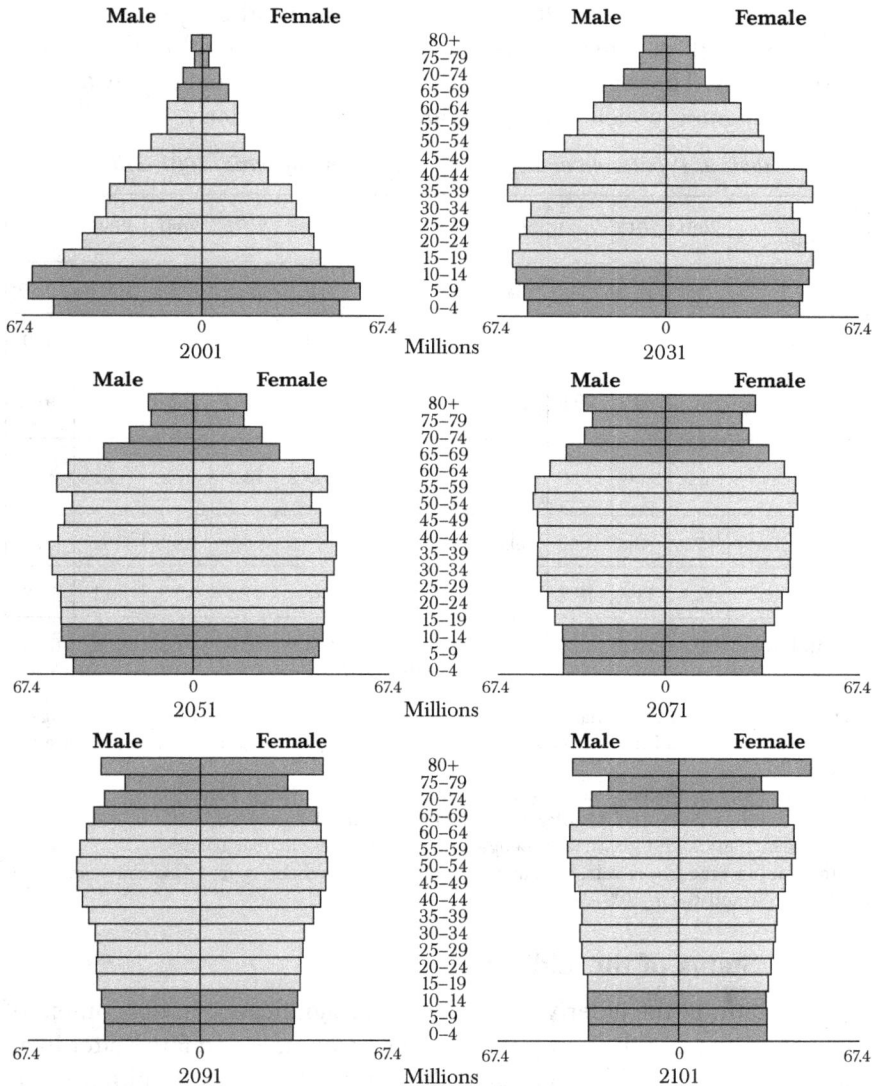

Source: Aliyar and Rajan, 2007.

As of 2001, one-fourth of the Indian elderly lived in south India (24.4 per cent), followed by central India (23.7 per cent) and the lowest proportion lived in north-east India. In 2051, the situation slightly changes; however, south India still leads with the highest proportion of the elderly (25.5 per cent) of all the regions in India. In 2101, two out of five Indian elderly persons (37.9 per cent) would live in central India, followed by east India (25.3) and south India declines to the third position with a mere 12.5 per cent. The same patterns are expected for old-old persons, age 70 and above and for oldest-old persons (age 80 and above) in the coming years in India. The regional ageing dynamics are expected to play a major role in designing policies and programmes for the elderly.

Table 9: Population ageing in different regions of India, 2001–2101

(In millions)	2001	2011	2021	2031	2041	2051	2061	2071	2081	2091	2101
India	76.8	96.5	133.0	184.1	233.3	298.2	346.5	377.2	422.3	463.6	504.7
North India	9.6	11.4	15.9	22.4	29.2	38.3	44.7	46.9	49.6	50.5	50.9
Central India	18.2	22.2	29.5	40.8	51.9	71.6	90.9	107.7	132.8	160.4	191.2
North East India	2.3	3.0	4.4	6.6	8.7	11.4	13.3	14.9	17.2	19.2	21.1
East India	15.9	20.3	28.3	39.5	49.1	63.2	76.6	86.9	101.8	115.5	127.5
West India	12.1	14.5	19.7	27.5	34.8	42.6	46.3	47.3	49.3	50.1	50.8
South India	18.8	25.2	35.0	47.3	59.6	71.0	74.6	73.6	71.6	67.8	63.3

Note :
North: Delhi, Haryana, Himachal Pradesh, Jammu & Kashmir, Punjab, Rajasthan and Chandigarh;
North East: Arunachal Pradesh, Assam, Manipur, Meghalaya, Mizoram, Nagaland, Tripura and Sikkim;
West: Goa, Gujarat, Maharashtra, Daman & Diu and Dadra & Nagar Haveli;
Central: Madhya Pradesh, Chhattisgarh, Uttar Pradesh and Uttaranchal;
East: Bihar, Jharkland, Orissa, West Bengal and Andaman & Nicobar Islands;
South: Andhra Pradesh, Kerala, Karnataka, Tamil Nadu, Pondicherry and Lakshadweep.
Source: Aliyar and Rajan, 2007.

Marital Status of the Elderly

Marital status of the elderly assumes special significance in the context of care in old age, as it is known that those who are married fare better in all economic and social aspects than those who are single (Holden et al., 1988; Zick and Smith, 1991). A major concern relates to the increasing proportion of elderly women, especially widows in the population. Two reasons are given for the marked gender disparity in widowhood in India (i) longer lifespan of women than of men and (ii) the general tendency in India for women to marry men older than themselves (Gulati and Rajan, 1999). Also, widowed men are much more likely to remarry and thus restore their earlier status than widowed women.

Figure 3: Incidence of widowhood among females and males in India (in percentage)

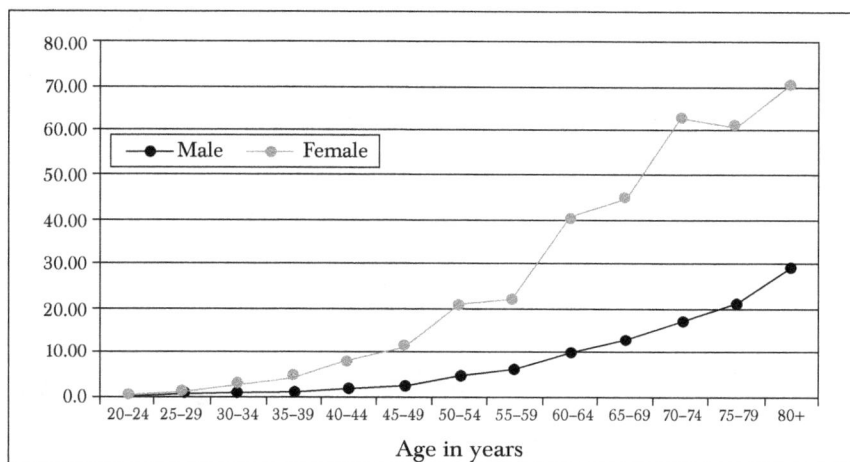

Note: Estimated by researchers based on the 2001 census.

According to the 2001 census, 33.07 per cent of the elderly in India live without their life partners. Widowers among old men form 14.98 per cent as against 50.06 per cent widows among old women. Among the oldest-old (80 years and above), widowhood is much more common. Almost half of them live without their spouse. Gender-wise analysis shows that 71.11 per cent of women were widows while only 28.89 per cent men in the oldest-old (80+) age group were widowers, according to the latest population census. Loss of the spouse is a major disaster in old age and such individuals who have undergone this trauma deserve suitable and adequate social safety nets. Designing policies to protect elderly females, particularly widows, should form a major welfare programme in the country, especially since it has been shown that old widows suffer much greater vulnerability to adverse outcomes like poor general health status, disability and poor utilization of health care (Sreerupa, 2006).

Living Arrangement

National Sample Survey (NSS) in its 60th round (January–June 2004) focused on many issues including economic independence, living arrangements and health status of the elderly population (60 years and above). This was a large-scale sample survey conducted throughout the country and its first report was published in March 2006. The elderly covered in the sample consisted of 17,750 males and 17,081 females. Here we have analysed the pattern of living arrangements among the Indian elderly by sex and place of residence. (Table 10)

Table 10: Percentage distribution of elderly by living arrangements, 2004

Living Arrangements	Rural			Urban			Total		
	Male	Female	Total	Male	Female	Total	Male	Female	Total
Living alone	2.8	8.0	5.3	2.1	6.5	4.3	2.6	7.6	5.2
With spouse only	13	8.7	12.5	13.3	7.5	10.4	15.5	8.4	12.0
With spouse and other members	58.9	28.4	44.2	64.9	29.4	46.8	60.9	28.6	44.8
Without spouse but with children	15.5	47.5	32	15.4	48.2	32.2	16.5	47.6	32.1
Without spouse but with other relatives	0.7	5.0	3.7	2.4	6.2	4.4	2.4	5.3	3.9
Without spouse but with non-relatives	0.2	0.6	0.5	0.5	0.5	0.5	0.3	0.6	0.5

Source: National Sample Survey Organization (NSSO), 2006.

Significantly, nearly 77 per cent of the elderly live either with their children without spouse or co-reside with spouse and children. This finding reflects the social convention of co-residence with children as the most preferred living arrangement for the elderly. Another 12 per cent of the elderly live with their spouses while only 5.2 per cent of them live alone and 4.4 per cent live with others – relatives or non-relatives. Although only a small percentage of the elderly live alone in India, results indicate that older women are more likely than men to be living alone (8 per cent vs 3 per cent) and that older men are more likely than older women to live with their spouses (15 per cent vs 8 per cent) or with spouse and other members (61 per cent vs 29 per cent). These gender differences, however, are almost entirely due to the differences in marital status. As we have already noted, there are more widows in India than widowers who form the majority of the elderly population living alone. In the absence of extra familial sources of care and support, they form a particularly vulnerable section of the aged population. Further, the much higher proportion of aged women who are widowed raises the share of aged women, as compared to that of men among the elderly, residing with their children but without spouse. Though much disparity in the rate of co-residence with children is not seen between the rural and the urban elderly, the differences continue to be pronounced between old men and old women.

Table 11: Percentage of elderly living with their children by regions of India, 2004

Region	Rural			Urban			Total		
	Male	Female	Total	Male	Female	Total	Male	Female	Total
South	72.2	69.8	71.0	77.4	74.3	75.8	73.5	71.2	72.4
West	73.7	73.1	73.4	81.8	74.4	77.9	76.3	73.7	74.9
N-West	84.2	86.2	85.2	83.9	83.6	83.6	84.2	85.6	84.9
North	75.1	75.8	75.4	84.8	79.2	81.9	76.6	76.6	76.5
East	83.9	81.3	82.7	83.0	82.1	82.6	83.3	81.2	82.4
NH	84.2	84.7	84.4	82.0	88.2	85.2	83.7	84.5	84.0
NE	78.4	77.7	78.1	81.0	84.8	82.5	78.9	78.1	78.6
UT	76.3	80.3	78.8	80.7	79.7	80.4	80.9	77.4	79.7
India	76.5	75.9	76.2	80.3	77.6	79.0	77.4	76.2	76.9

Note:
East Region: Assam, Orissa, West Bengal;
North East Region: Arunachal Pradesh, Manipur, Meghalaya, Mizoram, Nagaland, Sikkim, Tripura;
North Hill Region: Himachal Pradesh, Jammu & Kashmir;
North-West Region: Haryana, Punjab, Rajasthan;
North Region: Bihar, Madhya Pradesh, Uttar Pradesh;
South region: Andhra Pradesh, Karnataka, Kerala, Tamil Nadu;
Union Territories: Andaman & Nicobar Islands, Dadra & Nagar Haveli, Delhi, Lakshadweep, Pondicherry, Daman & Diu, Chandigarh;
West Region: Goa, Gujarat, Maharashtra.
Source: Tabulations made by the authors based on the NSS, 60th round.

Despite high levels of co-residence with children among the elderly in India, co-residence levels differ considerably by region, reflecting variations in the kinship system (matrilineal and bilineal system in the south and the patrilineal system in the north). Table 11 shows that co-residence levels are in general higher in the northern parts of the country, especially the north-west and the northern hills where 85 and 84 per cent respectively of the elderly live with their children. In contrast, the lowest level of co-residence is found in the southern region of the country at 72 per cent.

A sex disaggregated analysis of the living arrangements reveals that broadly a higher percentage of aged men co-reside with their children than aged women, with the exception of mainly the northern hill region. The gender difference in co-residence persists across rural and urban locations. Further, it was found that co-residence with children is higher in urban areas than in rural areas. The difference could be due to the higher cost of housing in urban areas.

References

Aliyar, Sabu and Rajan, S Irudaya, 'Population Projections for India, 2001–2101', Centre for Development Studies, Thiruvananthapuram, 2008.

Gulati, Leela and Rajan, S Irudaya, 'The Added Years: Elderly in India and Kerala', *Economic and Political Weekly*, Vol. 34, No. 44, WS46–51, 1999.

Guilmoto, Christophe Z and Rajan, S Irudaya, 'Spatial Patterns of Fertility Transition in Indian Districts', *Population and Development Review*, Vol. 27, No. 4, 2001, pp.713–38.

–, 'District Level Estimates of Fertility from India's 2001 Census', *Economic and Political Weekly*, Vol. 37, No.7, 2002, pp.665–72.

–, *Fertility Transition in South India*, Sage, New Delhi/Thousand Oaks, London 2005.

Holden, Karen C, Burkhauser, Richard V and Feaster, Daniel J, 'The Timing of Falls into Poverty after Retirement and Widowhood', *Demography*, Vol. 25, No. 3, 1988, pp.405–14.

Mari Bhat, P N, 'Changing Demography of Elderly in India', *Current Science*, Vol. 63, No. 8, 25 October 1992, pp.440–8.

–, 'Maternal Mortality in India: An Update', *Studies in Family Planning*, Vol. 33, No. 3, 2002, pp.227–36.

NSSO, 'Morbidity, Health Care and the Condition of the Aged', NSS 60th Round, (January–June 2004), Report No. 507, Ministry of Statistics and Programme Implementation, Government of India, 2006.

Rajan, S Irudaya, 'Aging, Pension and Social Security in South Asia' in Rajan, S Irudaya, ed, *Social Security for the Elderly: Experiences from South Asia*, Chapter 1, Routledge, London/New York/New Delhi, 2007, pp.1–38.

Rajan, S Irudaya, Mishra, U S and Sarma, P S, *India's Elderly: Burden or Challenge?*, Sage, New Delhi/Thousand Oaks/London, 1999.

Rajan, S Irudaya, Sarma, P S and Mishra, U S, 'Demography of Indian Aging, 2001–2051', *Journal of Aging and Social Policy*, Vol. 15, Nos. 2 & 3, 2003, pp.11–30.

Registrar General of India, *Population Projections for India and States, 1996–2016*, Census of India 1991, New Delhi, 1996.

–, *Ageing Population of India: An Analysis of the 1991 Census Data*, Census of India 1991, New Delhi, 1999.

Sreerupa, 'Gender, Ageing and Widowhood: Health Vulnerability and Socio-Economic Influences', M.Phil Disseration, submitted to the Jawaharlal Nehru University, New Delhi, 2006.

Sudha, S and Rajan, S Irudaya, 'Female Demographic Disadvantage in India 1981–1991: Role of Sex Selective Abortions and Female Infanticide', *Development and Change*, Vol. 30, No. 3, 1999, pp.585–618.

–, 'Persistent Daughter Disadvantage: What Do Estimated Sex Ratio at Birth and Sex Ratios of Child Mortality Risk Reveal?', *Economic and Political Weekly*, Vol. 38, No. 41, 11–17 October 2003, pp.4361–69.

United Nations, *World Population Aging 2007*, Department of Economic and Social Affairs, Population Division, New York, 2007.

Visaria, Pravin and Rajan, S Irudaya, 'National Family Health Survey: A Landmark in Indian Surveys', *Economic and Political Weekly*, Vol. 34, Nos. 42 & 43, 1999, pp.3002–7.

Zick, Cathleen D and Smith, Ken, 'Patterns of Economic Change Surrounding the Death of a Spouse', *Journal of Gerontology: Social Sciences*, Vol. 46, No. 6, 1991, pp.310–20.

Chapter 3

DISEASE, DISABILITY AND HEALTHCARE UTILIZATION AMONG THE AGED

S Irudaya Rajan
Sreerupa

Introduction

Decline in health and emergence of certain illnesses have been reported as the first category of cues or 'body reminders' of ageing in a study by Karp, 2000 (cited in Vincent, 2003) based on qualitative interviews with male and female professionals in America. Similar results have been found in studies on the aged in India, where decline in health status, restrictive activity pattern and being 'inactive' were associated with old age (Rajan et al., 1999). These perceptions of the aged are substantiated by empirical evidence which shows that a positive relation exists between age and morbidity among adults, i.e. at old age there is higher prevalence of morbidity implying that the risk of illness and morbidity is higher among the aged (Duraisamy, 2001). Further it has been found that as age advances the probability of disability also increases (Gupta and Sankar, 2003).

As men and women live longer there will be an increase in aged persons with chronic illness and disability which is a matter of concern for ageing individuals as well as health care planners of the society. Chronic morbidities and disabling conditions adversely affect the quality of life of the elderly. Poor health is a cause for concern among the aged as illness episodes have the potential to cause economic shock (Crystal et al., 2000), lead to financial dependency (Pal, 2004), loss of autonomy, reduced social contact and loneliness. Meanwhile, society has to deal with difficult issues like increasing demands on social and medical care as well as growing cost of providing prolonged health care services to chronically ill and disabled elderly. Thus, the health status of the aged should occupy an important place in any study of the elderly population.

The Nandal, Khatri and Kadian (1987) study found a majority of the elderly suffering from diseases like cough (cough includes tuberculosis of lungs, bronchitis, asthma, and whooping cough as per international classification of diseases), poor eyesight, anaemia and dental problems. The proportion of the sick and the bedridden among the elderly is found to be increasing with advancing age; the major physical disability consists of blindness and deafness (Darshan, Sharma and Singh, 1987). Shah (1993) in his study of urban elderly in Gujarat found deteriorating physical conditions among two-thirds of the elderly, consisting of poor vision, impairment of hearing, arthritis and loss of memory. Besides physical ailments, psychiatric morbidity is also prevalent among a large proportion of the elderly. An enquiry in this direction by Gupta and Vohra (1987) provides evidence of psychiatric morbidity among the elderly. This study also draws a distinction between functional and organic disorders in old age. It is found that functional disorders precede organic disorders, which becomes frequent beyond 70. Given the prevalence of ill health and disability among the elderly, Vijayakumar (1991) found that dissatisfaction existed among the elderly with regard to the provision of medical aid. The author also referred to the fact that the sick elderly lacked proper familial care while public health services were insufficient to meet their health needs.

The following section analyses the published tables of National Sample Survey (NSS), 60th round to assess the self reported health status, disease and disability profile among the elderly and the patterns of health care utilization. NSS in its 60th round (January–June 2004) focused on many issues including economic independence, living arrangements and health status of the elderly population (age 60 and above). The elderly module as well as the health module of the survey has been used for the purpose of this paper. The data on utilization of heath care services by the aged was generated from the health module which was administered to the population of all ages. This was a large-scale sample survey conducted throughout the country and its first report was published in March 2006. The following analysis and discussion are based on tables generated from the data available in the report. The elderly covered in the sample consisted of 17,750 males and 17,081 females.

Self Reported Health Status

Self assessed current health status is a subjective measure closely associated with the feelings of well-being and quality of life. In the survey, when asked to rate their health status (as 'excellent', 'very good', 'good/fair' or 'poor'), nearly 70 per cent of aged reported their health status to be ranging from 'excellent' to 'good/fair' while more than a quarter of the elderly reported their current health to be poor. Further, it was found that a slightly higher percentage of aged women report their health to be poor as compared to their male counterparts. The relative disadvantage faced by the older women in terms of health status has been found to become more intense when we consider only the older widows (Sreerupa, 2006). In line with the previous research findings, more elderly from rural areas report their health status as compared to those in urban areas.

Table 1: Self reported current health status of elderly by sex and location, in percentage, 2004

Current State of Health	Rural			Urban			Total		
	Male	Female	Total	Male	Female	Total	Male	Female	Total
Excellent	4.8	2.8	3.8	7.1	4.4	5.7	5.3	3.2	4.3
Good	65.0	62.1	63.6	69.1	68.2	68.6	66.1	63.9	65.0
Poor	26.6	31.3	28.9	21.6	24.9	23.3	25.3	29.5	27.4

Source: National Sample Survey Organization (NSSO), 2006.

Significantly, it has been noted in the analysis of the previous rounds (NSS 52nd round) that such a high percentage of positive assessment of general perception which associates old age with illness and health problems. To better understand the association of self reported health status with actual morbidity condition, the elderly respondent's perception about own health has been disaggregated on the basis of presence or absence of any ailment during the last 15 days prior to the interview in Table 2.

Table 2 reveals that more than 55 and 63 per cent of the elderly were reporting their health status to be 'good/fair' despite suffering from some kind of ailment in rural and urban areas respectively. On the other hand, nearly 17 and 13 per cent of the elderly in rural and urban settings respectively were reporting poor health status although they had no ailments. Further, it was found that a higher percentage of rural as compared to the urban elderly perceived their health status to be poor both when they were sick and were not ailing. Apart from the rural–urban difference in reporting, there were gender differences in reporting of health status; it appeared that more women reported their health status to be poor when suffering from an ailment as compared to their male counterparts, while more men reported good health status despite sickness. Similarly, more elderly women than men reported poor health status even when they reported to be not suffering from any ailment in the last 15 days.

The first impression that we get from Table 2 is that the rural elderly and older women tend to be pessimistic about their health status, whereas

Table 2: Percentage of elderly with sickness by own perception about health, 2004

Own perception about current state of health	Aged persons with sickness			Aged persons without sickness		
	Male	Female	Person	Male	Female	Person
Rural						
Excellent	1.9	1.4	1.7	8.1	4.3	6.2
Good/Fair	58	52.5	55.3	77.2	77	77.1
Poor	40.1	46	42.9	14.7	18.7	16.7
Urban						
Excellent	3.1	1.9	2.4	11.4	7.2	9.2
Good/Fair	64.1	62	63.1	77.5	78	77.8
Poor	32.7	36	34.5	11.1	14.8	13

Note: The proportions have been adjusted excluding the 'not reported cases'.
Source: NSSO, 2006.

the urban elderly as well as older men are more positive while assessing their health when the presence of an ailment in the previous 15 days is controlled. However, we need to take into consideration a few factors before interpreting the results. Apart from the obvious inference discussed above, the difference in reporting could also be rooted in the poor utilization of health services among older women and the rural elderly. So, when it comes to the reporting of ailments requiring formal diagnosis, it is quite possible that the female respondents may under-report (Sengupta and Agree, 2003). As a result, although these elderly felt that their health status was poor, they would not report any specific ailment. Meanwhile, there have been studies which have found self-perceived health to be a reliable predictor of future functional status and even mortality (Idler and Benyamini, 1997; Idler and Kasl, 1995). Hence there is a need for further research to take a closer look at the reasons for the differences in reporting health status.

Next, we examine the pattern of reporting the health status across monthly per capita expenditure groups in rural and urban settings to understand the association of income and self reported health status. The percentage of aged persons with sickness reporting their health status to be poor keeps falling as we move up the expenditure class and vice versa for those reporting their health status to be good. Similarly, the percentage of aged persons without sickness reporting poor health status diminishes, while those reporting good health status improves as we move up the expenditure class. These results are in line with previous studies which have shown a positive association between reported health and income, i.e. those with higher income report better health and fewer health problems (Mutchler and Burr, 1991).

Table 3: Percentage of elderly with sickness by own perception about health for each expenditure quintile class, 2004

MPCE	Aged person wih illness		Aged person without illness		Aged person with illness		Aged person without illness	
	Good	Poor	Good	Poor	Good	Poor	Good	Poor
	Rural				Urban			
0–225	41.2	54.5	70.9	17.8	42.9	56.5	54.5	27.5
225–255	40.1	55.9	67.6	21.5	53.9	41.1	55.5	27.9
255–300	43.4	52.5	73.4	16.6	52.0	46.1	68.6	23.4
300–340	47.3	50.9	68.1	20.0	46.1	50.2	75.8	16.0
340–380	53.0	42.6	71.7	18.4	57.3	42.1	69.0	12.6
380–420	52.3	45.3	72.0	16.5	49.8	46.6	79.8	10.1
420–470	51.5	40.4	73.3	16.2	59.6	36.2	78.7	10.2
470–525	55.1	41.1	72.0	17.0	67.8	29.2	80.6	10.5
525–615	54.3	43.1	74.9	13.1	64.6	33.1	75.7	9.9
615–775	60.3	36.7	76.0	13.3	72.1	23.2	76.6	10.2
775–950	60.7	34.5	77.5	11.2	61.3	35.7	76.8	9.8
950+	60.7	35.5	76.5	10.9	68.3	25.8	72.4	8.9
All	54.1	42.0	73.1	15.8	62.2	34.0	75.0	12.5

Source: NSSO, 2006.

Table 4: Percentage of elderly reporting poor health status by regions of India, 2004

Region	Rural			Urban			Total		
	Male	Female	Total	Male	Female	Total	Male	Female	Total
South	26.3	28.7	27.5	17.5	22.0	19.9	24.0	20.3	25.4
West	17.0	20.2	18.5	26.3	26.6	25.4	17.2	21.5	19.3
N-West	22.5	30.3	26.5	25.6	27.4	27.2	23.4	29.4	26.5
North	29.0	30.9	30.0	26.5	31.5	30.4	28.3	32.6	30.3
East	31.2	39.0	34.6	26.7	27.0	26.6	29.1	37.1	32.9
NH	26.5	36.4	30.7	22.7	14.6	18.5	26.1	33.9	29.4
NE	23.5	28.2	25.0	19.2	24.3	18.4	22.1	26.7	23.0
UT	21.2	19.8	20.5	24.7	25.0	25.2	22.3	23.6	21.8
India	26.6	31.3	28.9	21.6	24.9	23.3	25.3	29.5	27.4

Source: NSSO, 2006.

Further, a regional analysis of the reporting of poor health status has been carried out. In the eastern and northern regions of the country the highest percentage of aged persons report their health status to be poor (33 and 30 per cent respectively), while the lowest proportion of aged from the western regions report poor health status (19 per cent). However, when we consider the urban areas the pattern is slightly different, the north and the north-western regions top the regions with highest proportion of aged with a poor self rating of health status. The lowest percentage of aged persons from the north-eastern regions and the northern hills report their health status to be poor. The regional variation in reported health status could be due to regional disparity in the delivery of health care services, quality of these services or even awareness among the population of their health needs.

Physical Mobility

Moving on from the self perception about own health, we turn to the elderly who are either confined to their home or bed due to various health problems. Chronic morbidity and physical impairments in old age adversely affect mobility and the capacity of self care – this could be the culmination of much ill health in later life (Arber and Ginn, 1991). Disability and impairments leading to immobility among the elderly is a cause of concern for ageing individuals as it adversely affects their quality of life increasing their risk of dependence and loss of autonomy. Meanwhile, society has to address the increasing demands on social and medical care for such older persons.

Table 5: Per 1,000 distribution of elderly who cannot move and are confined to bed, 2004

Age group (years)	Rural			Urban		
	Male	Female	Total	Male	Female	Total
60–64	4	3	4	8	5	6
65–69	7	6	7	11	8	9
70–74	16	20	18	18	20	19
75–79	23	33	28	18	28	22
80 and above	49	69	58	69	69	69
All aged	12	14	13	17	17	17

Source: NSSO, 2006.

Nearly 8 per cent of the elderly in India have severely restricted physical mobility (they cannot move and are confined to bed or home), while a disproportionately higher percentage of women have restricted mobility as compared to men (9.1 per cent vs 6.8 per cent). There is a systematic gender difference across the age groups for both elderly who are confined to bed and home, as shown in Tables 5 and 6, however, it is more pronounced in the higher age groups. Numerous studies have shown higher prevalence of disability among aged women as compared to the men (Gupta and Shankar, 2003; Sengupta and Agree, 2003).

Table 6: Per 1,000 distribution of elderly who cannot move and are confined at home, 2004

Age group (years)	Rural			Urban		
	Male	Female	Total	Male	Female	Total
60–64	23	31	27	25	29	27
65–69	44	44	44	23	58	41
70–74	63	112	87	59	96	78
75–79	94	130	111	95	157	125
80 and above	171	257	211	170	254	214
All aged	55	74	64	51	83	67

Source: NSSO, 2006.

Results shown in Table 5 and 6 reveal that there is a sharp increase in the number of elderly who cannot move and are confined to bed or home as they grow older. In the age group of 80 and above, for every 1,000 elderly, 58 elderly in rural areas and 69 elderly in urban areas are bedridden, which is in contrast to four rural elderly and six urban elderly in the age group of 60–4 years. Table 6 shows similar patterns for those elderly who are confined to their homes. Another significant finding is that there is a slightly higher rate of immobility among the aged in the urban settings with the advance in age. This could be because the urban spaces, which have not been designed keeping in mind the needs of the disabled elderly, may be hampering the mobility of such aged persons.

Prevalence of Ailments

We start by analysing the prevalence of morbidity reported during the last 15 days prior to the interview.

Table 7: Percentage of persons reporting ailments during the last 15 days by sex and broad age groups, 2004

Age-group (years)	Rural			Urban			Total		
	Male	Female	Total	Male	Female	Total	Male	Female	Total
0–14	7.6	6.8	7.2	8.4	7.4	7.9	7.8	6.9	7.4
15–29	4.1	5.7	4.9	4.4	5.6	5.0	4.2	5.6	4.9
30–44	6.4	9.3	7.8	6.4	9.5	7.9	6.4	9.3	7.8
45–59	10.7	13.2	11.9	12.7	17.3	14.9	11.3	14.3	12.8
60 & above	28.5	28.2	28.3	35.2	38.3	36.8	30.1	30.7	30.4
All	8.3	9.3	8.8	9.1	10.8	9.9	8.5	9.7	9.1

Source: NSSO, 2006.

In the adult age groups (excluding 0–14 yrs), Table 7 shows that the prevalence of ailments shoots up as we move up the age groups. The prevalence of ailments is the highest among the elderly population (60 and above) with slightly more than 30 per cent reporting some kind of ailment. This signifies that the risk as well as the burden of morbidity is considerably higher for those aged 60 years and above. There are geographical variations in the prevalence of ailments, a substantially greater proportion of urban aged reported to be sick (36.8 per cent) as against rural elderly (28.3 per cent).

Table 8: Average duration of ailments (in days) reported during the last 15 days by sex and broad age groups, 2004

Age-group (years)	Rural			Urban			Total		
	Male	Female	Total	Male	Female	Total	Male	Female	Total
5–14	8.9	6.9	8.0	8.0	7.6	7.9	8.7	7.1	8.0
15–29	9.5	12.8	11.4	5.6	17.3	11.7	8.2	14.1	11.5
30–44	31.8	13.0	20.9	9.6	11.5	10.6	25.0	12.6	18.0
45–59	14.4	23.0	19.2	20.3	62.9	46.5	15.7	33.7	26
60 & above	38.3	46.1	42.3	104.5	96	99.6	50.9	57.5	54.4
All	16	15.6	15.8	16.2	27.5	21.9	16	18.6	17.3

Source: NSSO, 2006.

From Table 8 we have tried to understand the nature of the morbidity prevailing in the different age groups by examining the average duration of the ailment. The above table reveals that the average duration of the ailment climbs with the advance in age. The average duration of ailment is as high as 54.4 days among those aged 60 and above as against eight days in the 5–14 age group. The longer duration of ailment among the aged in general suggests the greater prevalence of chronic ailments among the elderly. Significantly, the urban elderly report a much longer average duration of ailment – 99.6 days as compared to the rural elderly who report 42.3 days of ailment on an average.

A regional analysis of the prevalence of reported morbidity reveals highest reporting of ailment in the western and southern parts of the country (39.6 and 39.4 per cent respectively) while the lowest prevalence was in the north-eastern and northern regions (18.1 and 18.6 per cent respectively).

A similar regional pattern of prevalence of reported morbidity has been found across urban and rural settings. Significantly, the reporting of ailments among older women has been consistently higher in the southern region of the country cutting across urban and rural settings. It is important to note that the higher reporting of ailments seems to be associated with regions having a relatively better health care delivery system. Hence, it appears that a higher reporting of ailments in such places is rooted in the increased awareness, better recognition and diagnosis of ailment rather than due to higher prevalence of morbidity in such regions.

Table 9: Percentage of elderly reporting ailments in the last 15 days by regions of India, 2004

Region	Rural			Urban			Total		
	Male	Female	Total	Male	Female	Total	Male	Female	Total
South	38.1	37.8	38.1	40.7	46.1	43.6	38.7	40.0	39.4
West	44.0	39.1	41.6	31.4	37.5	34.7	40.2	38.9	39.6
N-West	23.7	25.5	24.5	26.2	28.2	28.7	24.8	25.9	25.3
North	18.5	16.2	17.4	26.3	22.2	24.1	19.7	17.3	18.6
East	29.4	31.2	30.2	34.3	35.4	34.8	30.8	32.8	31.7
NH	31.3	30.7	30.9	35.0	31.1	33.2	31.7	30.5	31.1
NE	18.2	18.0	18.3	12.2	14.7	14.5	17.9	17.4	18.1
UT	24.7	30.0	27.9	27.3	29.0	28.2	25.1	30.4	27.8
India	28.5	28.2	28.3	35.2	38.3	36.8	30.1	30.7	30.4

Source: NSSO, 2006.

Pattern of Health Care Utilization

In the previous sections we had found that the morbidity rate increases with age among adults, making the aged a significant category of curative health care seekers. The following analysis confirms that with the advance in age, utilization of hospital care services increases.

The average hospitalization rate in the country per 1,000 aged persons is 76 as compared to 16 among those in the age group of 0–14 years. Among the elderly, there is a considerable gender difference in the rate of hospitalization as a much greater proportion of men are hospitalized as compared to their female counterparts (87 vs 67 per 1,000). This is contrary to our expectation of higher health care utilization among older females based on our previous analysis which revealed a female disadvantage in terms of various health indicators. This indicates towards a gender bias in utilization of health care services. Similarly, there is rural disadvantage in utilization of inpatient care services with only 66 rural aged persons being hospitalized as against 107 urban elderly per 1,000 elderly persons. The rural–urban difference in the rate of hospitalization stems from the lack of availability of hospitals with inpatient care facilities in the rural areas.

Next, we disaggregate the hospitalized cases by the nature of ailment. The diseases among the elderly for which there are more hospitalized

Table 10: Rate of hospitalization (number per 1,000) during last 365 days by sex and broad age group, 2004

Age-group (years)	Rural			Urban			Total		
	Male	Female	Total	Male	Female	Total	Male	Female	Total
0–14	18	11	14	24	18	21	19	12	16
15–29	19	22	21	19	28	23	19	24	21
30–44	26	30	28	32	34	33	28	31	30
45–59	46	43	44	59	53	56	50	45	48
60 & above	75	57	66	118	97	107	86	67	76
All	27	25	26	35	34	35	29	27	28

Source: NSSO, 2006.

cases than the rest are heart diseases, cataract and bronchial asthma. Other common health problems requiring hospitalization are accidents/ injuries/ burns/ fractures/ poisoning, diseases of kidney/ urinary system and diabetes mellitus. Among older women, cataract tops the list of diseases requiring inpatient care followed by heart disease. Among older men, heart disease followed by bronchial asthma has the highest reported cases of hospitalization. In urban areas, heart disease and cataract while in rural areas, cataract and bronchial asthma have the highest rates of hospitalization.

Most of India's elderly being economically dependent, the cost of treatment is often a burden on the household, especially in respect of poor households. Apparently, for this reason many of the elderly ignore their ailments unless they become too acute. Thus, there is a great need for an appropriate insurance scheme for enabling the elderly to meet their medical expenses. Evidently, such schemes should be made compulsory for all workers gainfully employed during their economically active years of life.

Conclusion

The main area of concern among the elderly is their health, which can in turn have a significant impact on their economic security, level of independence and social interaction. Our analysis of the NSS data revealed a huge 70 per cent of the aged reporting their health status to be ranging from 'excellent' to 'good/fair', while around a quarter of the elderly reported their current health to be poor. Our previous analysis had uncovered that such a high percentage of positive assessment of health status was despite a large number of the aged reporting to be suffering from at least one disability or chronic ailment. The present analysis has thrown light on the difference in self reported health status across sex, location, prevalence of ailment, income level and regions. Despite the female disadvantage in

Table 11: Per 1,000 distribution of hospitalized cases among aged during last 365 days by nature of ailment, 2004

Age-group (years)	Rural			Urban			Total		
	Male	Female	Total	Male	Female	Total	Male	Female	Total
Diarrhoea/ dysentery	33	62	45	22	33	27	29	52	39
Gastritis/gastric or peptic ulcer	37	54	44	30	24	27	34	43	38
Heat disease	95	59	80	165	162	164	118	96	109
Hypertension	23	53	36	50	59	54	32	55	42
Respiratory including ear/nose/throat ailments	25	25	25	21	34	27	24	28	26
Tuberculosis	42	18	32	11	5	8	32	14	24
Bronchial asthma	111	47	84	80	54	68	101	49	78
Disorder of joints and bones	30	40	34	26	45	35	29	42	34
Diseases of kidney/urinary system	78	28	57	89	33	63	82	30	59
Neurological disorders	40	35	38	51	33	43	44	34	40
Glaucoma	14	9	11	6	50	26	11	24	16
Cataract	77	132	100	64	94	78	73	118	92
Diabetes mellitus	30	52	40	68	36	53	43	46	44
Locomotor	17	20	18	22	16	19	19	18	18
Visual including blindness (excluding cataract)	12	14	13	5	7	6	9	11	10
Accidents/ injuries/ burns/ fractures/ poisoning	74	65	70	52	67	59	67	66	66
Cancer and other tumours	18	36	26	25	56	39	20	43	30

Source: NSSO, 2006.

reported health status and preponderance of older women among immobile elderly persons, a much greater proportion of men are hospitalized as compared to their female counterparts (87 vs 67 per 1,000). The diseases among the elderly for which there are more hospitalized cases than the rest are heart diseases, cataract and bronchial asthma.

Based on the observation made on the health status of India's elderly, it can be concluded that some definite health intervention measures are necessary to cater to specific health complications in old age. Further, with the ongoing fertility transition, the demand for maternal and child health services are expected to shrink, at the same time, in a not so distant future our societies are going to face the challenge of providing specialized health care services to the elderly population. This calls for specialities in geriatric treatment within public sector health facilities, special wards for treating the elderly people in the general hospitals throughout the country and specially trained personnel to treat geriatric disorders.

This vulnerable segment of society, like any other economically backward section of the population, needs to be provided with concessions specifically with regard to provision of health facilities. There is scope for tremendous positive intervention from the state as well as NGOs to improve the health care scenario of the elderly in a developing country like India. The need for such services becomes all the more acute in the absence of appropriate insurance schemes for life protection with regard to medical expenses in old age. Since the majority of elderly in India are economically dependent, the cost of treatment becomes a burden on the household, especially the poor households. Hence, there is a need to introduce schemes to provide health insurance to all citizens of the country so that they can get some financial and medical support in their old age.

References

Arber, S and Ginn, J, *Gender and Later Life: A Sociological Analysis of Resources and Constraints*, Sage, London, 1991.
Bordia, Anand and Bhardwaj, Gautam, eds, *Rethinking Pension Provision for India*, Tata Mcgraw Hill, New Delhi, 2003.
Crystal, S, Johnson, R W, Harman, J, et al., 'Out-of-Pocket Health Care Costs among Older Americans', *Journal of Gerontology,* Series B: *Psychological Sciences and Social Sciences*, Vol. 55, No. 1, 2000, pp.51–62.
Darshan, Salilesh, Sharma, M L and Singh, S P, 'Health Needs of Senior Citizens' in Sharma, M L and Dak, T M, eds, *Aging in India*, Ajanta Publications, New Delhi, 1987, pp.207–13.
Duraisamy, P, *Health Status and Curative Health Care in Rural India*, Working Paper, Series No. 78, National Council of Applied Economic Research, 2001.
Gupta, I, and Sankar, D, 'Health of the Elderly in India: A Multivariate Analysis', *Journal of Health and Population in Developing Countries*, 24 June 2003.
Gupta, Punam and Vohra, Adarsh K, 'Pattern of Psychiatric Morbidity in the Aged' in Sharma, M L and Dak, T M, eds, *Aging in India*, op. cit., pp.214–21.
Idler, E L and Benyamini, Y, 'Self-rated Health and Mortality: A Review of Twenty -Seven Community Studies', *Journal of Health and Social Behavior*, Vol. 38, No. 1, 1997, pp.21–37.
Idler, E L and Kasl, S V, 'Self-Ratings of Health: Do They Also Predict Change in Functional Ability?', *Journals of Gerontology,* Series B: *Psychological Sciences and Social Sciences,* Vol. 50, Issue 6, 1995, pp.344–53.

Kinsella, Kevin and Velkoff, Victoria A, *An Aging World,* Series P95/01, US Census Bureau, Washington D C, 2001.

Liebig, Phoebe and Rajan, S Irudaya, eds, *An Aging India: Perspectives, Prospects and Policies,* The Haworth Press, New York, 2003.

Mutchler, J E and Burr, J A, 'Racial Differences in Health and Health Care Service Utilization in Later Life: The Effect of Socio-Economic Status', *Journal of Health and Social Behaviour,* Vol. 32, No. 4, December 1991, pp.342–56.

Nandal, D S, Khatri, R S and Kadian, R S, 'Aging Problems in the Structural Context' in Sharma, M L and Dak, T M, eds, *Aging in India,* op. cit., pp.106–16.

NSSO, 'Morbidity, Health Care and the Condition of the Aged', NSS 60th Round, (January–June 2004), Report No. 507, Ministry of Statistics and Programme Implementation, Government of India, 2006.

Pal, S, *Do children act as old age security in Rural India? Evidence from an Analysis of Elderly Living Arrangements,* 2004, [http://129.3.20.41/eps/lab/papers/0405/0405002.pdf].

Rajan, S Irudaya, 'Chronic Poverty among Indian Elderly' in Mehta, Asha Kapur and Shepherd, Andrew, *Chronic Poverty and Development Policy in India,* Sage, New Delhi, 2006, pp.168–96.

Rajan, S Irudaya, Mishra U S and Sarma, P S, *India's Elderly: Burden or Challenge?,* Sage, New Delhi/Thousand Oaks/London, 1999.

Sengupta, M and Agree, E M, 'Gender, Health, Marriage and Mobility Difficulty among Older Adults in India', *Asia-Pacific Population Journal.* Vol. 18, No. 4, December 2003, pp.53–65.

Shah, V P, *The Elderly in Gujarat,* Department of Sociology, Gujarat University, Ahmedabad (Mimeographed), 1993.

Sreerupa, 'Gender, Ageing and Widowhood: Health Vulnerability and Socio-Economic Influences', Unpublished M.Phil. Dissertation, Centre for Development Studies, Trivandrum, 2006.

Strauss, J, Gertler, P J, Rahman, M O and Fox, K, 'Gender and Life-Cycle Differentials in the Patterns and Determinants of Adult Health', *Journal of Human Resources,* Vol. 28, No. 4, Special issue: *Symposium on Investments in Women's Human Capital and Development,* 1993, pp.791–837.

United Nations (UN), *World Population Ageing, 1950-2050,* Department of Economic and Social Affairs, Population Division, UN, New York, 2002.

Vijayakumar, S, 'The Family and Health of the Aged' in Jai Prakash, Indira, ed, *Quality Aging,* Association of Gerontology (India), Varanasi, 1991, pp.108–12.

Vincent, J, *Old Age,* Routledge, London, 2003.

World Bank, *India: The Challenge of Old Age Income Security,* Finance and Private Sector Development, South Asia Region, Report No. 22034-In, Washington, 2001.

Chapter 4

EMPLOYMENT AS OLD AGE SECURITY

E T Mathew
S Irudaya Rajan

Introduction

In a society like India, where it has not been possible for the state to extend social security to all its citizens, people tend to work as long as they can so that they may be able to support themselves during periods when they have no gainful employment. This applies to interruptions in employment caused by retrenchment, sickness, disablement, as well as advanced old age. Obviously, as old age advances into the seventies and eighties, opportunities for gainful employment get increasingly limited.

The need to engage in gainful employment, even after formal retirement from a given employment may arise due to a variety of reasons:

(a) There are specific instances where employees are not entitled to any retirement benefits; eg. casual workers and self-employed persons;

(b) In respect of several categories of regularly employed salaried persons, they may be entitled to, at the time of retirement, a one-time payment of gratuity based on salary last drawn and a provident fund based on contributions made during the period of service;

(c) In a relatively limited number of cases, salaried employees are entitled to a regular monthly pension in addition to the normal gratuity and provident fund payments.

It is important to note that the maximum pension which civil servants in India are currently entitled to is one half of the basic pay last drawn (plus dearness relief based on cost of living index). The actual basic pension, of course, may fall short of 50 per cent of the pay last drawn if the period of service put in by the retiree is less than the stipulated period. The crux of the old age financial problem consists in the fact that a family, which has been accustomed to a certain lifestyle based on a pre-retirement income, is all of a sudden faced with a sharp fall in income. The negative impact of retirement on income can be overcome only if the family has other sources of income to fall back upon, such as interest on bank deposits, rental income, dividend from equity shares or mutual funds, etc.

The scenario portrayed above applies to regularly employed salaried workers only. Such workers, however, constitute only a small proportion of the workforce. For instance, according to the results of the 55th National Sample Survey (NSS), (1999–2000), among the usually employed (principal and subsidiary combined), regular workers constituted at the all-India level only 9 per cent of rural males, 3.9 per cent of rural females, 41.9 per cent of urban males and 38.5 per cent of urban females of the workforce (Government of India, 2000). As far as the rest of the workforce, consisting of casual and self-employed workers, is concerned, their old age is characterized by varying degrees of hardship. Old age employment is, hence, a more pressing need with respect to such people. Since they have no formal retirement age, it may not be correct to refer to a pre or post-retirement period.

Be that as it may, there are specific circumstances, which worsen the financial status of the elderly regardless of their (pre-retirement) status of employment. One such contingency consists of serious illness. Health care being very costly nowadays, any major illness may wipe out whatever savings the elderly might have. In case the elderly are not in a position to lay their hands on any savings (or liquid assets) they would be constrained to depend on their children (if any) or other immediate relatives. The children or other close relatives, in turn, may not be able to afford the expenses of treatment of the elderly concerned. It may also happen that the children living far away do not respond positively to their parent's call for help.

In traditional societies, parents continue to support their children even after they have grown up and reached the working age. Besides, at least in limited cases, as a result of late marriage, parents find that the education of their children is not complete even while they are already old or that their daughters have not been given in marriage. To meet all these situations, the elderly may be compelled to engage themselves in gainful employment.

In extreme cases many persons, who stand at the doorstep of old age, realize, to their great frustration, that they do not have a house of their own. Being homeless adds to the agony of old age and they may desperately look for employment in such situations. (Of course, this is on the assumption that their children are not able to construct or buy a house which they can call their own.)

Levels and Statuses of Elderly Employment in India: A Review

We have in the preceding section briefly referred to the various circumstances which compel elderly persons to seek gainful employment. We shall now review the situation at the national level regarding elderly employment as revealed by the quinquennial surveys of the NSS on employment and unemployment in India This analysis is based on the raw data of the NSS (Worker Population Ratios (WPRs), workforce participation rates of the elderly).

We have used the concept of usual status (principal and subsidiary) for comparing the results of the different rounds of the NSS with respect to the elderly (age 60 and above). Age-specific WPRs of the elderly population for the different quinquennial surveys are presented in Table 1. Comparing the WPRs of the entire elderly population of India (usual status, principal and subsidiary) as shown by different NSS rounds, it is observed that there has been no consistent trend over the years. While the WPRs of the entire elderly population increased from 38.45 per cent in 1983 to 39.15 per cent in 1987–8 and to 40.82 per cent in 1993–4, it declined to 36.63 per cent in 1999–2000. This pattern broadly applies to male as well as female elderly. While male WPR increased from 58.79 per cent in 1983 to 60.46 per cent in 1987–8 and to 62.87 per cent in 1993–4, it declined to 56.79 per cent in 1999–2000. On the other hand, while female WPRs declined marginally from 17.96 per cent in 1983 to 16.80 per cent in 1982–8; it rose to 18.27 per cent in 1993–4, but subsequently fell to 16.32 per cent in 1999–2000. One major conclusion arising from this analysis is that compared to the previous rounds of the NSS there was in 1999–2000 a marked fall in the WPRs of the elderly population, male as well as female.

It is noted that the male WPRs is about three to five times as high as female WPRs. This difference is very significant as it goes to show that the male elderly are generally far more keen to work, and probably under greater pressure than the female elderly, to engage in gainful employment even in old age. The difference may partly be explained by the fact that although female life expectancy is higher, physical stamina of females may be lower than that of males and hence the elderly women may be less inclined to engage in gainful employment (frequent child bearing may be an additional debilitating factor particularly among the illiterate and the less educated sections). Another explanation may be that more among the elderly women attend to domestic duties, including looking after grandchildren. A further noteworthy characteristic of the WPRs of the elderly in India is that it has been declining with age, for males as well as females. The decline, however, has been sharper in the case of elderly females compared to elderly males.

Table 1: Age-specific worker population ratios of the elderly and aged 15 and above based on various NSS rounds in India

Round		Rural			Urban			Total		
		Male	Female	Total	Male	Female	Total	Male	Female	Total
38 (1983)										
Age	60–69	74.91	27.38	51.67	58.09	15.04	36.46	69.84	23.51	47.00
	70–79	47.91	11.05	29.63	35.01	7.24	20.41	44.12	9.83	26.80
	80 & above	25.29	4.57	14.92	19.80	4.97	11.76	23.75	4.70	13.98
Total elderly		63.06	20.74	42.24	48.74	11.91	29.86	58.79	17.96	38.45
Aged 15+		84.57	45.61	65.16	76.36	20.71	49.95	81.61	37.16	59.83
43 (1987–88)										
Age	60–69	77.43	25.19	52.30	55.74	13.73	34.81	71.06	21.66	47.04
	70–79	49.82	10.35	30.98	38.60	6.81	22.55	46.55	9.23	28.43
	80 & above	25.68	5.18	15.47	18.26	3.14	10.18	23.58	4.54	13.89
Total elderly		65.57	19.46	43.37	48.06	10.89	29.35	60.46	16.80	39.15
Aged 15+		83.37	43.81	63.81	75.47	21.31	49.67	80.60	36.29	58.97
50 (1993–94)										
Age	60–69	82.58	29.57	57.08	54.54	13.80	33.54	73.47	23.96	49.08
	70–79	57.28	11.33	35.02	34.90	5.97	20.14	49.65	9.38	29.77
	80 & above	24.67	3.90	14.50	15.01	1.61	7.66	21.54	3.03	12.10
Total elderly		71.17	22.60	47.73	45.93	10.58	27.66	62.87	18.27	40.82
Aged 15+		84.77	45.33	65.46	76.28	22.20	50.39	81.46	36.73	59.67
55 (1999–00)										
Age	60–69	77.20	27.10	52.37	49.79	11.82	30.44	67.56	21.54	44.52
	70–79	49.23	10.41	30.92	31.01	5.31	17.81	42.81	8.41	26.05
	80 & above	23.49	2.03	12.97	14.15	1.52	7.16	20.31	1.82	10.82
Total elderly		64.95	20.68	43.30	41.70	9.05	24.90	56.79	16.32	36.63
Aged 15+		82.70	42.89	62.92	74.52	19.62	48.09	79.39	33.84	57.04

Source: Estimated by the authors from the raw data of four rounds of NSS.

Yet another important dimension of the WPRs of the elderly consists in rural–urban differences. Rural workforce participation rates are much higher than the corresponding urban rates, the difference rising from about 13 to 20 percentage points during different NSS rounds. The only reason we can think of for this large difference is the higher level of poverty prevailing in the rural sector. Since poverty is so acute and pervasive among the rural households, even the aged are forced to seek gainful employment. It is well known that it is poverty which discourages people from retiring at an early age; the greater the level of poverty in a society, people are under increasing pressure to go on working till the very end, if possible. On the other hand, higher income groups in developed countries increasingly prefer early retirement so that they can devote their leisure to doing the things which they could not during their active lives.

Comparison of Elderly WPR and WPR of the Entire Population (Age 15 and above)

We know from experience that with advancing age people are normally less inclined to search for gainful employment. This tendency becomes pronounced when they reach the retirement age, whatever that may be. However, there will always be a limited number of persons who, out of sheer financial necessity, would want to engage in gainful employment beyond the retirement age. This may also apply to persons who, though not in dire financial need, are physically fit to work beyond the age of 60 or 65. Thus, the WPRs of the elderly as a group will always be less than that of the entire working population (age 15 and above). However, gender and rural–urban differences are likely to exist. These dimensions are also brought out in Table 1.

We observe that the workforce participation rate of the elderly as a whole is substantially lower than that of the entire population by about 20 percentage points. In the light of our earlier discussion, this difference should not be surprising. We also note that over the years, the rates for the elderly as a group and that for the entire working age population (age 15 and above) have remained almost constant, the rate for the elderly remaining close to 40 per cent and that for the whole population fluctuating within a narrow range between 57.04 per cent in 1999–2000 and 59.83 per cent in 1983.

As regards gender differences in workforce participation rate, we note that the rates for both elderly males and females are significantly lower than the corresponding rates for the entire population. In fact, the difference comes to about 20 percentage points for both male and female workers.

It may also be noted that rural–urban differences in the workforce participation rates of the elderly population and the entire population are large. However, between different NSS rounds we do not see any consistent pattern. The general tendency is for the rural workforce participation rates to exceed the corresponding urban rates by a large margin.

Employment Status of the Working Elderly

Earlier, we have compared the employment levels of the elderly population and the general population (age 15 and above). We have seen that the workforce participation rates of the elderly are substantially lower than the rates of the entire population, whatever basis or yardstick we might apply. In this section we discuss another dimension of employment, namely status. The employment status of the elderly at the national level is given in Table 2.

Table 2: Distribution of the employment status of the working elderly based on various NSS rounds in India

		Rural			Urban			Total		
		Male	Female	Total	Male	Female	Total	Male	Female	Total
Round 38	Self employed	79.23	73.48	77.84	71.07	58.86	68.58	77.22	70.42	75.64
	Regular employee	3.20	1.55	2.80	18.15	19.35	18.40	6.89	5.27	6.51
	Casual labour	16.69	24.51	18.58	9.86	21.53	12.25	15.00	23.88	17.07
	Others	0.88	0.47	0.78	0.91	0.27	0.78	0.89	0.43	0.78
	Total	100.0	100.00	100.00	100.00	100.00	100.00	100.00	100.00	100.0
Round 43	Self employed	81.48	78.11	80.75	72.64	64.65	71.15	79.43	75.40	78.58
	Regular employee	3.46	2.31	3.21	16.43	14.93	16.15	6.47	4.85	6.13
	Casual labour	12.76	18.45	13.99	9.09	19.44	11.02	11.91	18.65	13.32
	Others	2.30	1.14	2.05	1.84	0.99	1.68	2.19	1.11	1.97
	Total	100.0	100.00	100.00	100.00	100.00	100.00	100.00	100.00	100.0
Round 50	Self employed	80.63	74.00	79.11	75.41	63.57	73.07	79.37	71.83	77.70
	Regular employee	2.10	0.96	1.84	13.87	14.49	14.00	4.93	3.78	4.67
	Casual labour	17.28	25.04	19.05	10.72	21.94	12.94	15.70	24.39	17.62
	Total	100.0	100.00	100.00	100.00	100.00	100.00	100.00	100.00	100.0
Round 55	Self employed	82.27	73.95	80.33	76.95	67.88	75.25	80.90	72.69	79.08
	Regular employee	1.88	1.19	1.72	12.68	13.27	12.79	4.67	3.70	4.45
	Casual labour	15.85	24.85	17.95	10.37	18.84	11.96	14.44	23.61	16.47
	Total	100.0	100.00	100.00	100.00	100.00	100.00	100.00	100.00	100.0

Source: Estimated by the author from the raw NSS data.

The most striking aspect of the employment status of the elderly is that the vast majority of them are self-employed; the next highest proportion is accounted for by casual labour. Regular salaried/wage employment forms the least important. This is quite natural because old persons are seldom hired in a regular capacity. While they have better chances of being hired in a casual capacity, their last option is to be self-employed. NSS data shows that while the proportion of the self-employed elderly in India varied from 75.6 per cent in 1983 to 79.1 per cent in 1999–2000, the percentage engaged as casual workers ranged between 13.3 in 1987–8 (43rd round) and 17.6 in 1993–4 (50th round). The proportion of the regular employees varied between 4.5 per cent in 1999–2000 to 6.5 per cent in 1983. Though the general pattern applies to both male and female elderly, it is seen that a large proportion of the elderly males compared to elderly females are engaged in self-employment while the reverse is true of casual labour. The proportion of female elderly employed as casual labour is much higher than the proportion of elderly males.

With regard to rural–urban differences, a large proportion of the rural elderly are self-employed compared to the urban elderly. While the proportion of the rural self-employed has varied from 77.8 per cent in 1983 to 80.7 per cent in 1987–8, that of urban self-employed has ranged from 68.6 per cent in 1983 to 75.2 per cent in 1999–2000. On the other hand, the proportion of urban elderly engaged in regular salaried employment is much higher than that of rural elderly. While the proportion of rural elderly has varied from 1.7 per cent in 1999–2000 to 3.2 per cent in 1987–8, that of urban elderly has ranged between 12.8 per cent in 1999–2000 and 18.4 per cent in 1983. Since the urban sector is characterized by the predominance of non-agriculture, it is but natural that it offers greater opportunities for regular employment even for the elderly. Casual labour is more common among rural than urban elderly as indicated by the above table. It is well known that rural employment provides greater scope for casual labour.

The major difference in employment status between the elderly and the general population (age 15 and above) centres on the proportion engaged in self-employment. For both the elderly and the general population, self-employment is the most important category of employment but the proportion of the self-employed is much higher in respect of the elderly compared to the general population. While the proportion of the self-employed among the elderly has varied from 75.7 per cent in 1983 to 79.1 per cent in 1999–2000, that of the general population has ranged from 54.8 per cent in 1993–4 to 57.7 per cent in 1987–8. It shows that self-employment is the mainstay of the elderly at the national level. Similarly, casual labour is more predominant among the general population than among the elderly as seen from Table 4. Certainly, casual labour is a less preferred option among the elderly compared to the rest of the population. Further, regular salaried employment is less common among the elderly compared to the general population. In view of advancing age and the consequent deterioration of health, prospective employers will be normally hesitant to hire the elderly on a regular salaried basis.

To conclude, other things remaining the same, the older a person, the more inclined he/she would be to take things easy and relax. If somebody opts for gainful employment in old age, the overriding consideration must be financial. In such situations, it is most likely that the elderly chooses self-employment of some sort.

Employment of Elderly Revisited

In many situations, it has also been found that rural elderly continue to work though their number of working hours comes down with increasing age (Singh, Singh and Sharma, 1987). While examining economic self-sufficiency in another context, the same authors concluded that financial problems were more common among widows and among elderly in nuclear families. They also indicated that economic insecurity is related to class and caste. Another observation in this regard by Punia and Sharma (1987) finds economic insecurity to be the sole concern of the elderly in barely sustainable households in rural India. The major sources of worry for the elderly consist of stress and economic dependence. Worries arising from social intercourse are larger compared to economic worries for those who live in nuclear families or living alone (Shah, 1993). Detailed analysis indicates that more elderly men participate in economic activities than women. This may partly be due to the definitional problems related to women's work in the census (Gulati, Rajan and Ramalingam, 1997). In one of the group discussions organized among the rural elderly in Tamil Nadu, we were told: 'For us there is only one retirement, not from work, but from the world' (more details, see Rajan, Mishra, Sarma, 1999; Rajan, Mishra and Sarma, 1995). The Indian census also provides economic data on non-workers by categories such as household workers, beggars, students, pensioners, rentiers and others. As of 2001, around 40 per cent of Indian women were involved in household duties indicating their active participation in maintaining and caring for their children and grandchildren.

Evidence from NSS

In order to revisit the employment status of the elderly, we have used the raw data of the 50th and 55th rounds of NSS and the results are presented for the 55th round in this chapter. The NSS provides detailed break-up of different types of employment to capture the work intensity among the elderly. Among the 14 categories of employment, the following categories (own account worker, employer, unpaid family worker, worked as regular salaried, casual labour in public and other works, attending domestic duties and engaged in household work) are added to arrive at work participation rates of different age groups. Between the two rounds, the rural work participation rates for both males and females have shown a slight decline whereas the urban rates are almost constant for both males and females. The rural work participation rates among males and females were 59 and 66 respectively in the 55th round – seven points higher among females compared to males (Table 3).

Table 3: Workforce participation rates in India by sex and sector, 1999–2000

	NSS 55th Round (1999–2000)								
Work Category	**Rural**			**Urban**			**Total**		
	Male	**Female**	**Total**	**Male**	**Female**	**Total**	**Male**	**Female**	**Total**
NSS 55th Round									
11 Own account worker	24.6	3.6	14.3	19	2.7	11.2	22.4	3.3	13.1
12 Employer	0.9	0.1	0.5	0.8	0.1	0.5	0.9	0.1	0.5
21 Unpaid family worker	9.8	9.7	9.8	4.9	2.4	3.7	7.9	7	7.5
31 Worked as regular salaried	6.2	1.3	3.8	22.9	5.2	14.4	12.7	2.7	7.8
41 Casual labour in public works	0.2	0	0.1	0.2	0	0.1	0.2	0	0.1
51 Casual labour in other works	16.9	8.6	12.9	8.5	2.6	5.7	13.7	6.3	10.1
81 Available for work	1.5	0.5	1	2.9	1.2	2.1	2	0.8	1.4
91 Attending schools	29.4	22.4	26	31.1	28.3	29.7	30	24.6	27.4
92 Attending domestic duties only	0.3	24.1	11.9	0.4	40.3	19.5	0.3	30.2	14.9
93 Engaged in household work	0.2	18.2	9.1	0.1	8.9	4.3	0.2	14.7	7.2
94 Rentier and pensioner	0.7	0.4	0.6	2.4	0.7	1.6	1.3	0.5	0.9
95 No work due to disability	0.8	0.7	0.8	0.8	0.6	0.7	0.8	0.7	0.7
96 Beggars and prostitutes	0	0	0	0	0	0	0	0	0
97 Others	8.5	10.1	9.3	5.9	6.9	6.4	7.5	8.9	8.2
Total	100	100	100	100	100	100	100	100	100
94	0.7	0.4	0.6	2.4	0.7	1.6	1.3	0.5	0.9
95	0.8	0.7	0.8	0.8	0.6	0.7	0.8	0.7	0.7
96	0	0	0	0	0	0	0	0	0
81+91+97+NR	39.4	33.1	36.3	40	36.4	38.2	39.6	34.3	37

Note: Estimated by the author from the raw NSS data.

The rates were 57 and 62 for males and urban areas respectively. In general, work participation rates among females are higher than that among males in both rural and urban areas and the levels are slightly higher among rural areas compared to urban areas. We have also calculated workforce participation rates by age and sex for both rural and urban areas based on the 50th round as an example (Figure 1). The figures clearly indicate a decline in work participation rates among males and females beyond age 50; however, the rates still remain substantial. Even in the 80–4 ages, one-fourth of male elderly and one-sixth of female elderly continue to be economically active.

Table 4 provides the work participation rates among elderly aged 60 and above, 70 and above and 80 and above by sex and sector. According to the latest NSS data, 63 per cent of males and 58 per cent of females continue to work beyond 60. As they grow older, the work participation rate declines; however, even at 80 and above, 22 per cent of males and 17

Figure 1: Age-specific activity rate, NSS 55th round

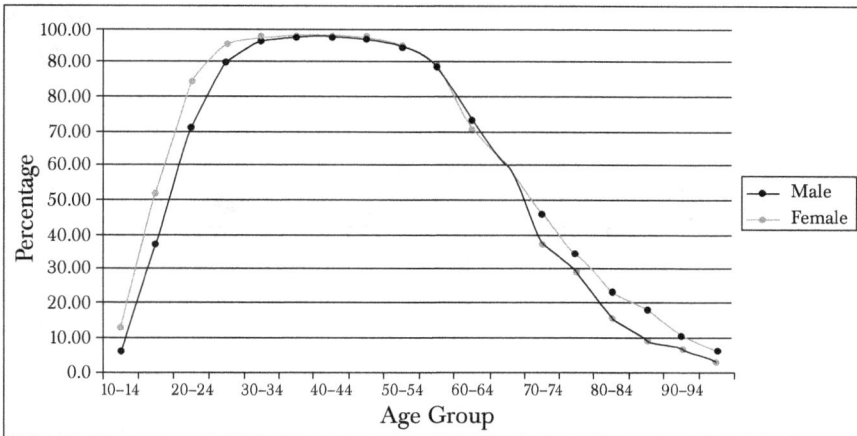

per cent of females continue to work in India. Higher work participation in old age is due to the lack of social safety nets and high levels of poverty.

State level work participation rates among elderly by sex in the different age groups revealed by the 50th and 55th rounds of NSS surveys are presented in Tables 5–7. Rural work participation rates among the elderly, aged 60 and above is much higher compared to urban areas. This is partly due to the predominant rural character of the population whose elderly continue to work. Among the major states, with the exception of Andhra Pradesh, Gujarat, Haryana, Kerala and West Bengal, work participation rates among the elderly are as high as 50 per cent and above among males. The highest work participation rate among males is reported for Uttar Pradesh (67) while the lowest rate is reported for Haryana. Among females, the situation is slightly different. All major states in the country except Assam and Haryana, show their female participation rates as high as 50 per cent or above. The highest work participation among females is reported for Punjab. Compared to 1993–4 sample survey, the 1999–2000 survey reports an overall decline in work participation rates among elderly 60 years and above.

In the case of the elderly 70 years and above, all states except Haryana reported work participation rates as high as 25 per cent or above. The highest percentage was reported for Himachal Pradesh for males and the lowest for Haryana. Though life expectancy at age 70 is just ten years for males, most of them continue to work for their economic survival. The same pattern exists for females too. Except in the case of Assam, Haryana and Orissa, other states report that one-fourth of elderly women aged 70 and above continue to work for a livelihood. In Andhra Pradesh, Assam, Gujarat and Punjab, male work participation rates among the elderly aged 70 and above in 1999–2000 was slightly higher than in the earlier NSS round. The same trend is reported for females in Maharashtra, Punjab and Tamil Nadu.

Table 4: Work participation rates among different groups of elderly

Age	NSS 50th Round								
	Rural			Urban			Total		
	Male	Female	Total	Male	Female	Total	Male	Female	Total
60+	70.8	59.4	65.6	45.9	55.3	51.1	62.6	57.9	60.3
70+	48.8	33.4	41.9	30.8	31.3	31.7	42.7	32.6	37.7
80+	24.7	17.5	22.4	15.8	15.6	17.1	21.8	16.8	19.2
	NSS 55th Round								
60+	64.4	56.0	60.3	40.9	52.7	47.0	56.2	54.7	55.5
70+	43.0	29.3	36.5	26.8	30.3	28.6	37.3	29.7	33.6
80+	23.7	12.5	18.2	13.4	12.9	13.1	20.1	12.7	16.3

Note: Estimated by the author from the raw NSS data.

Ironically, even among the elderly aged 80 and above, one-fourth of the males continue to work in states like Andhra Pradesh, Bihar, Himachal Pradesh, Jammu and Kashmir, and Uttar Pradesh. In a few states like Assam, Haryana, Karnataka and Punjab, one-fifth of the males, aged 80 and above continue to participate in several income generating activities. Around 20 per cent of females aged 80 and above were reported to be active in the states of Andhra Pradesh, Assam, Himachal Pradesh, Punjab and Uttar Pradesh.

One has to view these trends in work participation rates in the context of widespread poverty and inadequate social security systems in India. Only 2 per cent of men aged 65 and above participate in the labour force in some developed countries, whereas in certain developing countries, well over half of the elderly men are economically active. In richer countries, the elderly can afford to retire early because of the availability of pension schemes or social security programmes. These programmes are often lacking in poorer countries (Kinsella and Velkoff, 2001). Cross-national differences in levels of labour force participation rates are associated with societal wealth; countries with high Gross National Product (GNP) tend to have much lower labour force participation rates among the elderly than do low income countries (Clark, York and Anker, 1997).

Table 5: Work participation rate among elderly aged 60 and above, 1999–2000

State	NSS 55th Round								
	Rural			Urban			Total		
	Male	Female	Total	Male	Female	Total	Male	Female	Total
Andhra Pradesh	59.1	53.6	56.2	32.8	47.1	40.3	49.2	51.2	50.3
Assam	57.4	46.0	52.0	30.9	43.7	37.0	53.3	45.6	49.7
Bihar	74.4	62.1	68.8	49.1	57.3	53.1	69.2	61.0	65.4
Gujarat	57.1	54.1	55.5	40.1	46.9	43.9	49.1	50.5	49.8
Haryana	43.5	42.9	43.2	43.8	43.6	43.7	43.6	43.2	43.4
Himachal Pradesh	71.9	63.8	68.1	47.4	67.7	58.1	66.3	64.8	65.6
Jammu & Kashmir	76.4	50.7	63.9	40.5	53.9	46.8	62.9	51.9	57.6
Karnataka	63.4	52.1	57.7	34.4	47.9	41.2	51.0	50.3	50.6
Kerala	52.1	51.6	51.8	40.7	51.6	46.8	47.2	51.6	49.6
Madhya Pradesh	68.0	55.9	62.1	42.7	44.2	43.5	59.9	51.6	55.8
Maharashtra	63.3	61.2	62.2	36.0	49.1	43.0	50.9	55.6	53.4
Orissa	56.7	40.1	48.3	32.4	38.0	35.2	52.8	39.7	46.2
Punjab	59.6	63.9	61.7	48.6	67.6	58.2	55.7	65.3	60.4
Rajasthan	64.4	52.0	58.2	39.2	50.6	45.3	56.3	51.5	53.9
Tamil Nadu	61.2	57.9	59.6	42.9	60.8	52.0	52.6	59.4	56.0
Uttar Pradesh	71.2	61.8	66.8	53.0	57.0	55.0	67.0	60.5	63.9
West Bengal	56.7	49.6	53.2	35.4	58.6	46.6	46.7	53.8	50.2
India	64.4	56.0	60.3	40.9	52.7	47.0	56.2	54.7	55.5

Note: Estimated by the author from the raw NSS data.

Table 6: Work participation rate among elderly aged 70 and above, 1999–2000

State	NSS 55th Round								
	Rural			Urban			Total		
	Male	Female	Total	Male	Female	Total	Male	Female	Total
Andhra Pradesh	45.0	26.6	35.3	21.8	32.2	27.4	36.4	28.8	32.3
Assam	45.5	18.6	34.5	28.0	19.4	23.2	43.4	18.8	32.8
Bihar	51.8	34.9	44.7	38.6	41.9	40.1	49.1	36.5	43.7
Gujarat	33.7	32.0	32.8	23.6	23.7	23.6	29.1	27.6	28.2
Haryana	17.2	17.2	17.2	26.1	14.9	20.4	19.5	16.4	18.2
Himachal Pradesh	51.9	40.7	46.6	53.1	35.9	45.5	52.2	39.7	46.4
Jammu & Kashmir	55.4	26.0	41.1	32.8	39.7	36.2	47.2	31.2	39.3
Karnataka	37.0	19.9	28.2	20.5	31.3	26.2	30.2	24.7	27.3
Kerala	32.5	25.8	28.7	26.9	25.1	25.9	30.0	25.5	27.5
Madhya Pradesh	42.0	28.9	35.8	26.5	19.8	22.9	36.9	25.4	31.1
Maharashtra	40.8	26.2	33.3	21.3	26.8	24.3	31.7	26.5	28.9
Orissa	28.7	17.5	23.1	13.6	17.3	15.3	25.9	17.5	21.7
Punjab	36.9	40.2	38.4	34.1	43.2	38.3	35.9	41.3	38.4
Rajasthan	44.3	22.8	34.3	26.3	28.6	27.6	38.6	25.1	31.9
Tamil Nadu	35.5	32.2	33.9	28.8	34.5	31.7	32.2	33.4	32.8
Uttar Pradesh	52.0	35.8	44.9	37.5	33.2	35.3	48.8	35.1	42.6
West Bengal	35.5	27.9	31.8	20.7	37.1	28.7	28.1	32.5	30.2
India	43.0	29.3	36.5	26.8	30.3	28.6	37.3	29.7	33.6

Note: Estimated by the author from the raw NSS data.

Table 7: Work participation rate among elderly aged 80 and above, 1999–2000

State	NSS 55th Round								
	Rural			Urban			Total		
	Male	Female	Total	Male	Female	Total	Male	Female	Total
Andhra Pradesh	31.1	16.2	22.1	17.6	21.2	19.8	25.3	18.3	21.1
Assam	19.4	15.8	17.6	0.0	20.0	14.3	17.5	16.7	17.0
Bihar	25.9	11.7	20.0	30.4	15.8	23.8	26.9	12.7	20.9
Gujarat	18.6	10.4	14.3	14.0	9.3	11.5	16.1	9.8	12.8
Haryana	2.8	7.7	4.8	0.0	5.6	3.7	2.2	6.8	4.5
Himachal Pradesh	28.6	22.0	25.8	40.0	18.2	28.6	30.3	21.2	26.3
Jammu & Kashmir	33.3	13.8	24.2	23.8	13.3	19.4	29.6	13.6	22.4
Karnataka	20.0	9.3	14.8	18.2	8.1	12.9	19.2	8.8	13.9
Kerala	17.7	5.6	10.6	13.5	5.9	8.6	16.2	5.7	9.8
Madhya Pradesh	12.7	8.3	10.6	6.5	3.6	4.7	10.9	6.3	8.4
Maharashtra	19.7	13.3	16.2	3.4	10.1	7.2	11.7	11.7	11.7
Orissa	8.9	3.6	6.3	14.3	10.0	12.5	10.0	4.6	7.4
Punjab	19.8	18.3	19.0	18.8	29.4	24.2	19.5	21.6	20.5
Rajasthan	17.0	5.2	10.5	13.0	14.7	14.0	15.7	8.7	11.7
Tamil Nadu	12.7	15.1	13.9	14.3	12.3	13.3	13.5	13.6	13.6
Uttar Pradesh	34.3	17.8	27.5	18.2	16.9	17.5	31.3	17.5	25.3
West Bengal	18.0	8.5	12.8	7.0	15.3	11.2	12.1	11.9	12.0
India	23.7	12.5	18.2	13.4	12.9	13.1	20.1	12.7	16.3

Note: Estimated by the author from the raw NSS data.

References

Clark, Robert L, York, Elizabeth Anne and Anker, Richard, 'Retirement and Economic Development: An International Analysis' in De Jong, Phillip R and Marmor, Theodore R, ed, *Social Policy and the Labour Market*, Brookfield, Ashgate, 1997, pp.117–46.

Dandekar, K, *The Elderly In India*, Sage, New Delhi/Thousand Oaks, London 1996.

Government of India, 'Employment and Unemployment Situation in India: 1999–2000', Part I, NSS 55th round, (July 1999–June 2000), May 2000.

Gulati, Leela, Rajan, S Irudaya and Ramalingam, A, 'Women and Work in Kerala: A Comparison Of The 1981 And 1991 Censuses', *Indian Journal Of Gender Studies*, Vol. 4, No. 2, 1997, pp.231–52.

Jhabvala R and Subrahmanya, R K A, eds, *The Unorganised Sector: Work Security and Social Protection*, Sage, New Delhi/Thousand Oaks, London 2000.

Kinsella, Kevin and Velkoff, Victoria A, *An Ageing World*, US Census Bureau, Series P95/01-1, Washington DC, 2001.

National Sample Survey Organization, 'Socio-Economic Profile of the Aged Persons: 42nd round (July 1986–June 1987)', *Sarvekshana*, Vol. 15, No. 2, New Delhi, 1991.

Punia, Deepa and Sharma, M L, 'Family Life of Rural Aged Women' in Sharma, M L and Dak, T M, eds, *Aging In India*, Ajanta Publications, New Delhi, 1987, pp.145–51.

Rajan, S Irudaya, Mishra, U S and Sarma, P S, 'Living Arrangements among the Indian Elderly', *Hong Kong Journal of Gerontology*, Vol. 9, No. 2, 1995, pp.20–8

–, *India's Elderly: Burden Or Challenge?*, Sage, New Delhi/Thousand Oaks, London, 1999.

Shah, V P, *The Elderly in Gujarat*, Department of Sociology, Gujarat University, Ahmedabad, 1993, (Mimeographed).

Singh, Kanta, Singh, Raj and Sharma, M L, 'Problems of Aged Women in Haryana' in Sharma, M L and Dak, T M, eds, *Aging In India*, op. cit., pp.134–44.

Chapter 5

PROPERTY AND ASSETS AS ECONOMIC SECURITY

Praveena Kodoth
S Irudaya Rajan

Introduction

Where social or state protection for the aged is weak or inadequate in contexts of steadily eroding age-based hierarchies, secure property right over resources could turn into a crucial dimension of social security. Where age-based hierarchies were strong, dramatic, if highly uneven, social transformations since the colonial period have meant important shifts in family ideology and practices. In the Indian context, immovable property such as land and house have been owned largely by men and devolved among men, the only exceptions being matrilineal societies on the south-west coast and in the north-east (Agarwal, 1994). Despite differences in 'law' on a religious basis, which gained coherence through the use of religion to codify and evolve law during the colonial period, customs varied according to region and contiguity of communities. Thus, women's right to property under Islamic law, which provided daughters a lesser share than it did sons but protected that share against testation, was subject to the operation of custom which privileged the dominant practice in the region. Transformation of family relations among 'Hindus' through colonial legal interpretation and reform of personal law in the mid 1950s shifted the basis of women's property rights from the category of age to marital status i.e., unmarried daughters, wives and widows (Agnes, 1999). However, the process of transformation since the colonial period also weakened the position of aged men by allowing greater recognition of individual rights very generally over that of the corporate family, which gave aged men greater customary authority. Overriding customary practice, Christians have been brought under the Indian Succession Act, 1925, which not only recognizes individual rights to property, but also provides daughters rights equal to that of sons subject to testamentary rights of parents. Some regions – southern and western India – have experienced a more dramatic social transformation linked to advances in demographic transition and greater dispersion of social and economic changes, while customary hierarchies based on age, gender and caste are likely to have come under less dramatic social pressure in other regions – northern and eastern India. These factors have serious implications for the institutional framework within which the process of ageing is taking place, even as the process of ageing itself portends increasing numbers of aged people relative to those in younger age groups.

The social policy on ageing needs to be informed by the process of ageing usually captured in the context of demographic advance and in terms of the population base which determines the numbers of aged people. The proportion of aged people (defined in terms of those aged 60 and above in a population) is relatively low in developing countries compared to developed countries, where the population structure has already shifted towards the aged. However, some of the developing countries have larger numbers of aged people in absolute terms because of their large population base. For instance, though the proportion of the aged in the population of India was only 7.6 per cent in 2001, their absolute number is around 77 million which is larger than the total population of several developed countries (Rajan, Mishra and Sarma, 1996; Rajan, 2001; 2002a; 2002b). The projected increase in both the absolute and relative size of the aged population in many Third World countries is a major concern for policy (United Nations (UN), 2002; Risseeuw, 2002). In this context, the absence of even a minimal level of social protection for aged people is a serious problem.

In India, state policy has been concerned principally with managing population size through family planning as a core development/poverty concern, an emphasis that not only brought attention implicitly on to marriage as the defining social/sexual contract but also served to overlook long-term intergenerational concerns. Almost imperceptibly, this has meant that development practice has relied on strengthening the conjugal tie and the dyadic relation between spouses with little or nothing said about intergenerational contracts involving the aged. There is growing evidence of intergenerational tensions regarding the claims of the aged (Risseeuw, 2002; Yan, 1997). Recent explorations of the conditions that shape aged people's lives and their access to resources such as their living arrangements, marital status, child status, work status and property rights indicate that there is reason for concern on account of their greater vulnerability to poverty (Rajan, 2004). This paper seeks to analyse property and asset ownership of the aged according to gender, marital status and region to discern patterns and raise questions about the implications of differential access to property for the position of the aged.

Indeed, ownership of property and assets is strongly influenced by social disabilities, particularly restrictive gender norms, besides obvious economic factors (Agarwal, 1994; Chen, 1998; Dreze, 1990; Agnes, 1999). In documenting women's property rights, the literature differentiates between women's status as daughters and as widows, which entitles them to property in very distinct and asymmetric ways. There are strong indications that the basis of women's property rights, very generally, is not only weak but also eroding (Agarwal, 1994; Chen, 2000; Kishwar, 1990). Two factors seem important here: a) prospects of intergenerational transfers and b) access to paid work outside the home. One, for women there are severe constraints on the prospect of property rights through intergenerational transfers. Agnes (1999, WS51) has shown that colonial interpretations of Hindu law anchored women's property rights to martial status, a transformation that was built upon the erosion of the notion of *stridhanam* (women's separate property). Until recently, patrilineal inheritance rights continued to be protected in the Hindu Succession Act, 1956, in the *mitakshara* co-parcenary, which allowed only men birthrights in the Hindu undivided family property or ancestral property. An amendment to the Act in 2005 allowed women to be co-parceners at birth and has given women equal rights to inheritance of agricultural land in all states. However, accepting women as co-parceners rather than abolishing the co-parcenary has reduced the share that would go to the widow (Agarwal, 2005). These law reforms were built upon the interpretations of the colonial period, when property was concentrated in the hands of men. This, along with the continued recognition of unlimited testamentary rights, has made property absolute in the hands of Hindu men. Besides, the continued linkage of women's property to marital status (distinguishing women on the basis of whether they were married or unmarried daughters or widowed) underlined women's dependency in the family, a factor that is aggravated by age and widowhood (Agnes, 1999, WS52).

In addition to this, there is a significant gap between law and practice, which usually works against the interests of women (Chen, 2000; Agarwal, 1994, p.249). It is widely recognized that women's property as daughters continues to be transferred at marriage to their marital family – constituting dowry, a form of transfer that is legally barred. In the northern states, the possibility of women's inheritance rights is tied to their status as widows though this may not be translated into practice (Chen, 2000). The north-western states are known for the most severe customary restrictions on women's property rights, which could be expected to accumulate into old age disadvantage. In contrast, in the southern states, customary institutions endowed daughters with some rights over movable property of the natal family, particularly land (Mukund, 1992). The eastern states fall somewhere in between, conventionally allowing a greater extent of property rights for women as widows and daughters than the north and north-west (Agarwal, 1994). It is of particular interest to us that parts of India had strong matrilineal traditions of descent and lineage under which women's property rights were delinked completely from marriage. However, the colonial period marked the transformation of matriliny towards more marriage-centred property practices in these regions. Changes in family structure and the increasing tendency to link women's property rights to marriage despite legislation providing women inheritance rights (Kodoth, 2005) could have a cumulative dispossessing effect on women of age and widows, and this process and its implications need to be investigated. Significantly, aged women's property rights or its lack is likely to represent the accumulation of disadvantage (or capability) over the lifecycle.

Two, the confinement of women overwhelmingly to unpaid or household work constrains their access to incomes, which may be translated into property. The employment history of women cumulatively leads to aged women's relative deprivation vis-à-vis men as well as the young (Krishnaraj, 1999, WS75) and aged women's social security is more often than not mediated by marriage (Kodoth, 2005). A man's retirement dues from the organized sector jobs are protected against maintenance claims by a wife though a family pension cannot be willed away and older women have some security against transfer of their own property and on their claim of maintenance from their husband's property (Agnes, 1999).

The Data Analytical Categories and Household Context

We have analysed data from the 52nd round of the National Sample Survey (NSS), which had a special focus on the aged, defined as persons of age 60 and above.[1] The information on property rights was garnered from two very broad questions regarding the participation by aged people in: a) ownership and management of financial assets and b) ownership and management of property.

These questions were among the issues probed in Block 11 under 'particulars of family integration' and the responses were categorized into those who: a) own and manage; b) own but do not manage; c) do not own but manage and d) do not own or manage.

The survey defined property as land and buildings and financial asset as company shares, government securities, units from the Unit Trust of India (UTI), National Savings Certificates, etc.

The importance and limitations of this data need to be highlighted. The data on ownership and management tell us only the proportion of aged men and women who own property/financial assets and participate in management but not the extent of property/financial assets owned or managed. However, disaggregation by gender, marital status and other factors give us further insights from this data. Information on ownership of property and assets at the individual level has rarely been made available by the macro-level data collection agencies. Hitherto, we had to go by household level data on property status (such as in land ownership) or we have had to rely almost entirely on primary studies which are usually locality based. In fact, Bina Agarwal's seminal contribution to documenting women's property rights in South Asia and arguing its importance to women's well-being relies on an exhaustive compilation of primary and ethnographic studies from different parts of South Asia. The NSS data has the advantage of being able to provide an all-India and interstate picture on at least some dimensions of ownership of property and assets. The focus on the aged gives the issues a distinct importance as property rights of the aged could be a reflection of lifecycle factors (advantages or disadvantages over the lifecycle), and could highlight distinctions according to gender and marital status.

Property ownership is a sensitive issue and respondents may be cautious in revealing in-depth information. However, the NSS limits its questions to the first level of whether aged persons own and manage assets and property. Thus, the extent of ownership and nature of participation (except the proportion of persons who manage property/assets) is not directly available. It needs to be emphasized that we are dealing with data at a very general level. 'Ownership of any property or asset' could range from those with substantial to those with negligible property or assets. And yet, ownership of any property or asset could be a significant factor in aged people's ability to negotiate their needs.

Existing work on identity and demographic transition suggests that the experience of ageing is highly gendered and varies along dimensions of class, caste, marital status and region. The most obvious illustration of this is the feminization of the aged. Under 'normal' circumstances women have longer life expectancy than men, and thus greater representation among the aged. However, the higher proportion of widows than widowers is a reflection of social and cultural factors i.e., that overwhelmingly, women marry older men and there continues to be strong restrictions against widow remarriage. If we set aside for the moment the emotional aspects of the issues, it would be difficult to deny that widowhood constitutes a defining element of women's identity while being more of an inconvenience for men, prompting them to remarry far more frequently than women. Thus, the intersection of marital status and gender shapes rather different experiences of ageing for men and women. A third dimension that we will be concerned with is region. The process of ageing is embedded in socio-economic transformation and has been articulated very differently across different regions in India. As we have already noted, north and south India have long been regarded as distinct kinship regions, where the south was more favourable to women in terms of marriage and property practices and was ahead of the north in terms of demographic transition (Dyson and Moore, 1983).

There are very obvious indications of the gendered experience of ageing, the implications of which for power relations may be surmised. Most aged men, over 80 per cent of them, report as heads of the households they reside in as against a very small proportion of women, less than 15 per cent of them (see Table 1). In contrast, most women live in households headed either by their children or spouse. This implies that most women transit from households headed by their spouses to those headed by their children and this raises the issue of their greater dependency.

Table 1: Percentage of aged/widowed persons according to relation to the head of the household

Relationship to household head	All aged persons				Widowed persons			
	Rural		Urban		Rural		Urban	
	Male	Female	Male	Female	Male	Female	Male	Female
Self	82.74	13.15	82.06	16.69	40.68	12.84	33.75	15.83
Spouse	0.27	34.80	0.16	31.28	0.00	0.00	0.00	0.00
Parents, In-laws	0.36	0.91	0.51	0.82	1.37	1.12	0.31	1.00
Children	13.69	46.19	14.21	45.30	47.52	76.72	53.75	73.11
Other relatives	2.77	4.87	2.77	5.68	9.40	8.98	10.94	9.32
Non-relatives	0.17	0.08	0.28	0.21	1.03	0.09	1.25	0.48
Total	100.00	100.00	100.00	100.00	100.00	100.00	100.00	100.00

Source: Estimated by the authors using the Unit Level data of the NSS 52nd round.

Significantly, the findings in Table 1 differ considerably from a previous analysis of aged people's relationship to the head and living arrangements using National Family Health Survey (NFHS) data. Irudaya Rajan and Sanjay Kumar (2003, p.78) found that 57.76 per cent of aged men reported as heads of households as against 20.31 per cent of aged women.[2] In contrast, Table 1 shows that more than 80 per cent of aged men are heads of households as against 13 to 17 per cent of aged women. According to a previous analysis, 67.57 per cent of aged women lived in households headed by their children (*Ibid.*) as against only 45 per cent in Table 1. They found that 34.71 per cent of men lived in households headed by children as against only 14 per cent in Table 1. As the NSS is likely to have a more representative sample of aged persons, it is significant that the percentage of aged men reporting as heads is significantly higher than in the analysis of NFHS data and the percentage of aged women reporting as heads is slightly lower. The findings in Table 1 are reinforced by the pattern of living arrangements of aged people. It is significant that although only a small percentage of aged people live alone, there is a higher proportion (and much larger number) of aged women than men in this category (Table 2). Taking only the first two kinds of living arrangements, it is important that while similar percentages of men and women live in old age homes, a higher percentage of widowers than widows do so. As against this, there is a higher percentage of women living alone but not in old age homes.

Table 2: Living arrangements among the elderly in India

Living arrangement	All aged persons				Widowed persons			
	Rural		Urban		Rural		Urban	
	Male	Female	Male	Female	Male	Female	Male	Female
Alone in old age home	0.82	0.87	0.47	0.91	1.59	1.14	0.96	1.14
Alone but not in old age home	1.60	3.99	1.65	3.27	5.02	6.42	4.40	4.96
With spouse only	10.13	6.54	8.52	4.87	Not applicable			
With spouse and other members	63.01	33.59	68.29	31.71				
Without spouse but with children	19.88	48.11	16.37	51.23	77.43	78.90	78.59	80.20
With other relations sans spouse	2.92	4.76	2.98	5.82	7.59	7.48	9.27	8.06
Total	100.00	100.00	100.00	100.00	100.00	100.00	100.00	100.00

* gap in total on account of no response. *Source:* Same as Table 1.

Thus, Table 2 provides some indication of the greater lack of support for women and institutional failures to care for them. Taking into account that a small section of aged people are likely to have been childless, it is nevertheless important that women are over-represented in categories that do not conform to the traditional family units and modern institutional care. Thus, in the context of greater dependency within the family, well-defined property rights could form the basis of secure access to resources and thus could be crucial in ensuring social security of aged women.

Ageing and Property Rights: Some Patterns

Four aspects of aged people's property rights that emerge from Table 3 bear emphasis on the fact that striking gender differentials exist in ownership of property and assets and participation in their management. At the aggregate all-India level, aged women suffer from stark disadvantage in ownership of property and financial assets and participation in their management compared to aged men in both urban and rural India. If more than 75 per cent of aged men in rural and urban India owned property, less than half the aged women did so. Indeed women's disadvantage is reflected in all the important categories of ownership, whether we take those who own financial assets, those who own both property and financial assets or those who do not own anything.

Table 3 also shows that there is a significant gap between ownership of property and participation in its management by aged people in general and aged women in particular. The gender disparity in this category was most striking. As against 65 per cent of aged men who owned property and participated in its management in rural India, only about 20 per cent of aged women in rural India reported doing so – a female–male ratio of 0.33 as against 0.57 of ownership of property. While the significantly lower overall incidence of participation in management of own property could be a response to the inabilities of age, the pronounced disadvantage of women in participation in management of own property/assets is likely to be a response to gender constraints.

Spatial differences are muted, particularly when compared to gender differences. We generally find higher incidence of ownership of property and financial assets among rural men and women, except in the case of financial assets of urban men. Significantly, more urban (than rural) men also participate in management of financial assets, though this is not the case for women. However, lower incidence of ownership of property and participation in management among aged women in the urban (compared to rural) areas were accompanied by slightly more gender disparity. Gender disparity in ownership and management of financial assets is similar to that of property in rural India but slightly more in urban India. Rural–urban difference is less acute in participation in management of own property, than in ownership alone.

Table 3: Percentage of aged persons who own property and financial assets respectively and participate in their management by sex and sector, all India

Ownership of property and/or financial assets by aged persons	Rural			Urban		
	Male	Female	F/M	Male	Female	F/M
Own property	81.92	47.90	0.58	76.48	43.43	0.57
Own property and participate in management	65.65	21.64	0.33	62.29	20.02	0.32
Own financial assets	70.24	41.24	0.59	71.29	38.48	0.54
Own financial assets and participate in management	56.72	18.87	0.33	58.64	17.58	0.30
Percent owning assets of those owning property	84.26	83.28		89.27	84.62	
Own both property and financial assets	69.03	39.89	0.58	8.28	36.75	0.54
Own only property	12.89	08.01	0.62	08.21	06.97	0.84
Own only financial assets	01.21	01.35	1.16	3.02	01.73	0.57
Do not own property or financial assets	16.87	50.78	3.01	20.50	54.55	2.66
Total	100	100		100	100	

Source: Same as Table 1.

There is a significant overlap between those owning property and financial assets. Of the men and women who own property, more than 80 per cent also own assets. In the urban areas this goes up to nearly 90 per cent of men and suggests that ownership of property and assets tend to go together and is highly concentrated. Table 3 also indicates that ownership of property and assets is concentrated in the hands of men. Nearly 70 per cent of aged men in India own both property and assets whereas less than 40 per cent of aged women do so and about half of the aged women do not own either. Notably then, the gender disparity is lowest among those who own only property or only financial assets, which constitute a very small percentage of aged persons.

Thus, while far fewer aged women than men own property and assets and participate in their management in India, women are heavily disadvantaged in both. However, the gender dynamic is sharpest when we turn to the percentage of aged persons who combine ownership and management. If we take this, even tentatively, as a measure of 'effective' ownership, as it includes participation in management, we can see that women's disadvantage is compounded. Needless to say, these results are likely to be influenced by several social factors that distinguish aged people from other groups, particularly the differentiation within the broad age group of above 60 years and men from women, which we will make some attempt to investigate within the limits of the data.

Let us turn to the marital status in the position of widowed persons of age, important as it is in defining the position of women in patriarchal families. Table 4 shows that there is an overwhelming predominance of women among persons of widowed status in the country. Among aged people this is a complex of gendered institutions, which circumscribe the ability of widows to remarry while promoting the possibility of remarriage among widowers, and the greater survival capacity of women, particularly after the reproductive age, reflected in higher female life expectancy. It is widely recognized that widowhood is a source of particular vulnerability in the Indian context (Dreze, 1990; Chen, 2000).

Table 4: Widowed persons as a proportion of all aged persons by sector and sex

Age class	Rural		Urban		Total	
	Male	Female	Male	Female	Male	Female
60–69	0.17	0.48	0.11	0.48	0.15	0.48
70–79	0.25	0.71	0.20	0.75	0.23	0.73
80–89	0.36	0.83	0.35	0.87	0.35	0.85
90–99	0.58	0.92	0.45	0.95	0.54	0.93
Total	0.22	0.57	0.16	0.60	0.20	0.58

Source: Same as Table 1.

It is important to distinguish between young and aged widows. The oppressive institutional edge of widowhood applies far more to younger widows (Chen, 2000; Lamb, 2000). Focus on such institutional aspects, related in particular to sexuality, has meant relatively less scholarly attention on aged widows (Lamb, 2000). As the gendered institutional aspects of widowhood are centred on sexuality, it is not unlikely that the conditions of aged widows (or at least women widowed in old age) are more or less similar to the condition of aged women. Further, the law pegs women's inheritance rights to marital status and widowhood becomes an important node of inheritance. Thus, we would expect a higher proportion of widows in particular to own property than all aged women/currently married women. However, there is a big gap between law and practice (Agarwal, 1994; Sarkar and Banerjee, 1998). It has been noted that widows, separated and other single women are a highly vulnerable group when it comes to property rights over land (Chen, 2000; Dreze, 1990; Gupta, 2000). A summary of the ownership of property and financial assets by widowed people of age at the all-India level is presented below.

In order to interpret the figures in Table 5 meaningfully, we need to see them in relation to those in Table 3. When we do so, two points of significance emerge. Generally, widowed persons, irrespective of sex have lower incidence of ownership of property and assets and participation in their management than all aged persons. Thus, while more than 80 per cent of aged men (48 per cent of aged women) own property in rural India, only 74 per cent of aged widowers (44 per cent of aged widows) do so. The difference is perhaps all the more striking when we turn to aged men and women with no property or assets. As against 17 per cent of aged men, who are without property and assets in rural India, 25 per cent of aged widowers are in the same category. The direction of change is the same for women and for both in the urban areas as well.

Table 5: Percentage of widowed persons of age owning property and financial assets and participating in their management by sector and sex

Ownership of property and/or financial assets	Rural			Urban		
	Male	Female	F/M	Male	Female	F/M
Own property	73.57	44.00	0.60	66.06	39.8	0.60
Own and manage property	50.49	18.02	0.36	45.98	17.92	0.39
Own financial assets	64.22	36.06	0.56	62.62	33.32	0.53
Own and manage financial assets	44.92	15.13	0.34	44.74	15.15	0.34
Percent with assets among those with property	87.29	81.95		94.79	83.72	
Own both property and financial assets	62.89	34.85	0.55	59.27	31.72	0.54
Own property only	10.68	9.15	0.86	6.79	8.08	1.19
Own financial assets only	1.33	1.21	0.91	3.35	1.60	0.48
Do not own property or financial assets	25.10	54.79	2.18	30.59	58.60	1.92
Total	100.0	100.00		100	100	

Source: Same as Table 1.

However, the gender disparity is less among widowed persons compared to all aged persons, and consistently so, as the difference between all aged and widowed persons owning property and/or assets are higher for men than for women. Thus, while the direction of change in property ownership is the same for men and women, the intensity of the change is less for women. This is the case in rural as well as urban India. Thus, widowed men seem to experience a significantly higher incidence of disadvantage in property right than all aged men, widowed women are more or less in a similar position as all aged women.

Table 6 indicates that relative to all aged men, there is a greater concentration of ownership of property and assets in fewer hands among aged widowers. Thus, if 89 per cent of all aged men who own property in urban India also own assets, 95 per cent of widowed men do so, the direction of change being the same in rural India as well. However, the direction of change is not the same for women as there is slightly less concentration of assets in the hands of widows who own property than among all aged women.

We have pointed out that widowhood is a mode of inheritance and thus widowed persons may have been expected to have higher incidence of ownership of property and assets than all aged persons. The relative disadvantage of widowed persons, particularly widowed men could be on account of the specificity of gender based organization of marriage/family. That is, social restrictions on remarriage of widowed persons are applicable almost entirely to women. There are no such restrictions on men. On the contrary, it is likely that widowed men, particularly in the early aged groups, furnish a small but important segment of bridegrooms in contexts where women are unable to pay adequate dowries or for older unmarried women (Gupta, 2000; Sarkar and Banerjee, 1998). It is entirely likely that ownership of property and assets is a factor that shapes a widower's chances of making a remarriage, something we are unable to assert empirically from the NSS data. We are throwing up the possibility that among the widowers' captured in the survey there is a residue of men who have not been able to remarry. Of course, not all may want to remarry and yet it is likely that a significant section do. In contrast, institutional constraints would ensure that most women, who are widowed, at whatever age, are likely to remain so (Chen, 2000).

Could the disproportionate representation of widowed men in the category 'not owing property or assets', as well as the significantly lower incidence of ownership of property by widowed men than all aged men be shaped by remarriage of widowed men endowed with property? To take up this question, we turn to analysis of age and property status.

Property Status and Age

Table 6 shows the considerable influence that increase in age has on the percentage of men and women who own property and participated in its management. As age increases, there is a steady decline in the percentage of aged men and women who own property. The influence of age is even more significant in the participation of management of own property by aged men and women. Nearly 80 per cent of men in the 60 to 64 age group participate in management of own property in rural India, as against only 30 per cent of men in the age group above 85 years. The decline is just as steep in urban India i.e., from 73 to only 22 per cent of aged men.

Table 6: Percentage of aged persons by age groups, sex and sector who own property and participate in its management, all India

Age group	Ownership of property						Participation in management					
	Rural			Urban			Rural			Urban		
	Male	Female	F/M	Male	Female	F/M	Male	Female	F/M	Male	Female	F/M
60–64	88	54	0.61	82	50	0.61	79	29	0.37	73	27	0.37
65–69	85	50	0.59	81	46	0.57	72	23	0.32	70	22	0.31
70–74	81	44	0.54	73	40	0.55	61	17	0.28	56	17	0.30
75–79	78	44	0.56	74	40	0.54	51	14	0.27	52	15	0.29
80–84	71	39	0.55	67	38	0.57	40	11	0.28	39	12	0.31
85+	68	38	0.56	58	30	0.52	30	06	0.20	22	03	0.14
All aged	82	48	0.58	76	43	0.57	66	22	0.33	62	20	0.32

Source: Same as Table 1.

If ownership and management of property responds sharply to increase in age, sex differentials are even more prominent. Notice first that the percentage of women owning property in the 60–4 age group is less than the percentage of men owning property in the 85+ age group in both rural and urban India! As already pointed out, age has a more significant influence on participation in management of own property than on ownership alone. Here too sex is prominent. In the 60–4 age group in rural India, while 54 per cent of aged women own property, only 29 per cent (about half) participate in the management of own property. The decline is much less for men from 88 per cent to 79 per cent. With increase in age, there is a general increase in the gender disparity in ownership of property and participation in management of own property in both rural and urban India.

The spatial dimension too needs to be noted. Incidence of ownership is generally lower in urban India than rural India across age groups and gender disparity is slightly higher in urban than rural India across age groups. However, while there is only a slight difference among women participating in the management of own property in rural and urban India, in the higher age groups the difference favours urban women.

Thus, women seem to 'age' faster than men in relation to ownership of property and participation in management. The question remains, however, regarding whether this is on account of a 'natural' decline in ability to own or manage property or on account of intensification of social vulnerability with increase in age. In this context, the gender disparity is quite revealing. With increase in age, the increase in gender disparity is less in ownership of property when compared to participation in management, where the increase is steady and sharp. Thus, even while there is a sharp difference between the incidence of ownership and participation in management, as they grow older women seem to give up participation in management of property much more than men.

The percentage of aged persons who 'do not own property or financial assets' has been drawn by pooling together the data relating to ownership of property and financial assets respectively. Table 7 shows that the over-representation of widowed men 'not owning property or assets' is more a feature of the early age groups. As we can see in Table 7, the ratio of widowed to aged men 'not owning property or assets' decreases with increase in age in rural India. However, the pattern is not so clear in urban India.

When we turn to aged women, it is significant that the Widowed/Aged (W/A) ratio tends towards unity in virtually all age groups, suggesting similarity in position of women, whether currently married or widowed, a feature that corresponds to earlier patterns related to all aged women and widows. Otherwise, we notice that the percentage of all aged and widowed men and women 'not owning property or assets' increases with age. There is also little rural–urban difference. Thus, in contrast to widowers, the ratio of widowed to all aged women tends towards unity across age groups, indicating that there is a fairly even increase, with age, in the proportion of all aged and widows who do not own property or assets. A related factor is the lower gender disparity among widowed than all aged people in all age groups. Importantly, gender disparity is most pronounced among all aged people in the early age groups in both rural and urban areas. In contrast, the gender disparity tends to converge with increase in age, indicating again that widowed men in the early ages are at considerably greater disadvantage in property ownership than all aged men when compared to widowed women and all aged women.

The aged person's position in the household in which she/he resides may differ along several factors, which would be important in shaping his/her access to resources. Among the factors that we have examined are the economic status of the household they live in, whether they have children and of what sex, their relationship to the head of household and their living arrangements.

Table 7: Aged and widowed persons of different ages 'not owning property or assets'

Age class	All-India Rural							
	All aged persons			Widowed persons			W/A ratio	
	Male	Female	F/M	Male	Female	F/M	Male	Female
60–69	13.57	47.39	3.49	21.22	50.35	2.37	1.56	1.06
70–79	19.42	55.43	2.85	24.59	59.13	2.40	1.27	1.07
80–89	28.49	59.29	2.08	35.97	60.49	1.68	1.26	1.02
90+	36.9	65.57	1.78	38.89	65.48	1.68	1.05	1.00
Total	16.87	50.75	3.01	25.1	54.79	2.18	1.49	1.08
	All-India Urban							
60–69	16.86	50.62	3.00	22.82	53.82	2.36	1.35	1.06
70–79	23.76	59.14	2.49	31.46	61.12	1.94	1.32	1.03
80–89	34.07	64.56	1.89	45.66	67.49	1.48	1.34	1.05
90+	37.66	72	1.91	45.71	72.27	1.58	1.21	1.00
Total	20.5	54.55	2.66	30.59	58.6	1.92	1.49	1.07

Source: Same as Table 1.

Economic Status of Households and Property Rights of the Aged

Does aged women's/widow's ownership of property and financial assets/ or the lack of it, improve with the economic status of household (indicated by per capita expenditure class) they reside in?

The incidence of ownership of property by all aged men and women does not vary significantly over expenditure groups. Thus, around half the aged women across expenditure class do not own property or assets, as against less than a quarter of aged men in both rural and urban areas. Does marital status influence ownership of property/or its absence across expenditure class? We may draw fairly similar conclusions for widowed as for all aged persons regarding the incidence of propertylessness in different expenditure classes. Thus, across households belonging to different expenditure classes, a significant percentage of aged women and widows lack property ownership, as against only a much smaller percentage of aged men and widowers. The gender disparity tends to rise with expenditure class but declines in the highest expenditure class. In the rural areas the gender disparity is least in the lowest expenditure class. However, in the urban areas, gender disparity is least in the highest expenditure class for both all aged and widowed persons. Importantly, gender disparity is consistently lower in comparable expenditure classes of urban India among both aged and widowed persons. It is also less among widowed than all aged persons across expenditure classes in the urban and rural areas. Thus, all aged persons in the rural areas have the highest gender disparity.

Table 8: Persons 'not owning property or assets' and ratio of aged to widowed persons by consumer expenditure class

Age class	Rural							
	All aged			Widowed			W/A ratio	
PCCE	Male	Female	F/M	Male	Female	F/M	Male	Female
0–255	17.72	49.92	2.82	26.70	54.48	2.04	1.52	1.09
255–340	17.36	53.26	3.07	28.17	57.43	2.04	1.62	1.08
340–420	16.43	50.95	3.10	23.14	56.02	2.42	1.41	1.10
420–525	15.04	48.78	3.24	20.22	52.19	2.58	1.34	1.07
525+	15.90	49.3	3.10	21.30	50.50	2.37	1.34	1.02
Total	16.87	50.75	3.01	25.10	54.79	2.18	1.48	1.07
	Urban							
0–350	21.38	56.50	2.64	33.33	61.27	1.84	1.56	1.08
350–500	20.59	54.58	2.65	29.14	58.86	2.02	1.41	1.08
500–665	19.58	53.81	2.75	28.28	58.18	2.06	1.44	1.08
665–915	19.53	53.28	2.73	26.28	57.79	2.20	1.35	1.08
915+	21.68	52.64	2.43	36.89	52.03	1.41	1.70	0.99
Total	20.50	54.55	2.66	30.59	58.60	1.92	1.49	1.07

Source: Same as Table 1.

The disadvantage of aged widowers in property rights when compared to all aged men is spread across expenditure classes as is seen in the W/A ratios. In contrast, widows and all aged women are similarly positioned in terms of property ownership. A notable factor is the decline in W/A ratio with increase in expenditure class in rural India, indicating that widowers in households in the upper expenditure classes are less disadvantaged in terms of ownership of property. For women, in contrast, the W/A ratio is close to unity in all expenditure classes. The expenditure classes relate to the household in which the aged person/s reside and is not an individual characteristic of the aged person. Thus, the aged person may be living in a household in any of the various capacities, which may influence his/her property status and access to resources and power. We turn to analyse some of these factors in the following sections.

Child Status and Property Rights

Does having children and the sex of children have any influence on property status of aged/widowed persons? Table 9 indicates that variation in property status is once again on the lines of the gender of the aged/widowed person rather than whether or not the aged/widowed person has children and of what sex. As noticed in Table 8, gender disparity is higher for all aged than widowed persons and in rural than urban areas, indicating that women's property status is poorer in rural areas and is affected less by widowhood than the property status of men. The generally lower W/A ratios for women than men is a clear indication that women are less affected by widowhood than men, irrespective of child status.

A striking observation from Table 9 is that urban residents and widows, who do not have children, are considerably more disadvantaged, in terms of property status. The relatively lower W/A ratios in this category reflect the more or less general nature of this disadvantage. The lack of children is a likely indication of vulnerability as children (and the possibility of residing with and being cared for by them) constitute important aspects of social security for the aged. In this context, it is important that all aged men and women and widowers in rural areas are an exception to this. This, however, points to the lower incidence of propertylessness among currently married men and women in rural areas, despite lack of children, a situation not shared by widows. It may be pertinent to ask whether this is a reflection of wider traditional social networks in the rural areas, which privileges married women over widowed.

A second significant observation from Table 9 is the poorer property status (higher incidence of propertylessness) consistently in rural India of all aged men and to a lesser extent all aged women who have sons only. However, urban widows too, who have sons only show a higher incidence of propertylessness than is general among them. It may well be that a section of rural parents in their old age transfer their property to their sons. Does dependence on sons increase with widowhood and is this dependence realized in a loss of property right? It is significant that rural residents in the widowed category have poorer property status than all aged persons and that urban widows too have considerably poorer property status than all aged men and women and widowed men in urban India. The significantly higher W/A ratio among widowers and urban widows who have sons only is another indication.

A third observation is that urban widowers who have daughters only have significantly poorer property status than is general among them, worse than childless urban widowers' as well. The significantly higher W/A ratios indicate the wide difference between currently married men and widowers in this category. It is significant that this is not true for widows or all aged men and women in the urban areas. However, we can explore these issues further by taking up property status of the aged/widowed person in terms of their relationship to the head of the household in which they live and in terms of their living arrangements.

Table 9: 'Not owning property or assets' by elderly and widowed with child status

Child Status	All aged			Widowed			W/A ratios	
Rural	Male	Female	F/M	Male	Female	F/M	Male	Female
No children	17.56	50.97	2.90	20.69	58.43	2.82	1.18	1.15
Sons and Daughters	16.09	50.36	3.13	23.56	54.53	2.31	1.46	1.08
Sons only	20.45	52.99	2.59	33.09	56.37	1.70	1.62	1.06
Daughters only	18.02	51.07	2.83	22.76	54.22	2.38	1.26	1.06
Total	16.87	50.75	3.01	25.10	54.79	2.18	1.49	1.08
Urban								
No children	30.00	61.95	2.06	37.50	63.51	1.69	1.25	1.03
Sons and Daughters	20.06	54.11	2.70	29.78	57.83	1.94	1.48	1.07
Sons only	20.26	53.98	2.66	31.40	62.04	1.98	1.55	1.15
Daughters only	19.64	54.16	2.76	40.00	56.11	1.40	2.04	1.04
Total	20.50	54.55	2.66	30.59	58.60	1.92	1.49	1.07

Source: Same as Table 1.

Relationship of Aged/Widowed Persons with Head of the Household

The relationship of the aged or widowed person to the head of household is one of these factors. Indeed, Table 10 reflects the dynamics of power relations within the household in terms of gender and property status. Notice that only 13 per cent of aged men who are heads of households in rural India and 17 per cent in urban India lack ownership of property and assets. As against the above, a substantial section of aged men who live in households headed by their children in rural and urban India (35 per cent and 38 per cent respectively) lack ownership of property and assets. These two constitute the predominant section of aged men in the survey – more than 95 per cent of aged men in rural and urban India live under these two headship arrangements (Table 1). It is significant that only 14 per cent of aged men who live in households headed by their spouses, do not own property or assets in rural India, though it is 30 per cent in urban areas. However, the arrangement is seen only in the most exceptional of circumstances (Table 1). Though less than 5 per cent of aged men are distributed across other headship arrangements, they are significantly more disadvantaged in terms of property status. About 41 per cent of aged men living in households headed by parents, parents-in-law or other relatives and 61 per cent living in households headed by non-relatives do not own property or assets.

Table 10: Aged persons 'not owning property or assets' according to sex, sector and household headship

Household head	All aged			Widowed			W/A ratios	
Rural	Male	Female	F/M	Male	Female	F/M	Male	Female
Self	12.94	32.39	2.50	16.64	32.37	1.94	1.29	1.00
Spouse	13.79	43.36	3.14					
Parents and other elders	41.03	61.29	1.49	50.00	55.38	1.11	1.22	0.90
Children	34.56	59.49	1.72	37.22	60.31	1.62	1.08	1.01
Other relatives	41.08	67.61	1.65	44.35	69.30	1.56	1.08	1.03
Non relatives	61.11	87.50	1.43	66.67	75.00	1.13	1.09	0.86
Total	16.87	50.75	3.01	25.10	54.79	2.18	1.48	1.07
Urban								
Self	16.70	35.24	2.11	18.18	35.40	1.95	1.09	1.00
Spouse	30.00	47.00	1.57					
Parents and other elders	30.30	55.56	1.83	16.67	60.53	3.63	0.55	1.09
Children	37.75	65.17	1.73	47.25	66.56	1.41	1.25	1.02
Other relatives	37.08	66.93	1.81	46.67	69.81	1.50	1.26	1.04
Non relatives	72.22	78.57	1.09	57.14	84.62	1.48	0.79	1.08
Total	20.50	54.55	2.66	30.59	58.60	1.92	1.49	1.07

Source: Same as Table 1.

Women's position in rural and urban India presents a study in contrast. Even when the aged woman is head of the household, she is much less likely than men to own property or assets. Thus, less than 35 per cent of aged women in rural and urban India, who are heads of households do not own property or assets. Nevertheless, aged women's property status is best when they are heads of households (35 per cent or less without property or assets) followed by when they are the spouse of the head of the household. In any other relation to the head of the household, women's property status is poor. It may be noted that 80 per cent of aged women live in households headed by their spouses or children. Of those living in households headed by their children or parents/in-laws, nearly 60 per cent do not own property. As in the case with aged men, aged women who live in households headed by relatives or non-relatives seem to be most disadvantaged in property ownership but their disadvantage is at higher incidence than aged men.

Property Status and Living Arrangements

Table 11 shows generally lower incidence of lack of property among aged men and women, who live with their spouse only and spouse and other members as against those who live without spouse in both rural and urban India. These living arrangements account for most aged people. Significantly, the W/A ratios in the living arrangements without spouse but with children or other relations are close to one for men and women indicating similarity in the position of widowed and all aged persons.

Property status is best for all aged and widowed men and women living alone in old age homes in both rural and urban India, though it accounts only for a tiny section of aged people. Further, widowers in this category in urban India show greater advantage in property status. The W/A ratio for urban men indicates that widows have an advantage in property status over all aged men living in old age homes. The spatial difference is reflected in the significantly higher W/A ratio for rural men as against urban men.

Women and widowed persons living alone, but not in old age homes have better property status than in other living arrangements, with the exception of old age homes. In contrast, all aged men (influenced by the position of currently married men) register better property status when they live with their spouse only or with spouse and other members. Property status of aged men and women is worst among those living without spouse but with relatives. While less than 3 per cent of all aged men live in this category, it accounts for relatively higher percentages of aged women and widowed persons.

Our analysis so far at the aggregate all-India level indicates that gender and age are the most important factors that influence property status or the incidence of ownership of property and assets as well as participation in their management. Beyond this, we have seen that in its influence on property status, marital status is more important for men than for women, as W/A ratios are consistently lower and close to unity for women but not so for men. We also saw that gender disparity was generally lower in urban than rural India for all aged and widowed persons. Other factors that we have used to analyse property status are economic status, child status, relation of aged person to head of household and living arrangements. Women's and widows' generally poor property status improved significantly only when they were heads of household or when they were living alone in old age homes, particularly in the urban areas. The generally higher incidence of property or asset ownership among men and widowers declined significantly when they lived in households headed by other relatives or non-relatives. Additionally, the status of widowers worsened

Table 11: Percentage of aged persons 'not owning property or financial assets' in different living arrangements by sector, sex and marital status

Living Arrangement	All aged persons			Widowed persons			W/A Ratios	
Rural	Male	Female	F/M	Male	Female	F/M	Male	Female
Alone in old age home	11.36	25.84	2.27	16.22	26.87	1.66	1.43	1.04
Alone but not in old age home	19.19	36.12	1.88	23.08	36.34	1.57	1.20	1.01
With spouse only	15.81	43.86	2.77					
With spouse and other members	12.30	44.16	3.59					
Without spouse but with children	23.52	54.81	2.33	22.94	54.79	2.39	0.98	1.00
Without spouse but with relations	34.39	65.64	1.91	32.20	65.60	2.04	0.94	1.00
Total	16.87	50.75	3.01	25.10	54.79	2.18	1.49	1.08
Urban								
Alone in old age home	13.33	16.67	1.25	10.00	15.56	1.56	0.75	0.93
Alone but not in old age home	21.70	31.02	1.43	26.09	32.31	1.24	1.20	1.04
With spouse only	16.97	46.11	2.72					
With spouse and other members	17.07	47.80	2.80					
Without spouse but with children	27.16	59.41	2.19	28.83	59.89	2.08	1.06	1.01
Without spouse but with relations	36.98	60.94	1.65	42.27	62.78	1.49	1.14	1.03
Total	20.50	54.55	2.66	30.59	58.60	1.92	1.49	1.07

Source: Same as Table 1.

considerably in urban areas when they had daughters only or were childless. We now turn to state level analysis in order to get a picture of regional variations in the property status of aged persons according to gender and marital status.

State Level Analysis of Property Ownership

We have seen that more than 80 to 90 per cent of aged persons who own property also own assets. Given this considerable overlap, in further analyses we consider two categories of property ownership: a) aged persons who own property and participate in its management and b) aged persons who do not own property or assets.

We first analyse aged persons who own property and participate in its management across Indian states by sex, sector and marital status. A striking feature to emerge from interstate analysis[3] is that the states of southern India have noticeably lower incidence of ownership of property by aged men and participation in its management in rural and urban areas than other states, at levels considerably below the all-India average. While about 80 per cent of aged men own property in the rural and urban areas of most states, more than 90 per cent do so in the northern hill states.

In contrast, less than 75 per cent of aged men in rural areas of southern states and around 65 per cent in the urban areas own property. At slightly lower levels of ownership for men and women the pattern is similar in urban India as well, but with some significant exceptions. The incidence of men and women owning property is significantly higher in urban areas of Gujarat, Haryana and the North-east than rural areas. In the urban areas of Rajasthan and Bihar there is a higher incidence of women owning property and in West Bengal urban women are at par with rural women. There is a higher incidence of men owning property in the urban areas of Punjab.

When we turn to women, however, the picture is more differentiated. In the rural and urban areas of the southern states less than 45 per cent of aged women own property, at levels lower than the all-India average in the rural and urban areas respectively. This is comparable to the incidence of ownership by aged women in the north-western states, Maharashtra and West Bengal in both rural and urban areas and Madhya Pradesh in urban areas alone. On the other hand, more than 60 per cent of aged women in the north-eastern and northern hill states own property, in both urban and rural areas. The northern and eastern states and Gujarat fall in between. Corresponding to the incidence of ownership among women, the southern states, the north-western states, Maharashtra and West Bengal have higher gender disparity than all-India in the urban and rural areas, Kerala being a significant exception. However, in the rural areas gender disparity is more severe in the north-west and West Bengal than in the southern states. Gender disparity is least in the north-eastern and northern hill states followed by the northern states, Orissa and Bihar.

Now, let us turn to participation in the management of property. Reiterating from Table 3, gender disparity worsens significantly when we turn from ownership alone to participation in management of own property, own financial assets or both. We have also seen the variations over age groups – that both age and gender influence participation in management.[4] On the lower side, less than 60 per cent of aged men in the southern Indian states, Orissa, Assam and rural Punjab reported participation in management of own property, which is lower than all-India. Men fared better in rural West Bengal than all-India.

Table 12: Aged persons owning property and participating in its management by sector, sex and state

	Ownership of Property						Participation in management					
	Rural			Urban			Rural			Urban		
	Male	Female	F/M	Male	Female	F/M	Male	Female	F/M	Male	Female	F/M
Andhra Pradesh	66.13	33.83	0.51	62.87	27.90	0.44	48.13	13.12	0.27	47.52	11.83	0.25
Tamil Nadu	74.36	42.51	0.57	66.56	33.62	0.51	55.68	16.96	0.30	52.25	16.98	0.32
Kerala	75.45	45.55	0.60	67.19	43.67	0.65	61.61	19.97	0.32	52.86	18.16	0.34
Karnataka	75.77	39.39	0.52	66.25	30.97	0.47	54.65	13.89	0.25	49.38	12.09	0.24
Maharashtra	79.44	41.91	0.53	74.36	39.75	0.53	64.16	20.69	0.32	61.36	17.18	0.28
Gujarat	81.27	50.88	0.63	85.60	55.30	0.65	65.17	18.73	0.29	71.60	25.38	0.35
Rajasthan	85.53	41.14	0.48	81.40	44.07	0.54	73.42	16.36	0.22	68.18	20.00	0.29
Punjab	77.62	34.97	0.45	79.23	32.95	0.42	58.39	16.58	0.28	73.08	19.38	0.27
Haryana	80.41	36.45	0.45	80.79	43.21	0.53	65.54	17.06	0.26	68.56	18.93	0.28
Uttar Pradesh	87.00	51.44	0.59	85.43	51.19	0.60	73.58	27.82	0.38	74.20	28.30	0.38
Madhya Pradesh	78.86	48.23	0.61	75.89	41.03	0.54	66.38	26.51	0.40	64.03	24.79	0.39
Bihar	83.42	53.57	0.64	82.92	57.89	0.70	70.93	24.11	0.34	68.68	24.44	0.36
Orissa	84.10	52.20	0.62	78.01	46.20	0.59	56.49	13.00	0.23	58.87	17.09	0.29
West Bengal	87.85	41.25	0.47	80.17	41.23	0.51	71.88	12.82	0.18	60.67	16.49	0.27
Assam	88.92	51.10	0.57	80.53	45.71	0.57	61.79	9.09	0.15	58.41	10.48	0.18
Jammu & Kashmir	91.88	68.82	0.75	86.52	60.71	0.70	73.62	36.56	0.50	74.47	26.79	0.36
Himachal Pradesh	93.35	69.52	0.74	98.00	80.43	0.82	80.56	48.13	0.60	94.00	60.87	0.65
North East region	78.30	59.85	0.76	82.14	64.20	0.78	60.92	28.36	0.46	65.24	28.16	0.43
India	81.92	47.90	0.58	76.48	43.73	0.57	65.65	21.64	0.33	62.29	20.02	0.32

Source: Same as Table 1.

However, the lowest incidence of participation in management by aged women is in the eastern states, in both rural and urban areas, though they have a relatively higher incidence of ownership than women in the southern or north-western states. Women in the eastern states are followed by women in the southern and north-western states. In all these states, less than 20 per cent of aged women participate in management of property in rural and urban areas, but considerably below that in rural areas of the eastern states. In striking contrast are the significantly higher incidence of participation in management of own property by aged women and men in the northern hill states and aged women in the north-eastern states. The northern and western states fall in between. Not surprisingly, gender disparity is highest in the east and north-west followed by the south, with the exception of Kerala, and least in the north-eastern and northern hill states. Noticeably, there is a sharp increase in gender disparity when we move from ownership of property to participation in management of owned property.

At the aggregate all-India level, spatial differences are less sharp in participation in management of own property than in ownership alone. At the state level this is reflected in higher incidence of participation in management of property by men and women in the urban areas in several states – Gujarat, Punjab, Haryana, UP and Orissa; by women in Rajasthan, Bihar, West Bengal and Assam; and by men in Jammu and Kashmir and the north-east.

Let us now turn to the influence of marital status by analysing the position of widowed men and women relative to all aged persons across states. It is evident from Table 13 that very generally speaking, incidence of ownership of property and participation in its management is lower among widowed than all aged persons across states, with the significant exceptions of women in Kerala, Punjab, Assam and Himachal Pradesh. In rural areas, men suffer significant disadvantage as widowers, reflected in lower W/A ratios than all-India in ownership of property and participation in its management in several states, including the southern states, Bihar, West Bengal, Punjab and Gujarat. In urban areas, relative disadvantage of widowers is pronounced in Tamil Nadu, Karnataka, Gujarat and to a smaller extent MP. Besides, the incidence of ownership by widowed men in the southern states (Table in Appendix) is well below all-India in urban and rural areas, compounding their existing disadvantage among all aged persons.

The picture is significantly different for widows, as we observed in the case of all aged women relative to men. Despite the lower incidence of ownership in southern India, the relative position of all aged women and widows is not so different in the rural areas in ownership of property and participation in management. The W/A ratios in ownership of property are higher than all-India in the rural areas of the southern states, Punjab and West Bengal, but also Assam and the North-east. However, in the urban areas of the southern states, widows experience higher relative disadvantage than all-India in ownership of property, with the exception of Kerala.

Widows in the rural and urban areas of Andhra Pradesh are particularly at a disadvantage in management of property. In both rural and urban areas of the northern states, Rajasthan and Haryana widows register greater disadvantage relative to all aged in ownership of property as well as in participation in management. In the urban areas of Maharashtra, Punjab, Assam and West Bengal incidence of ownership of property by widows

Table 13: Ratio of widowed to all aged persons who own property and participate in its management

State	Ownership of Property				Participation in management of own property			
	Rural		Urban		Rural		Urban	
	Male	Female	Male	Female	Male	Female	Male	Female
Andhra Pradesh	0.79	0.99	0.89	0.89	0.74	0.79	0.76	0.88
Tamil Nadu	0.69	0.93	0.76	0.83	0.60	0.85	0.57	0.87
Karnataka	0.88	0.92	0.69	0.83	0.76	0.95	0.53	1.04
Kerala	0.87	1.09	0.89	1.05	0.61	1.20	0.88	1.22
Maharashtra	0.89	0.90	0.85	1.01	0.76	0.77	0.76	1.06
Gujarat	0.80	0.88	0.80	0.87	0.78	1.07	0.54	0.99
Rajasthan	0.96	0.80	0.93	0.87	0.88	0.62	0.73	0.64
Punjab	0.85	1.05	0.78	0.99	0.69	0.95	0.75	0.93
Haryana	0.96	0.84	0.92	0.79	0.79	0.88	0.71	0.87
Uttar Pradesh	0.94	0.85	0.89	0.93	0.83	0.77	0.76	0.83
Madhya Pradesh	0.87	0.75	0.78	0.81	0.77	0.61	0.72	0.70
Bihar	0.83	0.82	0.88	0.81	0.74	0.68	0.81	0.68
Orissa	0.91	0.92	0.94	0.93	0.70	0.76	0.98	0.88
West Bengal	0.88	0.98	0.92	0.96	0.72	0.87	0.76	0.90
Assam	0.91	1.03	0.98	1.01	0.64	1.00	0.73	1.29
Jammu & Kashmir	0.96	0.94	0.71	0.90	0.80	1.01	0.67	0.85
Himachal Pradesh	0.91	1.02	1.02	1.09	0.86	0.96	0.93	0.92
North East Region	0.93	0.98	0.95	0.90	0.68	0.87	0.78	0.87
Total	0.90	0.92	0.86	0.91	0.77	0.83	0.74	0.90

Source: Same as Table 1.

are above all-India (in Appendix). Thus, apart from Kerala and Assam, where widows have higher incidence of ownership and participation in management than all aged women, disadvantage of widows relative to all aged is significantly less than all-India in Punjab and West Bengal. Notably these were states that recorded low incidence of ownership among aged women and widows, along with the southern states.

To sum up, the relatively low incidence of ownership of property in the southern states, and Maharashtra to a lesser extent, is shared by men and women, while it is peculiar to women in the north-western states and West Bengal. Aged men and women in the southern and north-western states, register relatively low incidence of participation in management of own property as well, with the exception of Kerala, but here they are joined by women of the eastern states. Importantly, there is less difference between the position of aged women and widows in terms of property ownership than between widowed and all aged men in virtually all states. In the rural areas of the southern states, widows seem to be very similarly positioned as all aged women. Thus, keeping in mind the existing low incidence of aged women's property rights, widowhood has a somewhat greater effect on ownership of property by aged men than by aged women in most states. These broad patterns bear thinking about in the context of demographic transition and associated institutional changes, which have been articulated differently over these states. Before we do so, however, let us look at a more comprehensive measure of property rights among aged persons in the proportion of people who do not own any property or financial assets.

At significantly lower levels of propertylessness than women, men who lack property and assets in the southern states are three times more than in the northern hill states – ranging between less than 10 per cent in Himachal Pradesh, Sikkim and Jammu and Kashmir to about 30 per cent in Andhra Pradesh. As against this, aged men predominantly hold both property and assets across states (Table in Appendix). As in the case of aged men who do not own anything, the southern states fall well below all-India, in the case of aged men who own both. Aged men in Maharashtra and rural Punjab too fall below all-India but at higher incidence than southern India. As against the above, aged women who do not own property or assets range from 25 per cent in Himachal Pradesh to about 65 per cent in Andhra Pradesh. Corresponding to the pattern in ownership of property category, the percentage of aged women who lack property and assets in the southern states is comparable to women in the north-west, West Bengal and Maharashtra, and well below all-India in both rural and urban areas. The percentage of aged women who own both property and assets is well below all-India in the southern states, Punjab, West Bengal and Maharashtra i.e., about half or less than half the percentage of men in the urban and rural areas. The percentage of aged men and women who do not own property or financial assets is lowest in the northern hill states and the north-east, those who own both is highest in these states. Significantly, however, gender disparity is relatively low in the southern states, with female–male ratios less than 2.5 compared to more than 3.0 in the north-western states. However, the highest gender disparity is 4.5 in West Bengal and the lowest, not surprisingly, is less than 2 in the north-eastern states. Gender disparity is high in the northern hill states but at relatively low levels of propertylessness. Significantly, in the own both category, gender disparity is well below all-India and among the lowest in these states as against the southern and north-western states and West Bengal which have noticeably high incidence of gender disparity in rural and urban areas.

The striking inter-regional variation corresponds only partly with our received understanding of women's property rights in the country. The broader base of women's property rights in southern India should have translated into cumulatively higher incidence of ownership of combined assets in old age. However, the relatively low property status of the aged in the southern states is generalized for men and women, bringing to the fore the influence of the process of demographic transition. The process of ageing is more advanced in these states and in the north-west (except Rajasthan) than elsewhere in the country.

Table 14: Percentage of aged persons 'not owning property or financial assets' in Indian states by sector, sex and gender disparity

State	Rural			Urban			Total		
	Male	Female	F/M	Male	Female	F/M	Male	Female	F/M
Andhra Pradesh	31.73	64.51	2.24	31.19	69.87	2.03	31.50	66.94	2.12
Tamil Nadu	24.36	55.73	2.28	27.79	63.33	2.29	26.16	60.02	2.29
Karnataka	22.54	59.85	2.22	30.00	66.67	2.66	26.07	62.99	2.42
Kerala	22.73	53.63	2.02	27.34	55.31	2.36	24.52	54.30	2.21
Maharashtra	19.86	57.45	2.50	23.69	59.14	2.89	21.74	58.24	2.68
Gujarat	17.23	48.06	3.75	11.52	43.18	2.79	14.51	45.70	3.15
Rajasthan	13.42	57.27	3.39	16.12	54.58	4.27	14.47	56.19	3.88
Punjab	21.17	63.73	3.26	20.00	65.12	3.01	20.72	64.29	3.10
Haryana	19.26	61.54	3.46	16.16	55.97	3.20	17.90	59.04	3.30
Uttar Pradesh	11.11	46.97	3.65	13.07	47.69	4.23	11.62	47.18	4.06
Madhya Pradesh	20.08	50.10	2.46	23.32	57.26	2.49	21.21	52.45	2.47
Bihar	16.28	45.54	2.69	14.23	38.35	2.80	15.83	43.89	2.77
Orissa	15.36	47.20	2.33	21.99	51.27	3.07	16.72	48.18	2.88
West Bengal	10.32	58.23	3.73	15.29	57.02	5.64	12.79	57.63	4.50
Assam	10.61	48.28	2.87	18.58	53.33	4.55	12.29	49.53	4.03
Jammu & Kashmir	7.54	30.47	3.01	12.77	38.39	4.04	9.05	32.74	3.62
Himachal Pradesh	6.39	25.67	8.70	2.00	17.39	4.01	5.90	24.76	4.20
North East Region	19.83	37.38		16.43	34.37		18.55	36.07	
India	16.87	50.75	2.66	20.50	54.55	3.01	18.23	52.24	2.87

Source: Same as Table 1.

We have presented the ratio of widowed persons to all aged persons in the category 'not owning property or financial assets' in Table 15 as a more comprehensive measure of the propertied position of widowed people among all persons of the aged. Table 15 really substantiates the broad trends in the earlier tables.

Table 15: Ratio of widowed to all aged persons in ownership of property and assets

State	Not owning property or assets				Owning both property and assets			
	Rural		Urban		Rural		Urban	
	Male	Female	Male	Female	Male	Female	Male	Female
Andhra Pradesh	1.41	1.01	1.31	1.05	0.78	1.01	0.89	0.76
Tamil Nadu	1.92	1.05	1.56	1.09	0.65	0.85	0.74	0.79
Karnataka	1.48	1.05	1.52	1.08	0.92	0.90	0.72	0.75
Kerala	1.51	0.93	1.46	0.96	0.77	1.01	0.91	0.94
Maharashtra	1.47	1.07	1.47	1.00	0.96	0.86	0.85	0.99
Gujarat	1.88	1.13	2.56	1.16	0.88	0.87	0.85	0.82
Rajasthan	1.27	1.14	1.21	1.12	0.96	0.75	0.96	0.82
Punjab	1.54	0.98	1.90	1.01	0.90	1.04	0.78	0.91
Haryana	1.16	1.09	1.44	1.15	0.98	0.73	0.90	0.81
Uttar Pradesh	1.46	1.16	1.61	1.09	0.94	0.82	0.88	0.90
Madhya Pradesh	1.54	1.27	1.67	1.13	0.84	0.69	0.78	0.81
Bihar	1.84	1.21	1.72	1.29	0.80	0.79	0.93	0.77
Orissa	1.45	1.10	1.20	1.05	0.92	0.91	0.82	0.92
West Bengal	1.99	1.01	1.38	1.05	0.88	0.97	0.87	0.95
Assam	1.68	0.96	1.15	0.99	0.83	1.01	1.08	0.93
Jammu & Kashmir	1.22	1.14	3.05	1.14	0.98	0.95	0.78	0.92
Himachal Pradesh	2.09	0.94	0.00	0.69	0.90	0.98	0.83	1.09
North East Region	1.32	1.06	1.11	1.17	0.94	0.98	0.93	0.87
Total	1.49	1.08	1.49	1.07	0.91	0.87	0.87	0.86

Source: Same as Table 1.

The predominantly high levels of aged women's propertylessness (corresponding to low levels of property ownership) as against the predominantly low levels of aged men's propertylessness is reiterated in Table 16, which shows that almost all the states are below the diagonal. The exceptions as already noted are southern India, where the incidence of ownership of property or assets is low for both men and women and northern hill states and north-east, where the incidence of ownership of property or assets is relatively high for both.

Table 16: Aged women who do not own property or financial assets in the Indian states according to corresponding aged men in the same category[5]

Level of Demographic transition	Incidence of lack of property among aged women (%)		
	High (55 and above)	Medium (40–54)	Low(0–39)
Advanced	South, Punjab, Haryana		
Middle	Maharashtra, West Bengal	Gujarat	North East North Hill
Low	Rajasthan	North, Orissa, Assam	

Source: Same as Table 1.

If access to property is shaped by different cultural expressions of patriarchy in different regions of the country (as summarized earlier), the process of development, inclusive of demographic transition and ageing, may well alter or accentuate these cultural expressions significantly. To contextualize aged women's property status in terms of demographic transition, we have organized the states according to the level of demographic transition and the property status of aged women, considering the percentage of women who do not own property or assets in each of the Indian states (Table 17). The states are grouped into three levels of demographic transition – advanced, middle and low and the incidence of lack of property – high, middle and low.

Table 17: Aged women who do not own property or financial assets in the Indian states according to levels of demographic transition

Level of Demographic transition	Incidence of lack of property among aged women (%)		
	High (55 and above)	Medium (40–54)	Low(0–39)
Advanced	South, Punjab, Haryana		
Middle	Maharashtra, West Bengal	Gujarat	North East North Hill
Low	Rajasthan	North, Orissa, Assam	

Source: Same as Table 1.

Significantly, most of the states fall below the diagonal, suggesting the predominant tendency towards low property status or high propertylessness among aged women in the course of demographic transition. It is significant that all the states in the more advanced stage of demographic transition (South, Punjab and Haryana) show the highest incidence of propertylessness among aged women. At the middle level of demographic transition, states are distributed across three levels of property ownership. West Bengal and Maharashtra with middle levels of demographic transition show high incidence of propertylessness among aged women.

Given the overall picture, Gujarat, northern hill and north-eastern states are exceptional, with middle levels of demographic transition corresponding to middle or relatively low incidence of women's propertylessness. Again, it is significant that most of the states at the lower levels of demographic transition – the northern states, Orissa and Assam – have middle levels of propertylessness, only Rajasthan has high incidence of propertylessness among aged women. This may well be in accordance with cultural expressions of patriarchy in contexts where there has not been any dramatic transformation in patriarchal family structures and practices, such as would be expected to occur with the progress of demographic transition. Customary patriarchal family structures privileged age and women do gain power when they age.

As already noted in Table 13, the levels of property ownership are generally lower among widowed persons than all aged persons. As in Table 13, significant exceptions to this are Kerala, Assam, Himachal Pradesh and Punjab, which show an improvement in the property status of widows compared to all aged women. Table 18 substantiates this, as Kerala moves up to moderate levels of lack of property among widows.

Table 18: Aged widows who do not own property or financial assets according to level of demographic transition

Level of Demographic transition	Incidence of lack of property and assets among widows (%)		
	High (55 and above)	Medium (40–54)	Low (0–39)
Advanced	Andhra Pradesh, Tamil Nadu, Karnataka, Punjab, Haryana	Kerala	
Middle	Maharashtra, West Bengal	Gujarat	North Hill North East
Low	Rajasthan, Madhya Pradesh	Uttar Pradesh, Bihar, Orissa, Assam	

Source: Same as Table 1.

In contrast, the property status of widowers does not improve compared to all aged men, but it gets significantly worse in Gujarat, Punjab, Tamil Nadu and rural areas of West Bengal. Also widowers, as a group, experience a greater decline in property status in relation to all aged men than do widows in relation to all aged women in the states, with the exceptions of

Madhya Pradesh, Rajasthan, Bihar and Haryana (Appendix Table 7). The decline is sharp, with widowhood in Madhya Pradesh leading the shift from moderate lack of property or assets to high levels.

See Appendix for the tables in this chapter.

Notes

[1] We have used the sample data available in the raw form and not adjusted with weights for population.

[2] We need to keep in mind the sampling structure of the NFHS, which is tuned towards reproductive health concerns, particularly in selecting only those households that have women in the reproductive ages. Such a sample is far from likely to represent the generality of aged persons in particular.

[3] We have referred to states both individually and as part of regional clusters. The regional cluster are: South comprising Andhra Pradesh, Karnataka, Kerala, Tamil Nadu; West comprising Maharashtra and Gujarat; North west comprising Rajasthan, Punjab and Haryana, Northern hill states comprising Jammu and Kashmir and Himachal Pradesh; North comprising Uttar Pradesh, Madhya Pradesh and Bihar, East comprising West Bengal, Assam and Orissa, and the North east comprising Arunachal Pradesh, Meghalaya, Manipur, Tripura, Mizoram and Nagaland.

[4] Numbers will not allow disaggregation over states.

[5] As the percentage of aged people not owning property or assets varies on the high side for women and on the low side for men, low, middle and high are relative to the average for men and women respectively.

References

Agarwal, Bina, *A Field of One's Own: Gender and Land Rights in South Asia*, Cambridge University Press, Cambridge, 1994.

–, 'Landmark Steps to Gender Equality', *The Hindu,* 25 September 2005.

Agnes, Flavia, 'Law and Women of Age: A Short Note', *Economic and Political Weekly*, Vol. 34, No. 44, 1999, pp.WS51–WS53.

Chen, Martha Alter, ed, *Widows in India: Social Neglect and Public Action,* Sage Publications, New Delhi/Thousand Oaks, London 1998.

–, *Perpetual Mourning: Widowhood in Rural India,* Oxford University Press, New Delhi, 2000.

Dreze, Jean, 'Widows in Rural India', Suntory-Toyota International Centre for Economics and Related Disciplines, London School of Economics and Political Science, 1990.

Dyson, Tim and Moore, M, 'On Kinship Structure, Female Autonomy, and Demographic Behavior in India' in *Population and Development Review,* Vol. 9, No. 1, 1983, pp.35–60.

Gupta, Jayoti, 'Women, Land and Law: Dispute Resolution at the Village Level', Occasional Paper 3, Sachetana Information Centre, Calcutta, 2000.

Kishwar, Madhu, 'Codified Hindu Law: Myth and Reality', *Economic and Political Weekly*, Vol. 29, No. 33, 1994, pp.2145–61.

Kodoth, Praveena, 'Fostering Insecure Livelihoods: Dowry and Female Seclusion in Left Development Contexts in West Bengal and Kerala', *Economic and Political Weekly*, Vol. XL, No. 25, 18 June 2005, pp.2543–54.

Krishnaraj, Maithreyi, 'Ageing Women in a Welfare State: Cracks in the Utopia?', *Economic and Political Weekly*, Vol. 34, No. 44, 1999, pp.WS75–WS88.

Lamb, Sarah, *White Saris and Sweet Mangoes: Aging, Gender, and Body in North India*, University of California Press, Berkeley, 2000.

Mukund, Kanakalatha, 'Turmeric Land: Women's Property Rights in Tamil Society since Early Medieval Times', *Economic and Political Weekly*, 25 April 1992.

Rajan, S Irudaya , 'Social Assistance for Poor Elderly: How Effective?', *Economic and Political Weekly*, Vol. 36, No. 8, 24 February 2001, pp.613–17.

–, 'Home Away from Home: A Survey of Old Age Homes and Inmates in Kerala, India', *Journal of Housing for the Elderly*, Vol. 16, Nos. 1 and 2, 2002a, pp.125–50

–, 'Social Security for the Unorganized Sector in South Asia', *International Social Security Review*, Vol. 55, No. 4, 2002b, pp.143–56.

–, 'Chronic Poverty among Indian Elderly', Working Paper 17, Chronic Poverty Research Centre and Indian Institute of Public Administration, Indian Institute of Public Administration, New Delhi, 2004.

Rajan, S Irudaya and Kumar, Sanjay, 'Living Arrangements among Indian Elderly: Evidence from National Family Health Survey', *Economic and Political Weekly*, Vol. 38, No. 1, 2003, pp.75–80.

Rajan, S Irudaya, Mishra, U S and Sarma, P S, *'INDIA: National Aging Trends'*, in Life Long Preparation for Old Age in Asia and the Pacific, United Nations, ST/ESCAP/1684, New York, 1996, pp.79–104.

Risseeuw, Carla, 'Policy Issues of Inclusion and Exclusion in Relation to Gender and Ageing in the South', *The European Journal of Development Research*, Vol. 13, No. 2, 2001, pp.26–48.

–, 'Ageing: A Gendered Policy Concern in the South and the North' in *Sustainable Social Structures in a Society for all Ages*, Economic and Social Affairs, United Nations, 2002, pp.29–41.

Sarkar, Lotika and Banerjee, Narayan, 'Widows in a Tribal setting in West Bengal' in Chen, Martha, ed, *Widows in India: Social neglect and Public Action*, Sage, New Delhi, 1998.

UN, 'Sustainable Social Structures in a Society for All Ages', Department of Economic and Social Affairs, 2002.

Yan, Yunxiang, 'The Triumph of Conjugality', *Ethnology*, Vol. 36, No. 3, 1997, pp.191–212.

Chapter 6

PENSIONS AND SOCIAL SECURITY IN INDIA

S Irudaya Rajan
Syam Prasad

Introduction

In India, several mechanisms exist to provide economic and social safety nets to the economically and socially vulnerable groups. In broad terms, they are achieved through a formal or informal social security system that ensures equitable justice in society (Heller, 2003). This notion of the safety net enabled all societies to go in for the social security system. The International Labour Organization (ILO) has defined social security as 'the protection which society provides for its members, through a series of public measures, against economic and social distress otherwise caused by the stoppage or substantial reduction of earnings resulting from sickness, maternity, employment injury, unemployment, invalidity, old age and death' (ILO, 1942). Sir William Beveridge, father of the British social security system, defined it as, 'security of an income to take the place of earning when they are interrupted by unemployment, sickness, or accident; to provide retirement benefits, to provide against loss of support by the death of the other person and to meet exceptional expenditure such as those connected with birth, death and marriage' (Beveridge, 1943). According to Pierre Laroque, former president of the National Social Security Fund in France, social security represents 'a guarantee by the whole community to all its members of the maintenance of their standard of living or at least tolerant living conditions by means of a redistribution of income based on national solidarity' (Laroque, 1969). Leal de Araujo has viewed social security systems as 'supplementary machineries or economic agents for redistribution of income' (de Araujo, 1972).

Social security received widespread attention with the spread of the ideology of the Paternalist State and its welfare norms originating in the human mind as a part of its social, ethical and political consciousness. Social security as a system evolved first in the Western countries during the industrial revolution. The two models under which social security systems can be classified are the German model (Bismarckian model or social security/social market economy model) and the British model (Beveridgean model or the Basic-income model). The Bismarckian model focused on maintenance of living standards and the benefits were earnings related; on the other hand the Beveridgean model guaranteed only a subsistence income to all the elderly people at a flat, universal rate (Armingeon, Bertozzi and Bonoli, 1999).

The civil pension is considered an important component of the broader concept of social security provision paid to the elderly to enable them to maintain a comfortable life after retirement. Pension as a concept can be defined widely as retirement income contracts between the employee and the employer and represents the benefit payable, either as a lump sum or in the form of annuities, by an employer to an employee, for services rendered. Pensions are also viewed as means of transferring purchasing power from the working phase to the retirement phase of the lifecycle (Algoed and Spinnewyn, 2000).

The Supreme Court of India (1982) defined pension as 'a term applied to periodic money payments to a person who retires at a certain age considered age of disability; payments usually continue for the rest of the natural life of the recipient'. The pension provision should target at poverty relief, consumption smoothing and insurance in respect of longevity (Barr, 2000). According to the Asian Development Bank (ADB), old-age pensions are designed to meet the requirements of individuals when, due to ageing, their capacity for work declines to the point where they are unable to be self-sufficient (ADB, 2001).World Bank (1994) argues that pension should have an objective of consumption smoothing and the acceleration of social insurance in the context of extended longevity. In short, pension may be considered to be a means of livelihood for the elderly in their extended years of life.

In this chapter, we look into issues relating to the pension system in India in the context of a fast ageing society. The paper is divided into five sections besides the introduction. The second section gives the rationale of old age social security by looking at the economic conditions of the elderly. The next section looks into the pension system of the formal sector workers in India and identifies its important components. The fourth section deals with the pension system for the unorganized sector. The last section examines the need for reforming the system as it consists, in its present form, of several structural weaknesses.

Need for Social Security for the Elderly

In a poor country, the majority of the population lacks the capacity to save: given the ineffectiveness of extra familial welfare institutions, it would be worthwhile to note the level of economic dependence among the elderly population.

Table 1: Percentage of the elderly by level of economic dependence, India, 2004

Dependency status	Rural			Urban			Total		
	Male	Female	Total	Male	Female	Total	Male	Female	Total
Not dependent	51.3	13.9	32.7	55.5	17.0	35.9	52.3	14.7	33.5
Partially dependent	15.2	12.4	13.8	13.4	9.5	11.4	14.8	11.7	13.3
Fully dependent	32.0	72.0	51.9	30.1	72.1	51.6	31.6	72.1	51.8

Source: National Sample Survey Organization (NSSO), 2006

All the elderly in the National Sample Survey (NSS) were asked to state their nature of economic dependence, which was coded under three categories: not dependent, partially dependent and fully dependent. We have attempted an assessment of the level of economic dependence among the Indian elderly according to sex and place of residence in Table 1. Only 33.5 per cent of the elderly were economically independent; nearly 52 per cent were fully dependent predominantly on their children for their livelihood and economic support. Hence, it is seen that a considerable proportion of the elderly in India are economically vulnerable and require state led social security programmes.

As expected, sex-wise analysis of the situation reveals that a much higher proportion of older women (72 per cent) are fully dependent as against only 32 per cent of men. Dependency is thus found to be one of the reasons for the elderly to continue to work in their old age in spite of poor health. The marked gender disparity in the levels of economic dependence among the elderly is rooted in the social expectation of financial dependence of women on men and the gender division of labour, which restricts the participation of women in paid work. Further, rural–urban differences are not found to be significant although gender differences persist in this respect also. The poor economic condition of women in general in old age gets worse in the event of widowhood.

Widowhood is one of the major economic calamities in old age. Our analysis indicates that there is a marked difference observed between widowed males and females. This is one of the reasons why elderly women participate in household (invisible) work (Rajan 2006; Rajan and Mathew, 2008). India is a country that does not have either a universal pension system or a national insurance scheme for the elderly who are really under economic and social dependency.

The 2001 census showed that there were 631,000 elderly beggars (0.8 per cent of the elderly population) in India. It may be noted that only 0.4 per cent of the elderly in India were reported to be beggars by the 61st round of the NSS. The burden of care for the elderly is not equally distributed among households. The latest NSS of elderly persons (January–June 2004) report some relevant characteristics of elderly members in Indian society. Almost 5 per cent of India's elderly live alone and more than 12 per cent of them live with their spouse. Interestingly, another 5 per cent of the elderly live with relations or non-relations but not with their children or grandchildren. Again, during 2004, about 6 per cent of the elderly in India had no surviving children to look after them. Such conditions show the urgency for a comprehensive pension system in India to support its ever increasing elderly population.

The Pension System in India

In traditional Indian society, family relationships and ethical values maintained an informal way of caring for the elderly. The complexity of modern society and a paradigm shift in the demographic scenario have resulted in an inadequacy of the informal elder-caring system (Goswami, 2001). Available evidence suggests that the origin of social security in India dates back to the 3rd century BC. Different social assistance institutions and welfare centres used to be established during the ancient days in India, which were concerned with the relief and alleviation of sickness, poverty and distress (Srivastava and Suresh, 1985).

In modern India, no universal social security system exists for the protection of the elderly against economic deprivation. Perhaps, higher levels of poverty and unemployment act as deterrents to the institution of a state pension scheme financed by a pay-roll tax for all the elderly. Instead, India has adopted social insurance and the pension policy that largely hinges on financing through the employer and employee participation and restricts the coverage to the organized sector workers (Government of India, 1999). In this country, the most important state-sponsored (and also the unfunded Pay As You Go (PAYG)) pension system covers only civil servants.

Social Security for the Aged in the Formal Sector
The Indian Civil Service Pensions

In the history of a formal civil service, the pension system in India goes back to the colonial period. The first award regarding the pension benefits for the Royal Commission on Civil Establishments, went to government employees in 1881 (Goswami, 2001). This scheme was essentially contributory in character: members of the Indian Civil Service had to contribute 4 per cent of their basic salary to it. Apart from a pension, the civil servants were also entitled to a family pension under the Indian Civil Service family pension rules. Pensions and other benefits payable under these rules were of two types: those met from contributions of subscribers and those met from the exchequer.

On the recommendations of the Royal Commission presided by Lord Islington, the 4 per cent contribution that the employee had to make to earn the right of pension was abolished in 1920 and the government undertook to meet the full expenditure on the pension. However, in order to be entitled to the complete pension, a worker had to complete the full term of 25 years of service. In the Government of India Act, 1919, provisions were made so that retiring persons who had joined government service before 1920 as temporary employees were eligible to get pensions in proportion to the length of their service at the time of retirement.

In 1924, the Lee Commission recommended, apart from recommending an increase in the pension, that if and when a civilian recruited to a job was transferred, it should be optional for that employee to retire from service with a sum proportionate to the pension. Further, provident fund was suggested as an alternative to the pension system for all future recruits. Also, an Indian civil servant could, under certain conditions, commute his/her pensions for a lump sum payment of not more than half of the pension statutorily granted to him/her.

The Government of India Act, 1935 also protected the rights and privileges of the members of the civil services (Srivastava and Suresh, 1985). These schemes were later consolidated and enlarged to provide retirement benefits to all persons who retired from government employment, and later to entire public sector workers. They acted as guidelines to the sanctioning of civil service pensions in independent India.

The Civil Service Pension Scheme (CSPS) covers the entire gamut of salaried workers in central and state governments and Union Territory administrations in independent India. Within the central government, the pension schemes are organized for different departments and ministries under separate rules, each ministry having its own set of rules of eligibility. Thus, there exist separate schemes for railways, telecommunications and defence services. These programmes are typically run on a PAYG defined benefit basis. The schemes are non-contributory. And the entire pension expenditure is charged to the annual revenue expenditure account of the government. Table 2 gives an overview of the various pension provisions in vogue in India. In general, the basic pension amount is calculated with reference to the average of the basic pay drawn by the state government employee during the last ten months of service. The full pension amount is 50 per cent of the average pay, payable to employees who have completed 33 years of qualifying service.

Table 2: Types of Civil Service pensions in India

(i)	Superannuation pension: A Government servant who retires on attaining the age of superannuation is granted this pension (Rule 35).
(ii)	Retiring pension: A Government servant who retires or is retired prior to the stipulated age of superannuation or under FR 56 or Article 459 of Civil Service Rules (CSR) and also one who opts for voluntary retirement on being declared surplus, is granted this pension (Rule 36).
(iii)	Invalid pension: A Government servant who is retired from service on account of any bodily ornamental infirmity, which permanently incapacitates him/her for the service, is eligible for Invalid pension, which is granted only on the recommendation of a Medical Board constituted for the purpose (Rule 38).
(iv)	Compensation pension: A Government servant who is discharged from service owing to the abolition of his/her permanent post is granted this pension (Rule 39).
(v)	Compulsory Retirement pension: A Government servant who is retired compulsorily from service as a measure of penalty is granted this pension. A competent authority can sanction him/her either pension or gratuity or both at a rate not less than 2/3rd and not more than full compensation pension or gratuity or both (Rule 40).
(vi)	Compassionate Allowance: A Government servant who is dismissed or removed from service by a Competent Authority, and if the case deserves special consideration, is granted this allowance. Such allowance shall not exceed 2/3rd of pension or gratuity or both which would have been admissible to him/her had he/she retired on compensation pension (Rule 41).
(vii)	Pension on absorption in or under a Corporation/Company/Body: A Government servant who has been permitted to be absorbed in or under a corporation, company or body substantially owned or controlled by the central Government/state Governent in or under a body controlled or financed by central Government/state Government, is allowed this benefit.

Source: Report of High Level Expert Group on the New Pension System, Government of India, 2002.

There are three types of gratuity available to central and state government employees as retirement benefits from the government, which are financed by the state's revenue:

Retirement Gratuity

A minimum of five years of qualifying service is essential to make an employee eligible to get this one-time lump sum benefit. Retirement gratuity is calculated at the rate of one-fourth of the last basic pay for each completed six monthly period of qualifying service.

Death Gratuity

This is a one-time lump sum benefit payable to the nominee of the deceased employee.

Service Gratuity

An employee is entitled to receive gratuity (and not the pension), if his/her total qualifying service is less than ten years. The admissible amount is half-month basic pay for each completed six monthly period of qualifying service. There is no prescribed maximum or minimum monetary limit on this amount. This one-time lump sum payment is made, over and above the retirement gratuity.

The provision for the commutation of pension is an integral part of the pension provision in India and it is followed in almost every state. A pensioner has the option to commute a portion of his/her pension, not exceeding 40 per cent of the basic pension, for lump sum payment from the exchequer. Some state governments, however, limit the commutation amount to one-third of the basic pension. The lump sum amount payable is calculated with reference to the commutation table constructed on an actuarial basis. The commuted pension is deducted from the monthly pension and the full pension is restored on the expiry of 15 years from the date of receipt of the commuted value of the pension. Dearness relief on pension, however, continues to be calculated on the basis of the original pension, i.e. without reduction of the commuted portion.

Civil servants in India are eligible to receive other pension benefits such as provident funds. The pension coverage under the banner of state-sponsored pension system becomes more extensive if pension schemes under Employees Provident Fund Organization (EPFO), which are partially funded by either state or central government, are included. In all the states, the pension schemes cover all state government employees. In the case of employees of Grant-In-Aid Institutions (GIA), pension schemes differ across the states. GIA institutions, which are mostly educational institutions are fully covered by the government pensions in some sates. For example, in West Bengal, the number of the pensioners belonging to direct state government service is more or less equal to the number of pensioners belonging to GIA institutions and local bodies. As a result of

Table 3: Civil Service pensioners in India, 1991–2004

Years	Central government pensioners	State government pensioners	Government pensioners
1990–91	2594237	2568737	5162974
1991–92	2638184	2611933	5250117
1992–93	2716390	2689361	5405751
1993–94	2797200	2769367	5566566
1994–95	2880821	2852156	5732977
1995–96	2967202	2937677	5904879
1996–97	3105234	3074336	6179570
1997–98	3376717	3343118	6719835
1998–99	3430868	3396730	6827597
1999–00	3829218	3250000	7079218
2000–01	3938806	3365400	7304206
2001–02	4046396	3525000	7571396
2002–03	4152682	3855456	8008138
2003–04	4256062	4214228	8470290
2004–05	4403171	4554123	8957294
2005–06	4545213	4898737	9443949

Source: Calculated from Central Statistical Organization (CSO) abstracts.

increased coverage and rise in longevity, there has been a phenomenal growth in the number of pensioners in India.

Table 3 provides the coverage of the government pension system in India under civil pensions both at the Centre and states. In 2006, there were 94 lakh government pensioners under the Centre and the State governments taken together. The total number was around 52 lakhs in 1991 and nearly 60 lakhs in 1996. There has occurred a sharp increase in the number of pensioners in India both under the states and the Centre.

Contributory Schemes

Currently, India has a complex of different provident fund and pension schemes, targeted at different segments of the labour force:

The Organized Segment of the Private Sector

Participation in two social insurance programmes is mandatory for workers in establishments with more than 20 employees who earn less than Rs 5,000 a month. These workers constitute 49 per cent of the salaried workforce and slightly more than 7 per cent of the estimated total workforce. They participate in two types of funded pension schemes: (1) the Employees Provident Fund (EPF), a defined-contribution programme, and (2) the Employees Pension Scheme (EPS), a defined benefit programme, both overseen by the EPFO.

EPF Scheme

The EPF Scheme was launched in 1952 and participation is made mandatory for private and public enterprises in 177 specified sectors (excluding Jammu and Kashmir) that employ more than 20 persons. As of 2004, the EPF covered about 24.3 million workers in 339,271 establishments. The system covers those employees whose initial basic wages and 'dearness' allowances taken together are less than Rs 5,000. Workers whose wages later exceed this threshold are required to contribute only the first Rs 5,000 but may voluntarily contribute amounts in excess of this standard.

Table 4: Coverage of EPF and EPS, 1996–7 and 2005–06

	1996–97	2005–06
Number of establishments	277,555	339,271
Members of EPF (in thousands)	20,289	24,372
Members of EPS (in thousands)	18,324	21,275
EPF contributions (Rs in billion)	59.7	86.9
EPS contributions (Rs in billion)	27.9	40.5

Source: Annual Reports of EPFO.

Contributions to the EPF go into a fund managed by the EPFO, but the employers may seek an exemption to manage their own funds, as long as they meet regulatory requirements enforced by the EPFO (Table 4). With a few exceptions, employees are required to contribute 12 per cent of wages, with the employers making contributions of 3.77 per cent. Benefits are normally paid out as a lump sum upon retirement.

To cover administrative expenses, the employers contribute 0.65 per cent of wages, while those belonging to the exempt funds contribute 0.09 per cent of wages to cover expenses relating to their supervision by the EPFO. The difference in administrative costs provides a strong incentive to seek the exempt status. Prior to retirement, employees may make partial withdrawals for specified purposes like house construction, treatment of illness, assuaging of natural disasters and higher education of children. Employees may also withdraw 90 per cent of the balance in their accounts during the year immediately before retirement.

Returns paid on funds managed by the EPFO are set annually by the government and are announced around budget time; the rate was fixed at 12 per cent from 1990 but was reduced to 11 per cent from 2000. The government's budget for the year 2001–02 announced a further 150 basis point cut in returns. Exempted funds may not credit members with returns lower than that announced by the EPFO; shortfalls from investment income on fund assets must be made up from the employers' other income. Recent rates are as low as 8.5 per cent.

EPS

The EPS was established in 1995 by way of replacement of the Family Pension Scheme (FPS), which had provided survivor benefits. Its membership is lower than that of the EPF; as of 2006, it covered about 21.3 million workers. Establishments may be exempted from the EPS, if they provide benefits that are better than those exempted from it. However, the rules for exemption from the EPS are not entirely transparent, and there is currently a case pending before the Supreme Court regarding the conditions under which schemes may be exempted from the EPS.

The EPS is currently funded by the employer and government contributions of 8.33 per cent and 1.16 per cent respectively, of employees' basic wages plus dearness allowance. However, exempt funds do not receive the government's contribution. The EPS provides pension benefits that are calculated on the basis of a worker's average salary during the 12 months immediately preceding retirement, and a multiplicative factor calculated as years of service divided by 70. The maximum replacement rate is 50 per cent, and workers who have more than 20 years of service or have reached the retirement age of 58 years get credit for two additional years of service. Consequently, a 58-year-old worker with 33 years of service can retire with the maximum replacement rate. Finally, early retirement is possible at age 50 with a reduction in benefits for each year between the age of retirement and 58 years. A portion of EPS benefits is payable as lump sum at retirement. The tax treatment of EPS benefits is similar to that of EPF benefits. Survivor and disability benefits also are provided by the EPS.

Special Provident Funds

There are also some mandatory provident funds linked to specific occupations or states, such as the Coal Miners Provident Fund (1948), the Assam Tea Plantation Provident Fund (1955), the Jammu and Kashmir Provident Fund (1961), and the Seamens' Fund (1966). Although managed by different trusts and fund managers, they all generally follow the same investment and return rules as those of funds regulated by the EPFO. The total membership in these schemes is roughly 2 million.

Voluntary Programmes

There are also a number of voluntary group pension plans that exist primarily because of rules barring high earning employees from participating in the EPF system. These pension schemes are either privately run by managers appointed by the employers, or by the Life Insurance Corporation (LIC). The provisions of the Insurance Act 1938 and the LIC Act 1956 make LIC the only enterprise allowed to provide annuity schemes to the Indian public, since the annuity business is considered a part of the life insurance business. As a result, privately run pension schemes can accumulate and invest funds, but are required to purchase annuities on behalf of retiring employees from LIC. Although they are neither mandatory nor sponsored by the government, they are included here because they receive tax preferences and are subject to restrictive investment and annuity regulations. As of March 1998, the total accumulated funds for these group's pension plans were about Rs 65 billion (Gupta, 1998), of which the LIC managed Rs 49.7 billion on behalf of 4719 schemes. Annuity payments arising out of these schemes, covering about 210,000 persons, totalled Rs 3.1 billion in 2003. Voluntary individual annuity schemes also are eligible to receive preferential tax treatment. In 2003 there were about 670,000 such annuities, which paid out about Rs 14.5 billion.

Coverage of Social Security in the Formal Sector

Though different formal social security schemes are available to the elderly, the major one consists of pensions. Mainly there are two types of pension schemes: a defined benefit pension scheme for civil servants and schemes administered by the EPFO. Both appear to be suffering from structural and financial crises (Goswami, 2001). Such skewed coverage of the existing benefit schemes favour organized workforce during a period when informal employment is on the rise. With the growing pension liability of the

government, state finances are getting progressively weak. The majority
of other retirement savings schemes like the provident and pension funds
predominantly cover workers in the organized sector. Table 5 provides a
bird's eye view of the coverage of the pensions of EPFO schemes by
States for the year 2006.

Kerala leads the states with 18 per cent of elderly population covered
by pension, followed by West Bengal and Tamil Nadu with 13 per cent.
Bihar, Uttar Pradesh, Rajasthan, and Orissa stand below the national
average where the misery of the elderly is intensive. The pension system
on an average, covers 12 per cent of the total old age population who

Table 5: Percentage of elderly covered under the formal pension system, 2006

States	Civil service pensions (state)	Civil service pensions (Centre) EPFO and other schemes	Total
Andhra Pradesh	8.2	4.1	12.3
Assam	8.9	2.8	11.7
Bihar	6.0	6.0	12.0
Gujarat	8.4	5.1	13.5
Haryana	8.6	4.5	13.2
Karnataka	8.2	5.9	14.1
Kerala	12.1	7.3	19.4
Madhya Pradesh	7.0	5.1	12.1
Maharashtra	8.1	5.4	13.5
Orissa	6.7	4.5	11.2
Punjab	6.5	5.7	12.1
Rajasthan	5.9	5.1	11.0
Tamil Nadu	8.6	6.2	14.9
Uttar Pradesh	5.6	6.0	11.6
West Bengal	8.1	6.8	14.9
India	5.9	6.8	12.7

Note: Computed by researchers using CSO statistics on pension coverage contained in the *Handbook
of Statistical Abstract*, 2004, and information on the aged population based on the 2001 census.

had earlier spent their working lives for the formal sector. And the
remaining population (about 90 per cent), whose work cornered around
the unorganized sector, has no access to any formal system of old age
income security. This skewed coverage is likely to intensify further with
the growth of the informal sector, since the size of the formal workforce
has remained more or less stagnant according to CSO estimates. This

situation shows how the pension system is caught in a 'structural crisis' with limited coverage through pension system of the total elderly population. This structural crisis is likely to deepen in future as the process of population ageing gets underway in India.

Pension Expenditure in India

In an ageing society, the government has to bear a higher burden of expenditure on its welfare activities in the form of health and social security provisioning. The state administered pension system has been maturing alongside with the maturing of the population. The systems' stability is likely to get disturbed as the PAYG system is being affected by the increasing lifespan of the pensioners and contraction of the period of contribution by the workforce to the existing PAYG system as on intergenerational liability. The demographic phenomenon has thus put most of the pension systems under severe economic pressure. Pension systems all over the world are affected by the rapidly changing demographic regimes as a result of the rapidly ageing populations and the phenomenon of longer expectations of living (World Bank, 1994). The crisis of the pension system, which has traditionally been state-run, is largely due to the fact that pension accounts for a sizeable part of government expenditure. As the process of population ageing gets accelerated, the system grows under high incidence of pension expenditure, most of which is paid out of payroll tax. The change in the age structure affects the intergenerational distribution of the burden of pension schemes across the old (the pensioners) and the young (workers) (Atkinson, 2001). The balance between the two is also disturbed by the increase of the period of pension which exceeds the period of payroll tax contribution by an employee. As the ageing process advances, the state-sponsored pension system has to bear an increasing economic liability to be paid out of its fiscal resources. Thus, the pension system quivers on the verge of a crisis (World Bank, 1994). Various pension systems across the globe show an element of pension crisis as increase in life expectancy is a global phenomenon. Thus, the widespread notion of the unsustainability of the government-run defined benefits and the non-contributory pension system has become a matter of concern (Swain and Sen, 2004).

At present, the salary and pension bills of both the central and the state governments account for a large proportion of the public expenditure from fiscal resources. The total bill constituted 9 per cent of Gross Domestic Product (GDP) in 2003–04 while it had been only 7.9 per cent in 1990–91. The desegregation of the government liability for payment of salary and pensions shows that the share of pension expenditure came to about 2.5

per cent of total GDP in 2003–04 as against a mere 1.3 per cent in 1990–91. The pension expenditure of the government has been larger than most of the other items of social sector expenditure. The pension expenditure disaggregated to central and state expenditure shows an unprecedented increase since the beginning of the 1990s. Table 6 indicates that the total pension liability went up from Rs 6,870 crore in 1990–91 to Rs 57,855 crore in 2004–05. During this period, the pension expenditure of the country registered a growth of 16 per cent.

Table 6: Pension liability of both Centre and States (Rs in crore)

Year	Centre	State	Total
1990–91	3278	3592	6870
1991–92	3748	3715	7463
1992–93	4585	4379	8964
1993–94	5206	5107	10313
1994–95	5733	6123	11856
1995–96	6928	7813	14741
1996–97	8252	9826	18078
1997–98	11375	11667	23042
1998–99	15346	16166	31512
1999–00	19444	22679	42123
2000–01	20617	25453	46070
2001–02	21411	27849	49260
2002–03	22409	27133	49542
2003–04	24242	29456	53698
2004–05	26075	31780	57855
2005–06	27908	34103	62011

Source: Pension expenditure calculated by researchers based on Annual Budget and Economic Surveys of Government of India.

'Pension stringency' occurred in different states in India with different degrees of intensity, as the impact of demographic achievements and coverage of the pension system varied widely among them. The fiscal stress has been very high in states such as Tamil Nadu, Kerala, West Bengal, and Andhra Pradesh, where the life expectancy and the coverage of pension systems are considerably high. The extent of the fiscal stringency in the Indian states on account of the rapidly rising pension expenditure can be measured in terms of two fiscal indicators: the pension expenditure as a share of revenue receipts and the pension expenditure as percentage of the states' own revenue. Increase in pension expenditure as proportion of total revenue receipts is one of the most visible signs of fiscal stringency arising from the pension system. At the national level, pension expenditure as a percentage of revenue expenditure came to 12 per cent in 2004–5; it had been as low as 2 per cent in 1980–1 and 5 per cent in 1990–1. It may be noted that pension expenditure as a proportion of revenue expenditure went up sharply in the 1990s; it constituted a major fiscal constraint. Kerala ranks the highest among the states with more than 23 per cent of its revenue earmarked for pension payment as a part of the revenue expenditure in 2004–5.

Pension payment as proportion of 'States' Own Revenue (SOR)' shows the extent to which internal resources of a state are allocated for pension payment that covers less than 15 per cent of the workforce and the elderly. The drain of a state's resources' own account of pension payment has been increasing at an alarming pace in the past two decades. In the year 1980–1, the national average spending was 3.4 per cent of the SOR; it increased sharply in the 1980s and doubled to 7.9 per cent in 1990–1 in almost all the states. The latter part of the 1990s witnessed a further sharp increase and ended up at the national level of 18 per cent in 2004–5. In Bihar, the proportion went up to an unprecedented high of 63.5 per cent. States like Orissa and West Bengal reported figures around 30 per cent and Kerala allocated 28.5 per cent.

The rising fiscal crisis on both the demographic and macroeconomic front arising from pension payment is thus an indicator of 'Pension Crisis' in India. Here, the alarming pressure on the system through its intergenerational distribution makes it unsustainable.

Social Security for the Elderly in the Informal Sector

National Social Assistance Scheme

Until August 1995, no social assistance programme was in existence which was managed by the Government of India for its poor citizens. The announcement on 15 August 1995, of a National Social Assistance Scheme (NSAS) was a significant step towards the fulfillment of the Directive Principles enshrined in Article 42 of the Indian Constitution, which talks about public assistance in old age. On 19 March 1999, the Government of India announced another social assistance scheme called 'Annapurna' for the elderly destitutes.

The National Social Assistance Scheme has three components: National Old Age Pension Scheme (NOAPS), National Family Benefit Scheme (NFBS) and National Maternal Benefit Scheme (NMBS). Among the three schemes, NOAPS is meant for the poor and the elderly. This is a centrally sponsored programme with 100 per cent central assistance to the states and Union Territories in accordance with the norms, guidelines and conditions laid down by the central government. The scheme is managed by the Ministry of Rural Development, Government of India.

The following criteria strictly apply in the implementation of the NOAPS: (i) The age of the applicant (male or female) should be 65 or above; (ii) The applicant must be a destitute having little or no regular means of subsistence from his/her own sources of income or through financial support from members of his/her household or other sources. In order to determine destitution, the criteria, if any, currently in force in the state/Union Territory are to be followed. The Government of India reserves the right to review these criteria and suggest appropriate revised criteria; (iii) The amount of old-age pension will be Rs 75 per month under this scheme; (iv) The ceiling on the total number of old-age pensions for purposes of claiming central assistance will be specified for the states and Union Territories from time to time; (v) The benefit under NOAPS should be disbursed in not less than two installments in a year and, if possible, the benefit may be disbursed in more installments as per the direction of the state government. In 2006, the prime minister of India announced an increase in the allowance provided under NOAPS to Rs 200 from the existing rate of Rs 75 per month.

Annapurna Scheme

In 1999, the Government of India announced another social assistance scheme, namely, *Annapurna,* for the elderly destitutes who have no one to take care of them. Under this scheme, an elderly destitute is provided 10 kg of rice or wheat per month free of cost through the existing public distribution system. This scheme aims at covering destitutes who are otherwise eligible for old-age pension under the National Old Age Pension Scheme. The government has allotted a sum of Rs 1 billion for the first year of its implementation. It is expected that this scheme will benefit around 660,000 of the elderly destitute.

Structural Problems with the Current Pension System
Coverage and Equity

The most serious problem with the current pension system is that it fails to reach the vast majority of the population, and that no safety net exists for persons who are not covered by the system. Moreover, members of this left out group had far lower incomes while they had been working and far fewer resources on which to live after retirement. An equity concern also exists within the system as the average income of workers covered by the EPF, EPS, CSPS and the Integrated General Provident Fund (IGPF) is roughly Rs 2,900 per month. The average EPS (CSPS) benefit is in the order of Rs 1,000 to Rs 2,000 per month. On the other hand, NOAPS has a benefit scheme of Rs 200 per month and it reaches only a small proportion of the poor and the elderly. The strain on the budget is clearly an impediment to providing more formal assistance and larger benefits to the poor and the elderly. However, any reform programme must address this problem, either directly, with a plan to provide targeted assistance, or indirectly, with a plan to 'formalize' the informal sector so that the poorest workers could be given an opportunity to save for retirement.

In addition, net benefits of contributions and the implicit rate of return on contributions vary substantially across programmes, occupations and sectors. Such a situation is inequitable, when the differences are imposed by government regulation rather than as a result of freely made decisions about the structure of compensation. It is also one of the reasons why pension rights are not portable across these dimensions, thus creating impediments to labour mobility.

Fiscal Sustainability

Potential fiscal problems reflect a large unfunded liability of the system, and are concentrated in three areas: first the Civil Service Pension System. It creates a fundamental imbalance between wages and the pension benefits in the civil service. Given the high dependency, the pension age is almost certainly too low. Second, even with a low pension age, the average replacement rate is still over 45 per cent. Consequently, the pension bill is more than 25 per cent of the wage bill. This represents a huge 'hidden' cost. The situation is much more serious in the central government and in a few state governments where people's longevity is higher. It also creates a fiscal pressure with large implications for SOR and revenue expenditure.

Regulation and Administration

No statutory body supervises trustee-managed pension funds and funded gratuity plans and the data on their operations are made available only with substantial time lag. Also, although the EPFO supervises exempt EPF funds, there is relative paucity of data regarding the operations of exempt funds. In addition, an implicit conflict of interest exists in the matter of approval of EPFO and supervision of exempt provident funds, since the existence and growth of these funds reduce the resources under EPFO management.

The weak regulatory environment is reflected in the quality of service in the mandatory schemes. Delays in processing claims, crediting interest to members, and issuing annual account statements are common. These lags make the schemes not at all attractive to common people. Moreover, investment rules have constrained investment in corporate bonds and proscribed investment in equities, thus drastically reducing the return on investments to provident and pension funds.

Conclusion

In brief, the pension system in India is suffering from challenges posed by the demographic transition of ageing and increasing longevity. The pension system of the present kind targets a minority of the aged population and accounts for high government expenditure that leads to fiscal stringency. Thus, the system suffers from a structural crisis both on its delivery mechanism and its financing aspects. It is high time that the pension system is structured to provide basic security to the elderly at minimum cost on the part of the government. Thus, a structural reform of the pension system is urgently called for.

References

ADB, 'Social Protection in Asia and the Pacific', Manila, 2001.
Algoed, Koen and Spinnewyn, Frans, 'Pensions' in Bouckaert, Boudewijn and De Geest, Gerrit, eds, *Encyclopedia of Law and Economics,* Vol. 4 (*The Economics of Public and Tax Law*), Edward Elgar, Cheltenham, 2000, pp.311–27.
Amedick, Sigrid, 'Old Age Security in a Community Service Administration: the Example of the Bavarian State Railway, 1844–1914', Pension Systems for Public Servants in Western Europe, *Yearbook of European Administrative History* (JEV), Vol. 12, pp.55–75.
Armingeon, K, Bertozzi, F and Bonoli, G, 'Convergence towards a Unique Continental Model of the Welfare State in Europe? The Importance of Regional Integration for Swiss Welfare State Reform', 1999 (unpublished).
Atkinson, P, 'The Fiscal Impact of Population Change', Federal Reserve Bank, Boston Conference Series, 2001.
Auerbach A and Lee, R, ed, *Demographic Change and Fiscal Policy,* Cambridge University Press, London, 2001.
Barr, Nicholas, 'Reforming Pensions: Myths, Truths, and Policy Choices', IMF Working Paper No.WP/00/ 139, New York, August 2000.
Beveridge, William, *The Pillars of Security and Other War-Time Essays and Addresses,* Allen and Unwin, London, 1943.
Boldrin, M, Jimenez-Martin, S and Peracchi, F, 'Social Security and Retirement in France' in Gruber, J and Wise, D A, eds, *International Social Security Comparisons,* The University of Chicago Press, Chicago, 1999.
CSO, CSO abstracts of various years, New Delhi.
de Araujo, Leal, 'Social Security as an Instrument of Income Distribution in Developing Countries', *International Social Security Review,* Vol. 25, No. 3, 1972, pp.243–54.

Fox, L and Palmer, E, 'New Approaches to Multipillar Pension Systems: What in the World is Going On?' in Holzmann, Robert and Stiglitz, J E, eds, *New Ideas about Old Age Security – Towards Sustainable Pension Systems in the 21st Century*, World Bank, Washington D C, 2001.

Goswami, Ranadev, 'Indian Pension System: Problems and Prognosis', Paper presented in the IAA Pensions Seminar, June 2001.

Government of India, 'The Project OASIS Report Submitted by the Expert Committee for Devising a Pension System for India', Ministry of Social Justice and Empowerment, New Delhi, 11 January 2000.

Government of India, 'Report of High Level Expert Group on New Pension System', Vol. 1, Main Report, February 2002.

Government of Kerala, 'Kerala Service Amendment Rules', Various Reviews, Thiruvananthapuram.

Gupta, P C, 'LIC's Experience with Management of Pension and Superannuation Funds', Commissioned by Project OASIS (Old Age Social and Income Security), Ministry of Social Justice and Empowerment, Goverment of India, 1998.

Heller, Peter S, 'Who will Pay? Coping with Aging Societies, Climate Change and Other Long-Term Fiscal Challenges', International Monetary Fund, Washington D C, 2003.

ILO, *Approaches to Social Security*, Canada, Montreal, 1942.

Laroque, P, 'Social Security in France', in Jenkin, S, ed, *Social Security in International Perspective*, Columbia University Press, New York, 1969, pp.171–89.

NSSO, Morbidity, Health Care and the Condition of the Aged, NSS 60th Round, (January–June 2004), *Report No.507*, Ministry of Statistics and Programme Implementation, Government of India, New Delhi, 2006.

Rajan, S Irudaya, 'Social Safety Nets for the Vulnerable Poor and Elderly in India' in Srivastava, Nisha and Sharma, Pravesh, eds, *Protecting the Vulnerable Poor in India: The Role of Social Safety Nets*, Chapter 11, World Food Programme, New Delhi, 2006, pp.233–60.

Rajan, S Irudaya and Mathew, E T, 'India' in Rajan, Irudaya S, ed, *Social Security for the Elderly: Experiences from South Asia*, Chapter 2, Routledge, Taylor and Francis Group, London/New York/New Delhi, 2008, pp.39–106.

Srivastava, C and Suresh, L, *Treatise on Social Security and Labour Law*, Eastern Books, Lucknow, 1985.

Supreme Court of India (1982), cited in Prasad, Syam, 'A "Crisis in Making": The Pension System in India with Special Reference to Kerala', unpublished thesis submitted to Centre for Development Studies, 2005.

Swain, Sibani and Sen, Pronab, 'Pension Liabilities of the Central Government: Projections and Implications', Planning Commission, Government of India, 2004.

Prasad, Syam, 'A "Crisis in Making": The Pension System in India with Special Reference to Kerala', op. cit.

The Pensions Internationals, [http://www.pensions-research.org/].

World Bank, *Averting the Old Age Crisis: Policies to Protect the Old and Promote Growth*, Oxford University Press, Oxford, Washington D C, 1994.

Chapter 7

DEMOGRAPHIC AND SOCIO-ECONOMIC PROFILES OF ELDERLY IN SRI LANKA

Godfrey Gunatilleke

Introduction

Sri Lanka is among the societies which are ageing the fastest in the developing world. During the intercensal period, 1981–2001, the proportion of the population in the age group over 60 years has increased from 6.6 per cent to 9.2 per cent. According to the available standard projection, the elderly will account for approximately 20 per cent of the total population in 2026. This process of ageing, which is being witnessed in Sri Lanka is the outcome of policies and programmes which rapidly reduced mortality over a period of 50 years and increased the average lifespan from 46 years in 1946 to 74 years in 2001. Fertility reached the replacement level in the mid 1990s and has continued to decline further below this level, resulting in a corresponding decline in the share of the population under 15 years of age from 35 per cent in 1981 to 26 per cent in 2001.

Sri Lanka has undergone the demographic transition at a relatively early stage of economic development and at a low level of per capita income. The rapid changes that have taken place are imposing severe constraints on the capacity of the country's economy as well as its social institutions to provide the standards of economic and social security that should accompany the demographic changes and the process of ageing. While these problems affect the ageing population as a whole they become more acute in the case of elderly females. They face greater disadvantages in terms of both their economic and social status. Their participation in the workforce is about half of that of males. Their average earned income is again about half of that of males. The marriage laws, property laws and laws of inheritance are weighted against females in some systems of personal law that are in force. As a result, their condition of dependence in old age when measured in terms of financial and other assets tends to be much higher than that of males. This state of dependence has to be placed in the context in which females outlive males by approximately five years. In the census of 2001, for example, there were 471,429 widows of whom 288,682 were over 60 years of age. There were another 33,000 spinsters. The share of this segment of widowed or single females will continue to increase rapidly over the next few decades.

In the prevailing conditions, the care for the aged is borne by the family and the networks based on kinship. The institution of the family itself is undergoing far-reaching changes that tend to reduce its capacity to fulfil the traditional role it has played in the care of the aged. Meanwhile, the state has taken several initiatives to respond to the problems of ageing. It has established special institutions to deal with the problems of ageing and the needs of the old population commencing in 1982 following the Vienna World Summit on Ageing. A national policy and plan of action has been formulated and legislation has been enacted to protect and promote the rights of the elders. Various administrative measures had been taken in collaboration with voluntary organizations to address some of the specific needs of ageing. These include, laws relating to standards governing construction and buildings that take account of the special needs of the aged; issue of cards to senior citizens to enable them to get preferential treatment in the delivery of public services; old-age pension schemes to provide for the elderly in the informal sector; public assistance to the poor elderly through schemes such as *Samurdhi* and state assistance for institutions to care for the aged. However, the social security available to the elderly population through the state and state sponsored schemes is as yet very limited in its coverage and comprises mainly of the retirement benefits of employees in the state sector and the formal private sector. The government has still to evolve a comprehensive national policy that identifies the changing needs of the elderly population in the context of the rapid demographic and social changes that are taking place and the macroeconomic and budgetary challenges they pose.

There has been a considerable volume of writing on ageing in Sri Lanka. The Marga Institute produced two studies in 1989 and 1999 as part of a United Nations (UN) Economic and Social Commission for Asia and the Pacific (ESCAP) sponsored regional project which surveyed the trends in ageing and the emerging problems (UN, 1989; Marga Institute, 1998). Thereafter, there has been a wide range of studies on different aspects of ageing, including micro studies on the health conditions of the aged by health professionals and household surveys of the socio-economic status and the living arrangements of the old carried out by the Marga Institute. A recent full-length study on 'Ageing Population in Sri Lanka – Issues and Future Prospects' done by the United Nations Population Fund (UNFPA) in association with the Population Association of Sri Lanka (PASL), examines in some depth various aspects of ageing and presents the data available up to 2000 (UNFPA and PASL, 2004). More recent studies done by the Institute of Policy Studies and the Overseas Development Institute have examined in depth the macroeconomic implications of retirement schemes for the elderly and the policy options that are available. The present study, while drawing on the information and the analysis of issues in all this work has updated the situation analysis of the elderly population in Sri Lanka on the data available after 2000 in the Census of 2001 and other demographic and socio-economic surveys of the Department of Census and Statistics and the Central Bank. The study is organized into four sections. The first section analyses the existing demographic situation and the future trends relating to the elderly with particular reference to elderly females. It provides an overview of the changing needs of the elderly. The second section examines the policy framework on ageing, covering both the social development policies that produced the high social indicators which include the old population, as well as the age-specific initiatives to promote the well-being of the old taken within the UN framework of principles for older persons. The third section analyses the socio-economic conditions of the old population and the regional and gender disparities within them. The fourth and final section presents the conclusions and recommendations.

The Ageing Population: Past, Present and Future

The average life expectancy for 2003 is estimated at 74.1 years with female life expectancy at 76.8 years and male at 71.5 years – a differential which is in the expected region of five years and indicative of conditions of survival that are not discriminatory against women. The cohorts of the females aged 60 and over have been increasingly outnumbering those of men. In the 2001 census, females aged 60 and above outnumbered the males in this age group by nearly 100,000 for the population in the provinces that were fully covered by the census.

The table above provides the data for the age composition of the population at three points in time. The data for 1981 is taken from the 1981 census which covered the whole island. The data for 2031 are estimates provided in the population projections for Sri Lanka, 1991–2031 prepared by the Institute of Policy Studies (De Silva, 2007). We can now apply the available data to examine the emerging situation in terms of the three categories of the aged that have been used for the study – the young-old from 60–70, the 'old-old' from 70–80 and the very old above 80. In 1981, the young-old numbered 578,000 of whom 256,000 were females; the old-old 276,000 of whom 125,000 were females and the very old were 98,000 of whom females were 47,000. In all three age groups males outnumbered females. In 2001, the total number of young-old persons was approximately 990,000 of whom females were 518,000 outnumbering the males by 44,000. The old-old and very old together were estimated at about 738,000 of whom about 386,000 were females, again the females outnumbering the males. Of this, the very old above 80 years would be approximately 360,000 if we apply the proportions in the 1981 census.

Among the very old, females are likely to outnumber males by a considerable margin. The effects of the demographic transition resulting in higher life expectancy for females were not yet evident in the relative size of the male and female age cohorts in 1981. However, these were clearly reflected in 2001. In the population projections for 2031, the corresponding figures are 2.482 million for the young-old, of whom 1.306 million are females; 1.754 million for the old-old of whom 959,000 are females and 683,000 for the very old of whom 390,000 are females. In the rapidly changing age composition of the total population, the changes within the age structure of the population over 60 years are themselves striking. While the total population increased by a little more than a quarter between 1981 and 2001, the population above 60 years increased by 76.5 per cent. In 1981, there were six young-old persons to one very old person. This ratio declines from 2.7 to 1 by 2031. In the old age group, the very old are the least active and most dependent share of the population, and in the ageing of a society the most revealing indicator would be the increasing share of the very old. Many of the critical problems of ageing are linked to this variable.

The Dependency Burden

The ageing of the population can be measured by the increase in the share of the population over 60 years of age in the total population. In 1981, this share was 6.7 per cent. In 2001, it had reached 9.2 per cent. The proportion of the elderly will continue to increase rapidly as lower birth rates begin to take effect and the size of younger age cohorts begin to decline correspondingly. The IPS low projections extend to 2041 in which year the proportion of the old population would rise to 29.1 per cent.

Table 1: Trends in the age composition of the population in Sri Lanka, 1981–2031 (in thousands)

Year	1981			2001			2031		
Age Group	Total	Male	Female	Total	Male	Female	Total	Male	Female
0–14	5,226 (35.2)	2,662 (35)	2,564 (35.2)	4,926 (26.3)	2,516 (27.0)	2,419 (25.7)	3,059 (14.4)	1,552 (15.0)	1,507 (14.0)
15–59	8,638 (58.1)	4,383 (57.9)	4,255 (58.4)	12,082 (64.5)	6,002 (64.4)	6,089 (64.7)	13,307 (62.5)	6,642 (63.5)	6,665 (61.5)
60–64	340 (2.2)	183 (2.4)	157 (2.1)	543 (2.9)	260 (2.8)	273 (2.9)	1,308 (6.1)	626 (6.0)	682 (6.3)
65–69	252 (1.6)	133 (1.7)	118 (1.6)	449 (2.4)	214 (2.3)	245 (2.6)	1,174 (5.5)	550 (5.2)	624 (5.8)
70–74	180 (1.2)	97 (1.2)	83 (1.1)	337 (1.8)	159 (1.7)	179 (1.9)	1,015 (4.8)	465 (4.4)	550 (5.0)
75–79 (For 2001–75 and over)	106 (0.71)	56 (0.73)	50 (0.68)	395 (2.1)	168 (1.8)	207 (2.2)	739 (3.5)	330 (3.2)	409 (3.8)
80–89 (For 2031–80 and over)	86	45	41				683 (3.2)	290 (2.7)	393 (3.6)
90 and over	16	8	8						
Total of 60 and over	981 (6.6)	522 (6.8)	459 (6.3)	1732 (9.2)	802 (8.6)	904 (9.6)	4,919 (23.0)	2,258 (21.6)	2,657 (24.5)
Total Population	14,846	7,568	7,278	18,732	9,320	9,412	21,285	10,456	10,829

Notes: The age distribution for the 2001 census is available for five year age groups upto 75. In the projections for 2031, the five year age groups are given up to age 80 plus.
Sources: Department of Census and Statistics, 2000, 2001, 2005; De Silva, Indralal, 2007; Department of Census and Statistics, Sri Lanka, Demographic and Health Survey, 2000, Colombo, 2000; Department of Census and Statistics, 'Census of Population and Housing', Colombo, 2001; Department of Census and Statistics, 'Statistical Abstract 2005', Colombo; De Silva, Indralal, 'A Population Projection of Sri Lanka: For the New Millennium 2001-2101, Trends and Implications', Institute for Health Policy, Colombo, 2007.

Table 2: Dependency ratios, 1981–2041

(Per 1,000 persons)

	1981	2001	2021	2031	2041
Child dependency ratio	60.5	40.7	26.1	22.9	22.2
Old age dependency ratio	11.3	14.3	28.4	36.9	50.1
Total dependency ratio	71.8	55.0	54.5	59.8	72.3

Source: Same as Table 1.

Table 2 shows how the burden of dependency changes with the ageing of population. It should be noted that the dependency that is measured here is the demographic dependency in terms of the size of the age group – the ratio of the total number of dependents in childhood and old age to the total number in the economically active age group. Demographic dependency should be distinguished from economic dependency; this is examined in the section on the socio-economic status and living conditions of the old. Economic dependency will denote the ratios of the productively employed workforce to the dependent population groups. Demographic dependency has characteristics specific to the physical and personal burden of dependency – the component of care and family support. The economically inactive population who are excluded in computing economic dependency have a crucial role to play in managing the household and living conditions of the dependents and providing emotional and physical care. The economic dependency ratio on the other hand indicates the economic and financial resources that would be available for social security and services for the dependent population and is essential for examining the economic capacity of the household to support the dependents and the macroeconomic and fiscal implications of ageing. The economic dependency ratio is highly susceptible to change in response to a number of variables such as the participation rates. These are discussed in the section that follows.

The total burden of dependency in the region was 70 in 1981. It dropped sharply and remained within a range of 55 to 60 in the period 2001–31. In 2021, the proportion of the old population in the total population overtakes that of the child population and old age dependency rises to 28.4 per cent, more than 2 per cent above child dependency at 26.1 per cent. The total dependency ratio reverts again to the 1970s in 2041. Meanwhile, the weight of the burden of dependency shifts dramatically from the child population to the old, moving from a ratio of 60 in respect of child dependency in 1981 to 50 in respect of old age dependency in 2041. The old age dependency ratio rises from approximately 14 in 2001 to 36.9 in 2031 and 50 in 2041. This means that, whereas in 2001, there would be more than seven active persons in the age group 15–59 to every old person above 60 years of age, in 2041, there would be less than two (1.94). This is of course balanced by a sharp drop in child dependency and the number of child dependents. The average family will be released from part of the present burden of child dependents to provide for the care and support of the old.

Gender Differentials in Marriage, Divorce and Widowhood

Table 3 provides comparative data on nuptiality taken from the two censuses and depicts the trends over a period of 20 years when the demographic changes accelerated and the socio-economic impact of the economic reforms of the post-1978 period had time to take effect. The population over 30 years of age has been taken to ascertain the prevalence of marriage, as the average ages of marriage for males and females are about 28 and 24 years respectively. For the population above 30 years, the proportion of never married persons is in the region of 9.7 per cent in 1981 and 8.5 per cent in 2001. The lower figure for females in the married state has to be related to the much higher proportion of females who are widows. For the age group over 60 the total number of males who had remained single was about 45,000 (6 per cent) and that of females 36,000 (4 per cent). The total number of marriages has steadily risen from 125,223 in 1980 to 174,000 in 1999 which means that 250,000 males and females in 1980 and 354,000 in 1999 have entered the married state. These figures indicate that the trends relating to marriage have remained stable over time and that the large majority of the adult population continue to enter into legal marriages.

Monogamy is established by civil law with the sole exception of marriages contracted under Islamic law, but even here the incidence of polygamy is very rare. Monogamous family units therefore form the basic social unit for cohabitation and care during the entire lifecycle from childhood to old age.

The divorce rate in Sri Lanka is quite low. The 2001 census gives the total number of married persons as 7.4 million and the number of divorced persons as 23,820 – 0.32 per cent. The number of legally separated persons is 15,965. Those who are informally separated add up to another 78,866. The total number of people whose marriages have been disrupted in various forms would still be in the region of 1.6 per cent. According to the available global data on divorces, Sri Lanka has the lowest divorce rate of 0.15 per 1,000 people. The data for marriage and divorce over the period 1980–2001 indicate, that with the major demographic changes that are taking place, the basic social institutions of marriage and the family have remained relatively stable.

The 1981 census enumerated a total number of 468,000 widowed persons. Of these, the large majority, 377,000 (80 per cent) were females of whom 193,573 were over the age of 60 years. In the 2001 census, the total figure had increased to 549,000 of whom 471,429 (85 per cent) were females and of them 283,167 were over the age of 60. As stated earlier,

Table 3: Marital status, 1981 and 2001

	1981		2001	
	Male	Female	Male	Female
Population over 30 years of age	2,689,289	2,526,355	3,867,226	4,035,922
Married population over 30 years of age*	2,271,076	1,940,783	3,140,877	2,979,578
Divorced and Legally Separated	20,709	29,752	15,515	24,266
Not Legally Separated	–	–	31,413	47,453
Widowed	90,516	377,487	78,165	471,429
Widowed 60 & over	57,068	193,573	29,789	273,167
Never married population over 30 years of age	312,781	198,983	393,547	283,757
Never married over 60 years of age	34,889	21570	45,831	36,706
Average age of marriage	27.9	24.4	–	–

Note: These figures cover only the population fully enumerated in 2001 and exclude the seven districts in the north and east, where the population estimates are based on a sample survey. *excludes a total of 394,000 males and females who contracted customary marriages in 2001 Source: Same as Table 1.

the increasing number of widows among the elderly female population is an effect of the demographic transition and the gender differential in the average lifespan.

Trends in Fertility, Mortality and Family Size

Another important set of variables affecting the general living conditions of the female population and particularly the elderly segment in that population are those affecting the reproductive health of women.

The crude birth rate which declined slowly over a period of 30 years from 40 per thousand of population in1950 to 28.2 in 1981, dropped at a more accelerated pace to 16 by 2004. Infant mortality rate declined steadily from 82 in 1950 to 12 in 2001. Maternal mortality had declined from 55.5 per 10,000 live births in 1950 to 6.4 in 1980 to less than one (0.92) by 2000. The total fertility had fallen from 5.32 in 1953 to 3.45 in 1981 to 1.9 in 2004. The size of the household according to the socio-economic surveys conducted by the Central Bank and the Census and Statistics continued to fall from 5.75 individuals per household in 1963 to 4.61 in 1996–7 and 4.31 in 2003–4. All these indicators are closely inter-related. The drop in infant mortality and the improved chances of survival of children contributed to the reproductive behaviour that led to control of births and reduced the number of births per female. This in turn helped to improve the health status of women and extend their lifespan. Reduced number of births meant smaller families and smaller household size.

Table 4: Trends in birth rates, mortality and fertility, 1950–2002

(Per 1,000 persons)

	1950	1963	1971	1981	2002
Crude Birth Rate	40.5	34.1	30.4	28.2	19.1
Infant Mortality	82.3	56	45	30	11
Maternal Mortality	5.6	2.4	1.4	0.6	0.2 (1996)
Total Fertility Rate	NA	5.0	3.4 (1974)	3.7	1.9 (2000)
Family Size	NA	5.7	5.6 (1973)	5.23	4.3 (2003)

Source: Same as Table 1.

The impact all these demographic changes had on the family and its capacity to protect the well-being of its old members was, on the whole, positive in character. First, the total burden of dependency was being reduced substantially. It was declining from the high ratio of 71 in 1980 to levels ranging between 55 and 60 and will continue within this range till about 2031. Second, by reducing the burden of child dependency, these changes would be enabling the family to deal better with its old age dependents. As stated earlier, it is around 2041 that we return to the high level of overall dependency of around 70 that prevailed in the early 1980s, imposing severe strains on both the family and the economy. Therefore, the country needs to take advantage of the intervening period when the burden of dependency is comparatively low to develop strategies and policies that would be able to cope with the problems that will emerge in the long term.

Socio-Economic Profile of the Older Persons

Sources of Income and Ownership of Assets

If we assume that there are no wide disparities in life expectancy as between income deciles, the old population is likely to be distributed equally as members of households among the different income deciles and the socio-economic profile of the old population which relates to income will broadly correspond to the national profile of income distribution.

We are likely to find equal numbers of old people in the income deciles ranging from the first 2.5 income deciles which are below the poverty line to the highest income deciles which enjoy more than 40 per cent of the total household income. On an average, the old population will be found in equal numbers in households in each income stratum. Only minor adjustments will be needed for marginal variations in life expectancy, if any, as between income deciles as well as for regional variations. These adjustments are likely to reveal that the proportions of the old population are smaller in the disadvantaged groups for the obvious reason that lower life expectancies will result in lower proportions of the aged.

The macro-level socio-economic profile of the old population which emerges is still very aggregative in character and by itself does not tell us much about the intra-household distribution of resources and specific conditions of the old within these households. This distribution of the old population among the income deciles does not mean that the old persons in these households enjoy and have control over the incomes of the households in which they live. It only denotes the level of well-being of the household in which they live and in which they are likely to share. To some extent, it is an indicator of the economic capacity to bear the burden of old age dependency. To ascertain the incomes and other financial resources possessed by the old we need to go to other sources of data. The first UN principle states that older persons should have access to adequate food, water, shelter, clothing and health care through the provision of income, family and community support and self-help. Access to a source of income and possession of income earning assets is a fundamental prerequisite for a satisfying quality of life for the elders. The case studies indicate that the status of the elders range from a high degree of dependence both financially and physically to conditions in which they are relatively independent with adequate means to support themselves and in possession of the necessary physical and mental capabilities. In terms of these criteria, the majority of the very old would be in the former and the majority of young-old would be in the latter. For the very old, possession of a source of income may bring with it only nominal financial independence; their health status and physical dependence will deprive them of any effective control over these resources. They would eventually have to rely on the conduct of the caregivers for the quality of the care they receive. But, in all circumstances, income and self-help gives the old a measure of independence and autonomy which compensates for the growing physical dependence.

Employment Related Income of the Old

The financial independence of the old comes out of the sources of income they enjoy. These sources would depend on the nature of the income earning occupations the old had when they were economically active, the continuing sources of income they enjoy as a result of their retirement benefits, their savings and investments and their ownership of income earning assets and property.

The data from the labour force surveys enable us to draw some conclusions regarding the socio-economic status of the old population. In the Labour Force Survey of 1998, the labour force participation rate for the total population over 10 years has been 51.4 per cent with the male participation being approximately 67.7 per cent and the female 35 per cent – slightly more than half of that of males. The participation rates for males in the age group 20–49 years is about 94 per cent and for females 52 per cent. These rates are relevant for determining the proportions of the old population who were in the labour force during a large part of their economically active life. In 1998, the labour force participation rate for the old population over 60 years has been about 29 per cent – 45.9 per cent for males and 11.6 per cent for females. These data indicate that a significant proportion of the population over 60 years continue in employment and have a source of income. The major share of this workforce is in the young-old category – the 60–70 years age group. The demographic survey of 1994 has provided a breakdown of this workforce into five-year age groups which show that the major share of this workforce is in the 60–70 years age group with a small proportion extending into the age group above 70.

This old workforce raises a number of policy issues regarding the aged. First, the large majority of these persons are own account workers for whom there are no fixed age limits to their working life. There is no reliable data on the health status, working conditions and levels of earnings of this group. It is likely that many of the old workers are compelled by their indigent circumstances to continue working as they would have no other means of subsistence. These aspects need further investigation and study. On the other hand, this elderly workforce would include the old, who have the capacity to be economically active and who find self-fulfilment in work and continue to be gainfully occupied. The fact that there is a fairly high level of participation by workers above 60 years raises questions regarding the present age of retirement and the definition of the old. Should not both these be raised to 65? If nearly 30 per cent of the household population over 60 years is in the workforce, first, the problems of social security are to that extent reduced and second, the quality of life of the old population could be enhanced. What is needed are supportive measures that keep this workforce healthy and well-remunerated and promote opportunities for the old to be gainfully employed and actively contributing to society as long as they are in sound physical and mental health.

The data also indicate that compared to females, males with higher rates of participation and employment are much more favourably placed in regard to the retirement benefits and income support that they can expect from their employment during their old age. While the rate of participation of males during the working life between 20 and 60 years ranges between 84 per cent and 96 per cent, the rates for females range between 31 to 55 per cent. The male employed workforce is approximately double the female. The average estimated earned income of the female is half that of the male. Therefore, the male remains the principal provider for the household with greater access to and control over the household's resources.

The large majority of the old persons are not in the workforce. Of the total population over 60 years approximately 55 per cent have retired. It is this group who will enjoy retirement benefits of various kinds ranging from pensions in the public sector to one-time payment from provident funds in the case of employees in the formal private sector. Reliable estimates regarding the economic status of the old and data such as the number enjoying government pension and other retirement benefits require a survey of the elderly. In the absence of such data the employment status of the workforce will provide some useful information on how these benefits are distributed among the old population.

Table 5 gives the distribution for employed population by employment status and sex for 1981 and 2001. This profile of the employment status could be used to obtain some indicative estimates of the sources of income and nature of the financial support that the old could expect from their employment. According to the data for 2001, nearly 60 per cent are employees – about 13 per cent in the public sector and 46 per cent in the private sector. About 80 per cent of the public sector employees are in government institutions and are entitled to generous pensions. The remaining employees of the private sector are entitled to lump sum payments under the Employees Provident Fund (EPF) and the Employees Trust Fund (ETF). If the number of active member accounts in the provident fund are taken as a rough estimate of the coverage of the provident fund, approximately 2 million employees were covered in 2004. This coverage includes about 275,000 employees in the semi-government institutions and about 45 per cent of private sector employees.

Under the government pension scheme, government employees must be employed for a minimum of ten years to become eligible for a regular monthly pension during their lifetime after retirement. They are entitled to receive the pension when they retire on reaching the age of retirement, which is optional at 55 years and compulsory at 60 years. The maximum pension computed on this basis can amount to as much as 90 per cent of the average of the employee's salary drawn during the last three years of his service. The employee also has the option of commuting his salary and drawing a lump sum payment in which case he will draw a reduced

Table 5: Distribution and workforce by employment status

		1981			2001		
		Total	Male	Female	Total	Male	Female
Category		4,119,265 (100.0)	3,248,428 (100.0)	870,837 (100.0)	7,394,559 (100.0)	5,049,648 (100.0)	234,491 (100.0)
	Total	2,769,469 (67.2)	2,061,822 (63.5)	7,07,647 (51.5)	4,395,124 (59.4)	2973570 (58.8)	1,421,554 (60.6)
Employee	Public	1,354,184 (32.9)	905,399 (29.9)	448,785 (51.5)	963,852 (13.0)	600,381 (11.9)	363.471 (15.5)
	Private	1,415,285 (34.3)	1,156,423 (35.6)	258,862 (29.7)	3,431,272 (46.4)	2,373,189 (46.9)	1,058,083 (45.1)
Employer		71,062 (1.7)	63,789 (2.0)	7273 (0.8)	211,019 (2.9)	194,773 (3.9)	21,246 (0.9)
Own Account Worker		1,169,814 (26.4)	1,054,111 (32.4)	115,703 (13.3)	2,090,660 (28.3)	1,652,322 (32.7)	438,339 (18.7)
Unpaid Family Worker		108,920 (2.6)	68,706, (2.1)	40.214 (4.6)	692,756 (9.4)	228,983 (4.5)	463,772 (19.8)
Work Participation rate		33.8	49.4	17.1	48.8	66.3	33.9

Source: Department of Census and Statistics, *Annual Report of the Sri Lanka Labour Force Survey – 2004*, Colombo.

pension. In case of the pensioner's death, the spouse who survives the pensioner is entitled to the full pension. Therefore, the government pension scheme which provides a source of regular income, which at best amounts to 90 per cent of the income received at the end of the employee's career, would enable him to maintain or improve the standard of living he had when he was employed, given the fact that at this stage of life the pensioner would no longer have the household responsibilities of a growing family. Under the EPF, an employee contributes 8 per cent of his earnings and the employer matches this with 12 per cent making a total of 20 per cent. These contributions are held by the employee in an account in the EPF which earns interest. The accumulated money lying to the credit of the employee can be drawn at the time of his retirement after he reaches the age of 55. In addition, the employer has to contribute 3 per cent of the employee's earnings to an ETF which is invested on his behalf. These assets too can be drawn by the employee on his retirement. The EPF and ETF together enable the employee to save about 23 per cent of his total earnings which together with the interest earned is available to him on retirement. With the exception of daily paid casual workers who are not regularly employed by a single employer, the EPF is compulsory for all workers and employers in firms employing more than twenty workers. All employees are further entitled to a retirement gratuity of half a month's salary for every year of service. Of the two types of retirement benefits the old persons covered by the pension scheme have greater security of income than those benefiting from the EPF. The pension ensures a regular stream of income for the entire remaining lifespan of the pensioner regardless of his life expectancy. It is also adjusted for inflation. The one-time payment under the EPF can be substantial and can be converted into income earning investments. But the available information indicates that the majority of beneficiaries are unable to do this on a scale adequate to provide them with the income support they need in old age.

Detailed data on the economic status of the old population including the numbers covered by retirement are not available and would have to be collected through a national survey of the old population. According to the government data, for all retired government servants receiving pension there were 371,000 pensioners receiving government pension benefits in 2000. The number has been increasing at an annual average of about 10,000 during the last ten years. This figure, however, does not help us to ascertain the number of pensioners over 60 years of age as it includes all age groups – those who have retired at 55 at the optional age of retirement and the large number who were given the benefit of early retirement when services were restructured and their working conditions altered as a result of crucial policy changes such as the official language policy. We can derive some broad indicative estimates of the proportions of the population who enjoy employment related benefits by using the proportions of the employees covered by pension and provident fund when the present old population over 60 years of age were in the employed workforce. Old persons who reached 80 in 2000 would have reached the age of 55, the optional age of retirement in 1975 and the compulsory age of retirement in 1980. Old persons who reached 60 in 2000 would have normally retired in the period 1995–2000. The employment status of the workforce during 1975–2000 would help us to derive some indicative estimates of the old population who enjoy employment related benefits of either the pension or the provident fund. The economic status of the current generation of elders has to be compared to the employment status they enjoyed when they were economically active and left the workforce in the period following 1975. Unfortunately, we do not have a comparable set of data on employment status of the workforce covering the full period, particularly for the very old and old who would have joined the workforce in the 1940s and 1950s. The earliest data set is that of the 1981 census. According to the 1981 census, the number of employees in government services was about 12 per cent of the workforce and semi-government institutions about 20 per cent, approximately 32 per cent in all, and much higher than in 2004. This difference is due to the programme of privatization and retrenchment in the semi-government sector. The shift from the semi-government sector to the private sector would not have made any difference in regard to the conditions pertaining to retirement benefits as in both sectors employees would have been eligible for the same retirement benefits of the EPF and ETF. In 1981, there were approximately 1.2 million active accounts in the EPF for about 2.246 million employees in the semi-government and private sectors. This figure indicates a coverage of about 50 per cent of the total number of employees outside the government sector. This leaves approximately about 25 per cent of the employees who are not covered by any scheme that brings them retirement benefits. The differences between 1981 and 2004 for employment status are marginal. In addition to the EPF and ETF, there are a few private funds which had been established by some large private sector firms for the benefit of their employees. These were allowed to continue if the benefits they provided were not less than those of the EPF. These funds would cover a very small proportion of private employees. On these data, the proportion of the old population who would have been in the workforce as employees and who would be drawing a pension would be in the range of 10 per cent to 15 per cent, and the proportion who would have drawn provident fund benefits would be about 25 per cent to 30 per cent. The vulnerable group will be 25 per cent to 30 per cent, who were employees without any coverage for retirement.

In 2004, own account workers accounted to nearly 28 per cent of the workforce and 3 per cent were employers. In the 1981 Census, the proportions were 28 per cent and 1.2 per cent respectively. Own account workers – farmers, fishermen and the self-employed in other sectors will be among the most vulnerable segments of the old population. They will continue in employment as long as is physically possible and will constitute the major share of the workforce over 60 years of age. When they are no longer able to engage in income earning activity they would have to depend on savings and other income earning assets. The large majority of them would have to rely on the care that their families can provide. However, in the case of farmers, the ownership of agricultural land will give farmers considerable decision-making power over their living conditions in old age. The government initiative to provide voluntary contributory pension schemes for the farmers and fishermen is an attempt to provide social security to this category, but for a variety of reasons participation in these schemes has been very limited.

There is another category of employees whose status is relevant for their situation in old age. This is the category of unpaid family workers.

They would be generally working with own account workers, in family farms and other small household enterprises. In the 1981 census, they constituted 2.4 per cent. This is probably an underestimate due to inadequate coverage of this segment. In the labour force surveys that have been conducted from 1990 onwards, this figure has fluctuated widely both quarterly and annually. In 2004, they comprised approximately 9.4 per cent of the workforce; about two-thirds of these employees are females and the large majority of these females are in the agricultural sector. Apart from the aggregate data we have no age-specific or socio-economic data about this group. It is not clear to what extent family work is a transitory stage from which the large majority of workers improve their status of employment over time. In the case of workers who remain as unpaid family workers during their working life, unpaid family work would be one of the most vulnerable and dependent conditions. We need to gather more information about this group to identify the nature of the problems pertaining to it and formulate relevant policy responses.

Finally, there is the sizeable population of old females who have not entered the workforce and who have been engaged in household responsibilities as housewives. Given that the female rates of participation in the labour force are at best approximately 50 per cent, about half of the old females will fall into this category and will enjoy no employment related benefits. Any income and property these females would have in their old age, in their own right, would be what they brought with them at the time of marriage. But, as the large majority of the old population is married, the female old population will share in the employment related benefits of their spouses. However, the gender relations and the distribution of power and responsibility in old age will derive from the situation that prevailed when the old population was economically active and in the workforce. In this situation the decision-making power will be held by the males and the intra-family relations and the value system governing gender relations will determine the quality of life of the females. Therefore, housewives who have no independent means can be a particularly vulnerable category in their old age, especially in widowhood.

Ownership of Homes

One major source of security for the old is their ownership of their homes. As stated earlier, the state's policies on housing have enabled the largehousing conditions is given in Table 6.

The data indicate that nearly 90 per cent of the households own their home. With the exception of two provinces the central (76 per cent) and northern (63 per cent) all the provinces record a level above 85 per cent.

Table 6: Type of ownership of houses (As a percentage of households)

Type of Ownership	Six Month Household Income Quintile					All
	1	2	3	4	5	
Own House	85.7	86.6	90.3	91.6	91.7	89.2
Owned by Government / Employer	7.5	8.3	3.8	3.2	2.3	5.0
Leased / Rented	1.1	1.4	2.7	3.1	3.9	2.5
Free of Rent	5.4	3.6	3.1	2.0	1.9	3.2
Other	0.3	0.1	0.1	0.1	0.1	0.1

Source: Central Bank of Sri Lanka, *Consumer Finances & Socio Economic Survey – Sri Lanka 2003/04*, Part I, Colombo, 2004.

Over 80 per cent of all houses are permanent structures. The home is therefore a valuable asset and its owner is likely to enjoy both status and decision-making power. The proportion of those who own their homes in the population as a whole is most likely to apply to the old population as well. On this assumption, over 80 per cent of the old population are likely to own the home in which they reside. As the case studies have shown most old people retain ownership of their homes and children acquire ownership only after the death of their parents. The home and the property that goes with it, being vital capital assets for the household as a whole, their ownership continues to provide the old a certain measure of control over their living conditions. This has been borne out in the micro-level case studies that have been conducted.

Ownership of Land

Table 7 gives the most recent data available on land ownership from the Consumer Finances and Socio-economic survey of the Central Bank, 2003–4.

With the exception of the estate sector, the large majority of households in both rural and urban sectors own some type of land. As might be expected, land ownership is highest in the rural sector, where 93 per cent of households own homestead land and 41 per cent agricultural land. This is the sector which contains the largest proportion of own account workers. In the urban sector, 83 per cent of households own homestead land. The ownership of homestead lands goes together with the ownership of housing. The average size of land per household is 138.3 perches. As in the case of housing, the old population will normally retain their ownership of land during their lifetime and ownership of this asset will confer them some degree of security and control. In contrast, only a small minority of the households in the estate sector own any type of house or land. The

Table 7: Ownership of land by utilization and sector (As a percentage of households)

Type of Use	Sector			All Sector
	Urban	Rural	Estate	
Homestead Land	85.1	93.7	15.5	88.7
Agricultural Land	6.3	41.4	9.1	35.4
Commercial / Industrial Land	3.3	2.2	0.7	2.3
Unutilized Land	9.9	14.7	3.0	13.5

Source: Same as Table 6.

large majority of the old population in the estate sector will not therefore have the security and decision-making power that their counterparts in the other sectors have through their ownership of property.

Living Conditions of the Elderly Households

The elderly population will generally enjoy the living conditions of the households in which they live. The Consumer Finances and Socio Economic Survey (CF & SES) 2003–4 gives the latest data on the distribution of housing utilities and amenities. The quality of the houses in which people live is one of the most revealing indicators of their living conditions. If we assume that the proportion of the old in each income category is more or less the same as the national proportion, we can come to some broad conclusions regarding the general living conditions of the old population. The general quality of housing and how it is distributed among the different income groups is given in the recent CF & SES survey of the Central Bank (Table 8).

Nearly 85 per cent of the population lives in homes constructed with permanent materials. About 12.5 per cent live in wattle and daub houses with clay floors and cadjan or semi-permanent roofs. This component of substandard housing is concentrated in the lowest two income quintiles (bottom 40 per cent) of households, mainly in the rural and estate sector. In the lowest income quintile, the poor quality houses (with clay mud walls) are about 34 per cent, houses with mud walls and clay floors 27.8 per cent and houses of cadjan,12.5 per cent. The next quintile has smaller proportions of 21 per cent and 18 per cent to 8.4 per cent respectively. Living conditions in these households are likely to be the poorest and the old population in these households the most vulnerable. In terms of the utilities, water, sanitation, lighting and cooking facilities the living conditions of households have steadily improved. Approximately, 76 per cent of households have a protected source of drinking water, about 10 per cent have access to an unprotected well while about 5–7 per cent who are the most vulnerable use a river, tank or stream. These figures may,

Table 8: Types of construction by income quintile (As a percentage of households)

Category	Six Month Household Income Quintile					All
	1	2	3	4	5	
Wall Type						
Bricks	44.5	50.1	54.7	60.3	67.5	55.4
Cement Block	14.8	18.1	24.1	25.9	22.4	21.1
Cabook / Stone	7.6	9.8	7.7	7.1	8.1	8.1
Wattle and Daub / Mud	27.8	17.9	10.7	4.6	1.2	12.5
Wooden Plank / Metal Sheet	2.5	2.3	2.0	1.3	0.6	1.7
Cadjan / Palmyrah	1.2	0.9	0.3	0.5	0.0	0.6
Other	1.6	1.0	0.3	0.2	0.1	0.6
Floor Type						
Cement	60.5	74.6	82.7	88.4	83.6	77.9
Terrasso / Tile / Granite / Polished Wood	0.2	0.4	1.6	2.9	14.4	3.9
Prepared Clay / Mud	34.8	21.5	11.5	4.4	0.6	14.5
Wooden Plank	0.3	0.2	0.1	0.1	0.0	0.2
Unprepared Earth / Sand	3.8	2.9	3.5	3.5	1.0	3.0
Other	0.3	0.5	0.6	0.7	0.5	0.5
Roof Type						
Tiles	53.6	57.3	63.8	63.0	55.2	58.6
Asbestos	8.8	12.7	18.9	24.9	35.2	20.1
Metal / Tar Sheet / Amano	23.4	19.9	11.0	7.0	3.0	12.9
Cadjan / Palmyrah / Straw	12.5	8.4	4.7	2.0	0.3	5.6
Other	1.7	1.6	1.6	3.1	6.2	2.9

Source: Same as Table 6.

however, understate some of the seasonal variations and hazards that may arise in drought seasons in the dry zone. 5.6 per cent of households have no latrines, 7.8 per cent have pit latrines, and the rest of the households have latrines of satisfactory quality. Regarding lighting, 75 per cent have electricity supply, others rely on kerosene. For cooking, the large majority of households still rely on firewood. The use of kerosene and gas is confined to about half the households in the urban sector. Only about 30 per cent possess a refrigerator. The availability of radio and television, and access to a telephone will have an important impact on the leisure, recreation and social life of elders. In the recent past, access to a computer and use of it has made a significant difference to the quality of a small minority of the old population in affluent households. The availability of these facilities in households in 2003–4 is shown in Table 9.

Table 9: Availability of media/communication (As a percentage of households)

Item	Six Month Household Income Quintile					All
	1	2	3	4	5	
Radio	58.4	72.2	79.4	87.0	94.5	78.3
Television	38.5	57.7	74.6	87.2	95.9	70.8
Land / Cellular Phone (a)	1.5	4.3	13.8	32.3	70.4	24.5
Land Phone	0.6	2.2	7.0	18.3	55.3	16.7
Cellular Phone	1.0	2.3	7.5	17.5	38.3	13.3
Computer	0.1	0.2	0.7	1.7	17.9	4.1
E-mail	0.0	0.1	0.0	0.1	6.5	1.3

(a) Sub-category shares do not add up, as some households possess both categories of phones.
Source: Same as Table 6.

The data shows that the distribution of the amenities relating to media and communication has been progressing steadily. More than 70 per cent of the households possess radios and TV. More than half of the lowest quintile possess a radio and one-third a TV set. There is a considerable improvement as we move to the second quintile. The access to a telephone is as yet restricted to 24.5 per cent of the population. The survey also indicates that 4.1 per cent of households possessed a computer at the time of the survey. What is encouraging is that while the overwhelming majority of the users are in the highest income quintile the use of computers is reaching out to the lowest quintiles. There is one in a thousand households in the lowest quintile and two in a thousand in the second. While the coverage of radio and telephone is likely to increase rapidly the same cannot be said of the telephone and computer. Increasing the number of users of these two facilities will require not only rapid increase of household incomes but also access to cheaper services and greater marketing and promotional effort.

Educational Attainments of the Old Population

The educational attainment of the old, their capacity to access information and knowledge and by this means have some decision-making power will be an important determinant of the quality of their lives. It will affect their social life and their leisure time activity. Free education has produced a highly literate population and the old population would have participated in the benefits of free education which would help them to enjoy many of the conditions that are defined in the UN principles such as independence and dignity.

The age distribution for literacy and educational attainment is not yet available for the 2001 Census. They are however available from the CF & SES survey for 2003–4 and although the data is from a sample survey it is adequately representative for the purpose of delineating the educational profile of the aged (Table 10).

Table 10: Literacy rates by sector and age group 2003–04 (As a percentage of population in each age group)

Age Group (Years)	Sector			All Sectors
	Urban	Rural	Estate	
05–14	94.3	94.3	92.1	94.2
15–24	97.9	98.6	95.0	98.3
25–34	96.5	96.2	84.1	95.6
35–54	95.4	91.8	72.9	91.3
55–64	94.7	89.3	62.5	88.5
Over 64	82.3	75.7	54.1	75.7
All groups	94.8	92.8	81.3	92.5

Source: Same as Table 6.

The rates of illiteracy increase progressively with the older age cohorts. Here again, the female rates of illiteracy are more than double the rates for the males. The illiteracy that continues to be recorded is largely the result of the survival of persons who were not able to enter the school system in 1930–50. These rates will persist at a somewhat lower rate during the next two decades. The illiterate, particularly the females would be a highly vulnerable group among the elders. Their vulnerability will however be mitigated by the fact that the large majority of them will be living in households with members who are literate and educated. The data from the CF & SES survey give us more information on the educational attainment and literacy rates of the old population (Table 11).

The data for the population over 64 could be taken for our analysis as the preceding ten-year age group includes those between 50 and 55. About 25 per cent of the population over 65 has no schooling and is illiterate. The largest pocket of illiteracy is in the rural sector which has approximately 25 per cent of illiterates. The rate of illiteracy is highest in the estate sector with 54 per cent. The estate sector however contains only about 5 per cent of the population. 41.7 per cent of the population had a primary education, 25 per cent had seven to ten years of schooling and 7.9 per cent had reached the post secondary stage. Majority of the elderly have an educational background and are sufficiently literate to occupy themselves meaningfully in activities in the community during their leisure time.

Table 11: Attainment of education by age group and gender, 2003–04 (As a percentage of population in each age group)

Education Level	Gender	Age Group (Years)							All Group
		05–09	10–14	15–24	25–34	35–54	55–64	Over 64	
No Schooling	Male	11.1	0.7	2.0	4.3	7.5	7.6	11.8	5.8
	Female	13.7	0.6	1.4	4.9	10.4	16.8	36.6	9.7
	Both	12.4	0.7	1.7	4.6	9.1	12.2	25.3	7.9
Primary (a)	Male	88.9	50.5	7.1	14.5	25.8	35.0	49.5	31.6
	Female	86.3	48.9	4.8	11.5	25.1	33.9	35.2	28.3
	Both	87.6	49.7	5.9	12.9	25.4	34.5	41.7	29.9
Secondary (b)	Male	–	48.8	57.5	50.5	45.4	38.1	28.7	42.9
	Female	–	50.5	52.1	48.2	40.4	33.5	22.0	39.4
	Both	–	49.6	54.8	49.3	42.7	35.7	25.1	41.1
Post Secondary (c)	Male	–	–	33.4	30.7	21.3	19.4	10.0	19.7
	Female	–	–	41.6	35.4	24.1	15.8	6.2	22.5
	Both	–	–	37.6	33.3	22.8	17.6	7.9	21.2

(a) Completed Kindergarten to passed Year 6
(b) Passed Year 7 to passed Year 10 (up to G.C.E. Ordinary Level)
(c) Passed Year 11 to graduated (G.C.E. Ordinary Level and above)
Source: Same as Table 6.

Health Care for the Aged

One key determinant of the quality of life of elders will be their access to health care and the quality of the services available to them. Equally with other age groups, the old population will have access to the free health care services delivered by the state. The state services provide approximately 70 per cent of the services needed; the balance 30 per cent is provided by the private sector. Apart from micro-level studies on the efficiency and coverage of the health services which include a component of the old population, there are no large-scale surveys of the health status and health care of the old population. There are micro-level studies on self reporting and self assessment of health by elders and surveys of their functional ability to attend to basic Activities of Daily Living (ADL). There are no age-specific data for morbidity or hospitalization in the annual health bulletin. There is a set of data relating to age specific causes of mortality based on the Registrar General's statistics. The CS &SE survey data contains some information on age-specific rates of illnesses. These however are not classified according to the diseases in the international code for diseases and only describe the condition of ill health in general descriptive terms such as fever, cough, breathing problems (Table 12).

Table 12: Person in ill health by province and age group (As a percentage of population)

Age group (Years)	All Provinces
Below 15	14.2
15–34	8.7
35–54	14.1
55–64	18.4
Over 64	22.1
All Groups	13.3

Source: Same as Table 6.

The CF & SES data are useful for identifying the broad trends in age specific morbidity. They indicate how the main burden of morbidity has shifted from the infant and child group to the old population. In 1981–2, the rate of morbidity for the age group 0–4 was 19.78 per cent while the rate for the entire population group over 55 years was 18.64. In 2003–4, the rate below 15 years was 14.2 per cent while that of the age group over 64 years was 22.1 per cent.

The micro surveys on self assessment indicate that about 50–60 per cent assessed their health as excellent, good or fair. The ADL surveys dealt with daily activities relating to personal cleanliness, feeding, etc. as well as the use of instruments. The percentage of the old who were able to attend to their daily activities without difficulty ranged from 60–90 per cent in these surveys. The proportion of females with functional ability (76 per cent in one of the surveys) was less than that of males (82 per cent). A large proportion of the elderly consider themselves healthy and are able to carry out normal, everyday activities. As might be expected, instrumental ability was much lower. Functional ability declined sharply in elders over 80 years of age. The data in these studies need to be compared with some of the data on economic activity and labour force participation that indicate a considerable proportion of the old remain in active working life beyond 70 years of age.

The data set in the annual health bulletin on age-specific mortality and causes of death, although dealing only with the pattern of disease leading to death, enables us to identify the main diseases that affect the elderly and serves as a useful starting point. It should be noted that some of the conditions of chronic morbidity among the old which may not be a major cause of mortality such as asthma and arthritis may not be fully represented in Table 13.

The data for 2002 – the latest published data available – indicates the dramatic changes in the age-specific disease pattern as a result of demographic transition. Whereas in the 1940s, preventable deaths of infants

Table 13: Age and sex specific mortality rates per 100,000 population for selected diseases, 2002

Disease and ICD (10th Revision) Code	Sex	All ages	Under 1 year	1–4	5–14	15–24	25–44	45–64	65 & over
Neoplasms	Male	38.3	4.0	5.9	4.0	5.3	12.3	104.2	288.8
	Female	32.3	4.7	5.0	3.2	4.6	14.0	94.3	198.4
Anaemias	Male	2.5	3.3	1.6	0.4	0.4	0.9	4.9	20.9
	Female	2.7	2.7	1.4	0.4	0.9	1.6	5.7	16.1
Mental and behavioural disorders	Male	8.9	0.7	0.4	0.3	0.9	9.2	25.4	34.5
	Female	2.1	0.7	0.3	0.2	0.2	0.9	4.5	17.9
Hypertensive diseases	Male	16.6	1.3	0.0	0.1	0.6	2.7	40.6	167.7
	Female	21.1	0.7	0.0	0.1	0.3	1.9	22.0	142.5
Ischaemic heart diseases	Male	63.4	11.9	1.3	0.7	2.6	23.1	174.0	509.9
	Female	25.8	11.3	1.4	0.8	1.4	4.9	49.6	283.1
Diseases of the respiratory system	Male	49.4	123.0	13.6	3.9	5.5	15.9	106.6	417.5
	Female	28.8	97.5	12.8	3.2	5.5	9.9	48.6	250.8
Diseases of the digestive system	Male	37.7	22.5	3.7	1.4	2.2	38.3	116.3	121.0
	Female	6.5	12.7	3.5	2.1	1.0	3.2	14.5	38.6
Transport accident	Male	15.5	3.3	2.2	3.7	12.3	19.8	25.8	39.4
	Female	3.8	2.0	1.5	1.4	2.7	2.9	7.1	15.0

Source: Department of Health Services, Annual Health Bulletin, Colombo, 2002.

and children below the age of five posed the biggest challenge to health care, the incidence of mortality has shifted as might be expected to the oldest age cohorts, following the natural path of physical ageing and degeneration. This also represents an epidemiological transition from infectious parasitical and other external pathogens that are microbial in origin to non-communicable diseases which result from organic disorders of the human body, which are caused both by the degenerative processes of ageing, unhealthy lifestyles and heath hazards of the environment. Sri Lanka developed a health care system, both preventive and curative which was very well equipped to deal with the first category of health hazards and diseases. It was remarkably successful in improving child and maternal health and in controlling major communicable diseases such as malaria, tuberculosis, hookworm and typhoid. The system has not yet been able to adjust and acquire the new capacities needed to deal with the problems that have emerged with the ageing of the population and the rapidly increasing incidence of Non-Communicable Diseases (NCD) in the older age cohorts – heart diseases and diseases of the circulatory system, cancer, diseases arising from the malfunctioning of various vital organs of the body, diseases of the nervous system and mental illnesses. The deaths caused by these diseases per 100,000 of population double when we move from the 50–9 age group to the 60–9 age group; in the age group over 70 it is eight times those of the 50–9 age group.

The inadequacies in the present health care system in relation to the NCDs have been documented in several studies, notably the Marga study on NCDs.

- In general, NCDs are significantly different in the way they affect household incomes. The nature of the illness, the need for long-term care and vigilance, the recurrence of acute episodes and the regime of continuing medication imposes strains on the household economy in a way that other diseases such as infectious diseases and parasitic diseases do not. The latter group of diseases are usually episodic and of shorter duration, and when the cause of the illness is identified and treated, leads to full recovery. NCDs have a continuing grip on the household and households normally are required to allocate both financial and human resources on a regular basis for the management of these illnesses.
- Early diagnosis, self-care and health behaviour, control of the diet, the lifestyle of the patient and household are all critical determinants in the management of the NCDs and the path they take. In such a context, special care has to be given to programmes of health education that must form part of the health care of NCDs.
- In the case of NCDs, apart from the continuous management and control of diseases, certain conditions can arise where the patients are physically or mentally disabled to the extent that they cannot function without the assistance of others. In these circumstances they require continuous attention and supervision of other members of the household. In developed countries, either such households would have domiciliary assistance to handle the situation or such patients would be provided institutionalized care in appropriate institutions specially established for the purpose. In Sri Lanka, in the majority of these cases the responsibility would fall on the nuclear family and the closest relations.
- Interventions are required at two levels. First, diagnostic services and appropriate care must be provided closer to the household if the disease is to be controlled at an early stage at lower cost both to the state and to the household. Second, the serious gaps in knowledge on the part of patients in regard to their illnesses as revealed in studies draw attention to the deficiencies in the existing system of

health care for NCDs. There is a vital need to enhance the capacity of the household and the patient through a sustained and systematic programme of health education specially designed for the NCDs, and this must reach all parts of the country and all income levels. General knowledge of NCDs must be a readily available resource at the household and community level. The health education required for the NCDs is of a significantly different order than that for the infectious and parasitic diseases and child and maternal health that had hitherto been the dominant concerns of the health care system. Patients and households need to be educated so that they adopt the appropriate health behaviour and lifestyles and acquire the capacity for extended periods of basic self-care and for managing the disease throughout the lifetime of the patient. Health education for management of the disease and appropriate self-care will in all probability be of greater significance in dealing with the ill health of the present and future stages of the health transition than direct medical interventions by doctors. For such a health education initiative to be successful and effective the relationship between provider and household/patient has to be a continuing long-term one in which the rights of the patient to information is fully respected.

- The treatment of NCDs involves a long-term relationship between the provider and the patient. To produce successful health outcomes, such a relationship has to be caring and attentive in a sustained manner. The present system of health care is not fully designed to create and sustain the appropriate relationships between provider and patient that are demanded for the treatment of NCDs. The normal processes governing the treatment of patients have many of the attributes of a long-term relationship. The patient is registered for treatment in clinics and the history of the patient is maintained by the provider for continuing treatment. The patient is also given a document, which contains the basic information and enables the patient to report regularly on appointed days. Although these formal procedures lay the basis for the long-term relationship, the mode of treatment in actual practice fails to build up to the interactive relationship in which the patient remains the continuing subject of care and attention by the provider team and acquires the capacity for the management of the illness with the self-care and discipline needed.

These shortcomings affect victims of NCDs in general regardless of age but the hardships are accentuated in the case of old people. There is another dimension to the disease burden of the old – the gender dimension. Females significantly outnumber males and most of them are widows. The physical and mental health of the female elderly requires special attention. Although the burden of disease and mortality is shifting rapidly to the old population, the health care system has not yet adopted an age-specific approach to the treatment of disease. The government has not yet developed specialized services for geriatric care. It has, however, appointed a director who has been assigned the functions of planning, implementing, monitoring and co-ordinating the delivery of health care services to the elders. This director combines these duties with responsibilities for youth and disabled. One important initiative, which the Ministry of Health (MOH) has taken is the pilot project in which two to three areas have been selected from a district for implementing a holistic programme for improving the health care and well-being of the elderly. This programme aims at enhancing the care giving capacity of the family through trained health volunteers, promoting community participation, raising awareness of the public concerning the needs of the old population, providing health education and training, and improving tertiary health care for the elderly. This may provide the basis for an expanded and accelerated programme of care and enhancement of well-being of the old. This programme, however, still does not appear to be a significant element of national health policy. The latest available *Annual Health Bulletin* for 2002 does not refer to it.

There is no geriatric branch of the health care services or special facilities for the preventive and curative services for the old population. The deployment of specialists in the curative care services does not include any geriatric specialists. Hospitals do not have geriatric wards. The Post Graduate Institute of Medicine does not include any courses on geriatrics; neither has the social sciences given a special place to gerontology and the study of the special problems of ageing. There is also no provision for formal training for the paramedical professionals for geriatric care or home visitors who are the equivalent of midwives for child and maternal care. Such training forms part of the curricula of higher educational institutions in developed countries. The approach to health care which is generic and not age-specific in the case of the old population is probably based on the evidence of fairly high rates of mortality caused by NCDs in the age groups 40–59 who are in their productive age and whose claims on the health care system are higher than those of the old population. It might be argued that in such a situation the heath care services cannot afford to be age-specific and that heath care for the NCDs have to be organized on generic lines which will include the aged among other segments of the population. However, the data in the table indicate that not only is the rate per 100,000 much higher for the older population but that the number of cases for the old population far exceeds the number of cases for the 40–59 age group. The nature of ill health, health risks and needs, and the quality of care for the two age groups will differ significantly. It is possible that an age-specific system will not only enhance the quality of care for both groups but may also be more cost effective. The experience of geriatric health care in other countries with ageing populations appears to demonstrate this. These aspects of the health care system will need further study. Policymakers will need to pay greater attention to these aspects in developing a health policy that is better attuned to the needs of an ageing society.

There are a number of medico-legal problems pertaining to the old that require special attention. The rights of elders who suffer from various types of mental impairments are not adequately safeguarded under present laws and the procedures for medical treatment. Under guardianship and custody they lose their standing as a legal person even though in many cases they retain their faculties to the extent that they can be consulted and their wishes ascertained. With ageing and the high incidence of mental illnesses, the present medico-legal framework needs to be re-examined and appropriately amended to take account of these problems.

Poverty and the Old Population

In the earlier discussion on the distribution of the old population in different income classes and socio-economic categories, it was pointed out that this distribution of the old population will broadly correspond to the national distribution. A proportion of the elders will be included in the segment of the population who are in absolute poverty. However, the size of this segment is likely to be less than the national average, which is 22 per cent. As higher life expectancy would normally go with better living conditions, the rates of survival are likely to increase marginally with income and the higher income deciles are likely to contain a proportion larger than the national average. These broad conclusions are borne out in the most recent data from the 2002 Household and Income Expenditure Survey (HIES) showing the proportions of households in poverty in all the districts excluding those in the north and east.

The largest pockets of poverty in terms of numbers are in Kurunegala, Ratnapura, Kandy and Badulla which have over 300,000 people who live below the poverty line. The deepest pockets are in Monaragala, Ratnapura and Badulla which have more than 30 per cent in absolute poverty. The most vulnerable households in which the burden of care for the elderly are likely to be heaviest and in which the poverty trap becomes inescapable are likely to be in these districts.

Institutional Care of the Old and the Role of the NGOs

Institutional care is seen as a residual that looks after the old who do not have the support of the family – mainly the very poor destitute and abandoned old. There is no reliable information on the total number of voluntary and private institutions as all of them are not registered. The government runs four national homes and several cottage homes accommodating approximately 1,200. The registered homes for the elderly number 158 and provide accommodation to about 5,500. The registered homes receive a government grant and they come under government supervision for maintenance of the required standards. A major voluntary and philanthropic contribution from a large number of NGOs and the private sector has gone into this effort. Religious bodies and Helpage Sri Lanka have taken leading roles. However, as is evident from the figures the coverage is small. There have been no reliable surveys which have assessed the need and demand for these facilities. With the exception of a few micro-studies there has not been a full independent evaluation of the performance of these institutions. Many institutions such as Helpage, however, are recognized for the quality of their work and receive public support. In the past, institutional care of the aged had been associated with the destitute and the poor. In the recent past, however, the need for institutional care at all income levels has been recognized and is receiving attention. Few elder homes and residential facilities providing middle and upper class living conditions and care for elders have been established. These facilities are costly and are generally in the range of Rs 10,000 to Rs 15,000 per month. This component of residential facilities for elders is another facet of the needs of an ageing society that cut across income groups. This part would normally be met through the market and the private investment that would be generated. However, there would have to be a framework of regulations to protect the old population against exploitation and ensure standards that take care of the needs of the elderly.

The care of the aged has shown the capacity for mobilizing both generous philanthropic support and voluntary work. It seems to be strongly motivated by the traditional value system and religious ethos. In this context the NGOs have a special role to perform. Many of these NGOs are linked to religious institutions and are well equipped to maintain the balance between a family-centred system and institutional care where it is essential. The government has recognized and provided mechanisms for consultation and close collaboration. The national programme for the old would have to build on this partnership and promote NGO participation on a larger scale.

References

De Sliva, Indralal W, 'A Population Projection of Sri Lanka: For the New Millennium 2001–2101', *Trends and Implications,* Institute for Health Policy, Colombo, 2007.

Marga Institute, 'Sri Lanka's Population Future and its Implications for the Family and Elderly', Colombo, Sri Lanka, 1998.

UN, *Emerging Issues of Population Aging in Sri Lanka*, ESCAP, Bangkok, 1989.

UNFPA and PASL, *Ageing Population in Sri Lanka: Issues and Future Prospects*, Colombo, 2004.

Chapter 8

INSTITUTIONAL PROVISIONS AND HEALTH SECURITY FOR ELDERLY IN SRI LANKA

Myrtle Perera

Introduction

The goal of this chapter is to provide guidelines for public policy for social security and health care of the aged. The varied needs and experiences of the aged were obtained from clusters of populations that were probed as distinct groups in which key aspects of ageing were likely to differ from one another. This study envisaged an interest in understanding the significance of shifts in intergenerational contracts, in emerging institutional failures to cope with the process of ageing and it's implications for social security and health of a highly heterogeneous ageing population in Sri Lanka.

Research Design and Methods

Both time and budget constraints were considered in designing techniques and selecting the sample. Responding to the underlying concerns to capture the dimensions, characteristics and trends related to ageing among different social and economic groups of the aged, the sample was stratified into population clusters from selected locations that used to advantage intra-cluster homogeneity. Four clusters captured the ethnic variations. The sample of majority ethnic group of Sinhalese was drawn from two locations, one in and around the hill country with its main town, Kandy, which is home to a community that is upholding its own set of traditions, the other from the southern area in and around Galle, from a rural population that has entrenched traditions of its own. Rural agricultural society is represented by a sample from an interior rural location, which continues with traditional peasant agriculture while adopting non-traditional methods as well. The Fisheries Cluster reflects the norms of the coastal communities with fishing as their main occupation.

Urban population groups were picked from a spectrum that included a specific low income community in the capital Colombo and a mix of low, middle and high income households from Colombo and its suburbs. Details of the cluster characteristics are given in the ensuing section. (See Figure 1)

Figure 1: Distribution of the sample among population clusters

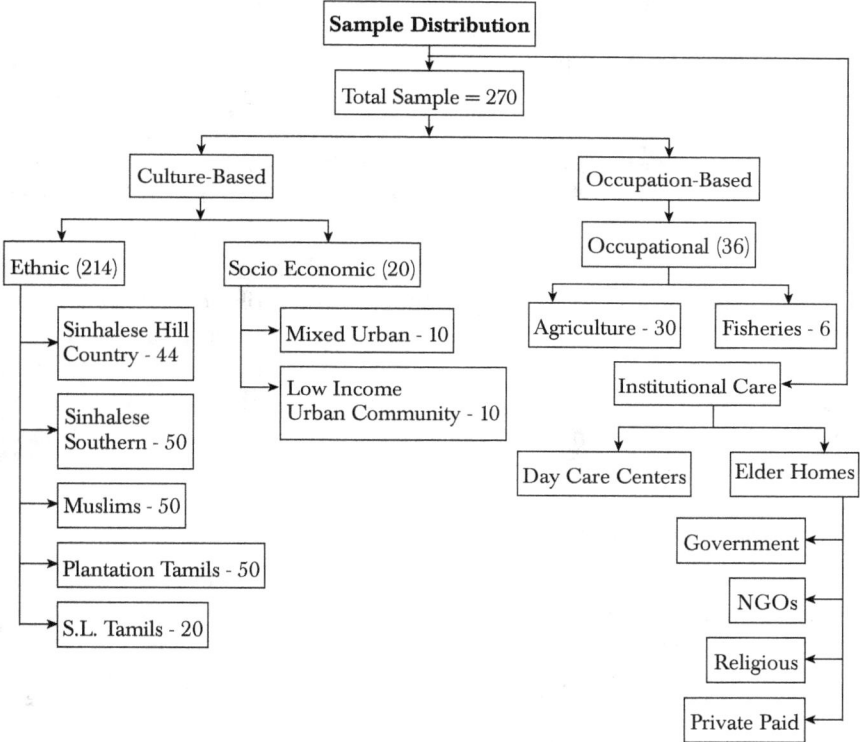

Figure 2: Sample distribution by age, gender and household income

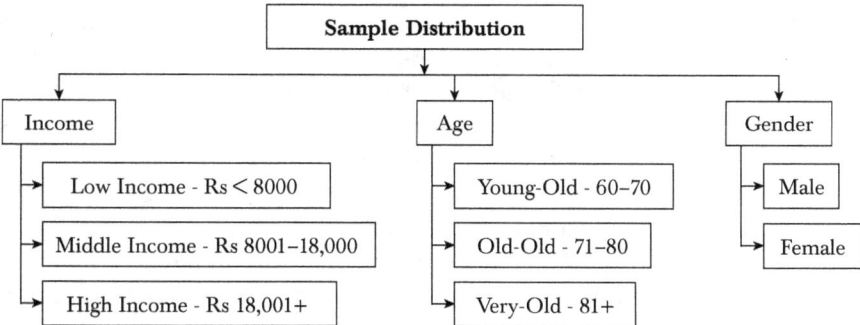

Sinhalese–Rural Hill Country Residents and Residents in the Rural South

Some of the clusters represent the major ethnic groups in the population. The Sinhalese ethnic group (about 80 per cent in Sri Lanka) has two distinct communities residing in the hill country and others in the rural south. Historically, the Hill Country Sinhalese maintained a separate kingdom with their own monarch and were the last to fall to the British who captured the entire country in 1815. The coastal belt had been under the Portuguese and the Dutch from 1505 and experienced early exposure to the western cultures that diluted the traditions of the multi-ethnic groups that live in the coastal belt. Social contracts such as marriage and property ownership and inheritance rights were embedded in tradition and formalized in a compendium of Kandyan Law. The sample was drawn from the residents with traditional roots in these locations and adhered to conventional social mores in the essentials of family structure, roles and social values.

The Southern Sinhalese who live in the rural areas and the coastal belt have absorbed the varied laws and practices of each of the western colonial powers. The Roman Dutch Law that became the common law of the country was, however, subject to the Kandyan Law on aspects such as marriage and inheritance as they applied to the Kandyan Sinhalese, to the Muslim personal laws in respect of Muslims and the Thesavalamai laws for property rights and inheritance for the Hindu Tamils.

Muslim and Tamil Clusters

Two other ethnic groups that comprise about 20 per cent of the population have specific differences based again on their cultural, religious and legal systems. The Tamils have two distinct ethnic groups. The plantation Tamils were of south Indian origin and were brought as plantation labour to work exclusively on the tea estates by the British. They formed a separate sector with their own traditions, but mostly governed by the economic contract that confined them to a geographic area of the plantation with Indian citizenship. They have been given Sri Lankan citizenship only recently. The other sector of Sri Lankan Tamils, as they were termed, are citizens of Sri Lanka who have lived traditionally in the north and parts of the east of Sri Lanka but it's members have settled all around the country mostly in the urban towns. They mix freely with the other populations outside the north and the east and have less rigorous ethnic-based values and perceptions compared to their members living in the north. Nevertheless, the study could not access the dwellers in the north owing to the conflict and instead selected a cluster that had migrated to the south and settled as permanent residents in the suburbs of the capital Colombo.

A similar restriction prevented a typical sample from being selected of Muslims who live in the east of the country. However, a traditional Muslim community that has settled in a cluster in one location in the Western Province was selected to represent the Muslim perspective.

Urban Clusters

A mixed urban cluster contained a random sample of a mix of ethnic and economic groups who have lived in and around the capital of Colombo. They are deemed to have diluted their separate cultural traditions and values, absorbing more of the common values of an urban culture.

The Low Income Urban Cluster formed a conglomerate of their own. They are a mixture of ethnic, religious and cultural groups, who share a common culture of an erstwhile slum and shanty community but now more accurately described as a Low Income Urban Cluster, who have shed some of the environmental and housing features of the typical slum environment. They had been given ownership of their small plots of land in the capital Colombo, where they lived in slums, given assistance to build permanent housing, provided basic urban services such as community latrines and water taps in a policy of upgrading of these communities by the government of the late 1980s and early 1990s.

Agriculture and Fisheries Clusters

Differences were expected in clusters of populations that were grouped around the main occupations of agriculture and fisheries. The Agriculture Cluster presented the typical rural peasants' situation with traditions going back in history to the agrarian civilization that was the major social and economic base in Sri Lankan society. The sample in the Fisheries Cluster placed on the seafront along the coast is small since the field work was going on when the tsunami struck. A few insights were gathered from this sample that could be typical of that sector.

Living Arrangements and Co-Residential Patterns

Cultural Issues

Co-residential patterns more than other variables have been placed on the agenda for change with the changing demographic and economic structures. An uncritical acceptance of co-residence of the aged with children and kin as being synonymous with elders' well-being would fail to take cognizance of the importance of relationships within that arrangement that would in fact determine the quality of life of elders.

Little is understood of the changes that are taking place in intergenerational tensions that are inevitable consequences of social and economic change. The management of these tensions may be a key aspect of well-being of both the aged and the young adults in the household. The extent to which such tensions could be forced on the aged who have no options for living arrangements would be a relevant aspect in studying living arrangements as they function as a determinant of aged welfare.

Steven Ruggles (2001) argues that social security in fact grew up in response to needs arising from the decline in multi-generational families, which was a consequence of broad economic and social changes. Ruggles thus contests the view of scholars that the enhancement in the social security system had provided an impetus for the decline in multi-generational living arrangements.

In the Asian context, nevertheless, there appear to be compelling factors that combine to maintain multi-generational families. Young persons do not find it easy to obtain employment with sufficient remuneration for their upkeep, housing is a key impediment for young families and persons to live and work independent of their parents. Coupled with this is the necessity for elders to depend on children's support both financially and for care. The fact that most elders live with children is being used by the state to defer formulation of a national policy that recognizes state responsibility for at least a part of elders' well-being.

Configurations of Living Arrangements in the Study

Diverse types of co-residential structures were captured in the study. These are described in the section that follows. This subject is considered sensitive to socio-economic and cultural differences and, is, therefore, analysed according to individual clusters. The study identified three configurations: nuclear, extended and multi-generational within the broad typology of co-residence with family and kin.

Co-Residence with Family or Kin

A nuclear family is defined for purposes of this study as one that comprises parent/s and unmarried children, a married couple or a single elder living alone. An extended family includes elder or young kin members living with a nuclear family. A multi-generational family contains parents with or without unmarried children but having one or more married children and their families living together in one household.

According to our survey, among 270 aged, nearly half (45 per cent) lived in multi-generational families, that is with families of married children.

Near equal proportions, (of 29 per cent and 26 per cent respectively), lived in extended and nuclear families. Although the majority of elders living in nuclear families were in the 'young-old' age group i.e. between 60 and 70 years, the 'old-old' – of 70–80 and the 'very old' – 80+ too were found in this type of household but in smaller proportions. This could be evidence that children who could be much over 25 years of age and who remain unmarried continue to reside with parents. Likewise, the parental home provides a refuge for children whose marriages have failed or have been terminated by death of the spouse.

Much as these arrangements have been a traditional norm in Sri Lankan society, it was stated earlier that, according to national level data this was not a universally and unreservedly preferred arrangement. Then, what factors led to the continuation of such arrangements? Some studies suggest that living alone or as two elders could be feasible only as long as health and mobility permits. Debility and advancing age would see elders moving into residences with children. Traditional cultural mores placed obligations on both children and aged parents in mutual caring relationships that had underpinnings of practical considerations.

Cultural differences could determine the variations among clusters. The Muslim Cluster had a high proportion (62 per cent) of elders living in multi-generational families, more of them (30 per cent) in extended families and only a small proportion (8 per cent) in nuclear families. This is commensurate with their known cultural patterns of co-residence. The Hill Country Resident Sinhalese Cluster too with it's bent towards traditions, had a relatively low proportion (23 per cent), but much higher than in the Muslim Cluster of elders in nuclear families; the majority lived in extended families.

The next conservative community was the non-plantation Tamil Cluster, the majority of them residing in the northern and eastern provinces. However, with the upheavals in their society consequent on the ethnic conflict, those who lived in the north have migrated and settled in the suburbs of Colombo – samples were taken from this group. It had half the elders living in nuclear families, which is a shift away from conventional patterns among this ethnic group. This is not surprising since these families are likely to be parts of extended or multi-generational families that were able to leave their villages, break away from their conventional lifestyles and migrate to the south. Nevertheless, half of them retained their conventional family structure of extended and multi-generational families in their new residences in the south. The southern Sinhalese Cluster form the rural south, though not less conventional than the Sri Lankan Tamils in the north, which had elders living in a mix of nuclear and non-nuclear families. The relatively high proportion – 46 per cent of elders – in nuclear families was evidence of the exposure of this community to the economic changes that gave opportunities to females, in particular older children, to engage in work and postpone marriage.

Among the other clusters, the Plantation Tamil elders lived for the most part (90 per cent) in extended and multi-generational families. This appeared to be more an economic fallout rather than culture related, and sprang from the peculiar labour contract that provided housing within the plantation for the families of workers for as long as a family member worked in the plantation. Married children continued to work and live in the estate house while elders who moved out from work continued to live with them. The small proportion of elders in nuclear families could have unmarried children living with them who continued to work in the plantations.

Similarly, in the Low Income Urban Cluster, a high proportion (70 per cent) of elders living in extended and multi-generational families is likely to arise from a housing shortage in the geographical locations they live in, rather than from care needs of elders. The Mixed Urban Cluster too is likely to reflect in their predominance of elders in non-nuclear families, the high cost of urban housing that would preclude young families moving out readily to seek independence from elderly parents.

Altogether, 97 per cent of elders in the sample lived with children only or with children and spouse; 1.1 per cent lived alone and 1.9 per cent lived with the spouse only. Some of those who lived with their spouse only appeared to have no option because children had married and left the home while others upheld their ownership of their house and property by residing there. Yet another reason that underscored deprivation of the elder is that children could not afford to support them if they lived with them. Those who lived as a single elder alone owned the house and so did not wish to leave it to move in with children or because they relished their independence.

The rural Agriculture and coastal Fisheries Clusters differed from each other in that half of the elders in the Agriculture Cluster lived in nuclear families. These were primarily the 'young-old' elders with unmarried adult children, the majority belonging to the low and middle income households. The low income of the clusters compared with extended and multi-generational families could be explained by a shortage of family labour on the one hand or cultivation of small home-gardens or *chena* land (slash and burn) on the other. Rural agriculture continues to depend largely on family labour and, therefore, the combination of young and old members was one that typically supported an economically feasible family support system for elders.

The Fisheries Cluster differed with high prevalence of extended and multi-generational families, and only 17 per cent of elders lived in nuclear families. The nature of their work appeared to be the determining factor in this community when the men are out at sea most of the day and the young families seek protection from older members be they male or female within the living arrangements in their homes.

One or two elders living alone have been found in small numbers in Sri Lanka. That some of these have been picked up by the sample gave an opportunity to probe their conditions of living and quality of life.

Female elders living alone were widows found mainly in the Hill Country Sinhalese and Low Income Urban Clusters; all of them had low incomes and the majority was in the 'old-old' age group of 70–80 years. They probably owned their homes but had only very small incomes. Both care and support would be lacking in their lives. In general, more female elders were living in non-nuclear families (82 per cent) compared to males (69 per cent).

Among elders who lived with family, over half (59 per cent) were widows or widowers living with children; a high percentage (76 per cent) of them were widows. Widowed elders living with families were spread fairly evenly among the low (28 per cent) and the high (32 per cent) income groups while they predominated (40 per cent) in the middle income group. The considerable proportions of widowed elders in all three age groups living with family affirms the general tendency for more female elders who are widowed to find security with children.

Elders Perspectives on Social Support Systems

Elders' opinions on aspects of care and support being closely related to the cultural mores, their responses could differ according to population groups. Among the elders as a group, nearly half affirmed the greater obligations of sons to provide financially for old parents; lesser proportions (29 per cent) placed the obligation on both equally. But, in a non-typical response, about a quarter placed this obligation on the daughter. This response signified an attitude towards elder care irrespective of the presence of sons and daughters in the family. Gender disparities could be significant, yet overall, the obligation of the son was affirmed in near equal proportions of male and female elders, more females placed the obligation on daughters while more males left it in the hands of children of either sex.

Significant cluster-wise differences were found. In three clusters half or more in each felt that sons should take over financial provision of the aged, more markedly so in the Plantation Tamil elders – 76 per cent, Sri

Lankan Tamils – 60 per cent and the Hill Country Sinhalese. The only cluster that comprised of substantial proportion (about 50 per cent) and which felt that daughters should provide was from the Low Income Urban Cluster. Interestingly, the Plantation Cluster was divided firmly between sons and daughters as in the case of Low Income Urban Cluster. A somewhat peculiar response from the Mixed Urban Cluster left out a role for daughters specifically; all clusters accorded a low preference for daughters fulfilling this role with the agriculture and fisheries clusters giving the lowest preference. The next highest preference for children without a gender distinction had high proportions in the Agriculture, Fisheries, and the Mixed Urban Clusters.

More females in the Low Income Urban Cluster opted for daughters. The Agriculture and Fisheries Clusters and the Mixed Urban Clusters stood out in opting for children of either gender.

Moving into the area of general care of parents, the pattern was significantly different. A higher preference for both sons and daughters as caregivers was evident in 44 per cent of the responses; the preference for sons in general care of parents was maintained but more muted, with only 23 per cent saying so while 14 per cent opted for daughters. However, most significant was the belief held by a relatively small but significant proportion of 19 per cent that aged parents should be independent of their children, with similar proportions of males and females agreeing.

Individual clusters showed the strong cultural and social differences in the way in which general care was allocated to the offspring. First, the view that old parents should not depend on children was highest in the Plantation Tamil Cluster – 46 per cent, with both males and females thinking alike. This preference was expressed by around 20–30 per cent of elders in three clusters – the two Sinhalese, and the Low Income Urban Cluster. The Agriculture and Fisheries had about 15 per cent subscribing to independence of elders. The Sri Lankan Tamil, and the Mixed Urban Clusters had not subscribed to this idea, while in the Muslim Cluster in an unexpected response, 4 per cent of females said the aged should be independent. None in the Mixed Urban Cluster and very few in the Sri Lankan Tamil, southern Sinhalese and Agriculture Clusters had seen a role for daughters but most in all clusters perceived children as caregivers. There were no marked gender differences in these responses, which is rather surprising when compared with earlier studies.

The emerging attitudes that foster independence of elders, is probed in an inquiry about what elders think is the best way for them to live. All who expressed a view that old parents should not be dependent on children for care were, however, not opting to live by themselves. Only 6 per cent said it was best to live alone. Significantly more of them – 12 per cent – were from the low income households. The proportion that thought it best to live with 'children' – 46 per cent – was consistent with those that thought children should care for parents. So it was with those who preferred sons – 24 per cent and daughters – 14 per cent. A new option of rotating among children was introduced by 11 per cent and could include some of the 19 per cent who felt that 'aged parents should be independent' of care by children. That a distinction has been made between living alone and being independent of children for care needs is evident in the cluster division too. The small proportions that thought aged parents should be independent as the best option were distributed among six clusters with Hill Country Sinhalese having the highest (16 per cent among males and 18 per cent among females), 15 per cent among Low Income Urban Cluster (10 per cent and 14 per cent among males and females respectively), the Muslim Cluster (8 per cent among males and 4 per cent of them females) - and the lowest among the Southern Sinhalese, Plantation Tamil and Agriculture Clusters. The Sri Lankan Tamil, the Mixed Urban and the Fisheries Clusters had no responses to this. The Low Income Urban Cluster and the Mixed Urban Cluster were uppermost among those who suggested rotating residence among children, although lesser proportions agreed in other clusters.

An elder's perception of the attitude of young persons in the matter of care of the aged was an indirect attempt to gauge the tension that might prevail between the generations in the matter of elder care. The query was specific; did elders feel that caring for aged had become a burden. Two in the high income group avoided a direct response saying 'it is difficult to say'. There did not appear to be a very decided opinion among elders on this issue; 57 per cent agreed that it is a burden and 42 per cent did not think so. There did not appear to be an economic reason behind the response since although 70 per cent of the low income households affirmed that it was a burden the proportions were high in the middle – 62 per cent and not much lower in the high income households – 43 per cent. It was not a significant gender perspective either.

Among the clusters, the Plantation Tamils (84 per cent) and the Low Income Urban Cluster (80 per cent) were foremost in affirming it is a burden along with the Mixed Urban Cluster, the Fisheries and, by a lesser proportion, the Muslim Clusters. The two Sinhalese Clusters were divided equally between the two opinions. This left the Sri Lankan Tamil and the Agriculture Clusters with a majority view that the burden of care was heavy on the young.

An attempt to substantiate caregiving was made through an inquiry into specific 'providers' of stipulated needs. Four categories of needs – basic, monetary, physical, and emergency were provided by children, with hardly any difference in gender of the elder, as detailed below:

- Basic needs   -   89 per cent
- Monetary needs   -   84 per cent
- Physical needs   -   70 per cent
- Emergency needs -   88 per cent

A new provider entered the arena of emergency needs in the form of the 'domestic help' cited by 12 per cent of elders, 12 per cent of male and 10 per cent of female elders. The other notable finding was the provision of needs by the spouse as stated by the male elder but not by the female elder, whose dependence on 'self' as the provider was fairly high particularly for physical needs. A related aspect of elder's satisfaction with current care arrangements by children was probed. Only about a quarter – 24 per cent stated they were 'largely' satisfied and this was supported by a higher proportion in the upper income households and by the 'very old' – 62 per cent with a substantial 73 per cent saying that they were 'somewhat' satisfied, only 2 per cent expressed dissatisfaction.

A deviation from the normal co-residence pattern for elders, that is, the institutional home is emerging as a feasible option for elders. In this study, a majority of 56 per cent stated it was not a good option but the margin was small since 43 per cent were certain of this being a 'good' option. This option gained favour with more males – 47 per cent than females – 36 per cent, and among the males 2 per cent left it to the wish of the elder. When cluster differences were analysed it showed that the Mixed Urban Cluster was totally rejecting the option. The other clusters had some elders agreeing for institutional living arrangements as given below:

- Muslim cluster- 16 per cent
- Hill Country Sinhalese- 39 per cent
- Plantation Tamil- 38 per cent
- Low Country, Sri Lankan Tamil, Low Income Urban- 70 per cent
- Agriculture and Fisheries- 80 per cent

The proportion of females that favoured elders living in elder's homes was low only in the Muslim Cluster – 9 per cent while in the others notable gender differences were seen in the Sri Lankan Tamil – 29 per cent females and 61 per cent males and the Agriculture and Fisheries Clusters – 33 per cent females and 85 per cent males agreeing to the idea of old age homes for the aged. The option was sought at a more personal level. In a very curious but fairly typical turnaround, from 43 per cent of elders who believed old age homes were good for the aged when it came to their personal option only 6 per cent would actually go into one.

Institutional Living Arrangements as Alternative
Day Care Centres

A compromise between family and institutional care has been achieved in a system of day care in formal private institutions or, it's a more informal type of Community Day Care Centres (DCC). These appear to provide relief to both the elders as well as the family. Information was obtained from a case study of a DCC in the urban capital of Colombo. Established through a Trust Fund this is run for both male and female elders who are paid a monthly allowance of Rs 1,000 and cared for during the day. Elders preferred this system to living in an elder's Home. The allowance was important for some since it would take care of the elder's personal needs and relieve the family of that burden. But in other instances the family itself used this allowance as an input into household income. Other benefits to the household that flowed from the DCC included food for an elder's spouse who was at home alone, which the wife took back with her each evening. Still others found relief from tensions at home. These arose from children, from a son or daughter-in-law or even from a wife who was nagging the male spouse when he was at home. That it was not always a matter of material comfort was evident when one female elder insisted it was not financial gain that she valued but an escape from loneliness when left in an empty house all day – 'no one will know even if I happen to be ill or fall and injure myself'. Another could not stand the noise with small children at home – 'they will not let me eat my lunch or have my tea but take my food from me. Here I eat what I am given and I have peace of mind all day – I go home in time to sleep'. The peer group interaction was greatly valued and 'keeps me free of illness'. Community centres have been strongly recommended preferably combined with day care for children where the grandparent–grandchild relationship can be replayed and mutual interaction benefit both elders and children.

Elder's Homes

The DCC catered to elders who had a home to return to in the evening and to those who were in good health. Though considered more restrictive and formal, the elder's home had its benefits for elders whose children could pay for their sojourn in comfortable homes or for those who could not pay at unpaid homes run by the government or by religious and secular organizations. The monotony, the feeling of being abandoned, with nothing to look forward to at the end of the day, same food, peer group irritations, a sense of isolation from normal living were the negative features that were highlighted. Yet, there were elders in these homes who went out to work, gave tuitions, worked on crafts for sale and lived a reasonably full life. The generation gap in their families made for friction, which told on the elder's health and happiness, so the elder's home was a better option for such elders.

Provision for them to be taken to clinics or hospitals when they fell ill while in an elders' home gave them a sense of security which they did not have in their own home, even when they had children. Access to knowledge and entertainment through newspapers, radio and TV, leisure time activities, religious activities and regular trips were some of the positive features provided for elders' well-being in the better managed and funded elders' homes. One witnesses through these narratives an increasing acceptance of the institutional living arrangement as a completely rational alternative to family care.

Homeless Elders

Another group of elders were found to fall in between these arrangements; these were ejected from their family homes and also failed to gain entry to institutions. Their 'home' was the street. No count has been taken of such abandoned elders that are seen begging in the streets of urban townships. This study investigated a group of such elders living in towns in the hill country. The research probed the lives of six such elders who were living on the streets and begging for food and clothing. These are presented as case profiles. There were a variety of types of elders in this group. One type was elders who had been plantation workers who had been given a house tied to the labour contract but had lost it when they retired. Only recently given citizenship, these were originally Indian Tamils who were confined to the plantations. Usually, the children carried on work in the plantation and the house was given to them; the parents lived with the children. However, three of the street elders who belonged to the Plantation Tamil group had been thrown out of the house, two of them from a house now given to the children and one who had lost the house because the son moved out of plantation work and refused to keep the elderly father. Among the other two, one was a male and the other a female. Another elderly female came to the street as a child when the mother who was a domestic was thrown out when she became pregnant. After she was born the mother continued begging but died when the current elder was 13 years old. She had worked as casual labour while living as a street beggar. With advancing years she continues to eke out a living by begging during the day and sleeping on the doorstep of the post office. Two male elders, Sinhalese, were begging for a living; both were sleeping at night in a squatter shack on state land, but their circumstances differed. One had occupied a shack as a squatter, but was married and had children, he was earning from casual work. At age 70 he was incapable of working and the children who were married refused to accommodate him in their home. He has since been a beggar. The other elder was abandoned as a child and lived by doing odd jobs. He is now unable to work and can only beg.

Not having a permanent place of residence disqualified them from benefiting from the charity allowance given to indigent elders. They had to live and die as beggars, as seen from their narratives summarized below:

Sinnamma, age 64, worked in a tea plantation in the hill country while living in the small house given by the plantation. Her husband drank heavily and died before he retired. She too was ill and had to retire when she was only 50 years old even though she could have continued till 60 years. She got her provident fund of Rs 72,000 which the children took from her. She gave her gold chain to her daughter. When the money was over she was asked to leave the house. She tried working in homes but fell ill with asthma. So she began to sit at the entrance to the kovil and got paid for looking after the shoes of the worshippers. She collected the coconuts which worshippers split for the ritual and sold the coconut halves to the boutiques (shops that sell coconuts). She has made this her living now. People give her food when they go to the temple. When she fell ill recently, the kovil priest sent her to the government hospital. When she recovered she came back to this place and continued to beg.

Somapala, came to town with his father when he was 12 years old. His father was a trader. When his father left him to look after two bags of spices he had purchased and went to transact another deal, a man took him by force into a boutique and left him there. When he escaped he found the two bags were missing – stolen by the man who tricked him. He hid from his father because of fear of reprisal. He never saw his father again. He worked in boutiques and did odd jobs all his life until he could not work anymore. He begs during the day and sleeps in an unauthorized shack.

Elder's Contribution to the Household Economy

Financial needs of the aged have greater significance in the light of the changes in the family structure alluded to in the earlier section. The presence of smaller families with fewer children is associated, in the Sri Lankan context, with greater demands for financial outlay for young children's education and investment in skills perceived as critical in a highly competitive job market, which could leave little surplus for expenses for the aged members in the family. Added to the longer lifespan of elders that require longer periods of care by the children, the increasing presence of long-term chronic ailments that require costly treatment places additional burdens to old age care. The economic burden, therefore, has more salience in a discussion on elders' well-being within the family than perhaps a decade ago. This aspect is accorded considerable importance in this study. This section uses a set of indicators that attempt to assess, from several different stances, the economic capability and conversely, the vulnerability of the elder, within the economy of the household. Indicators use data that indirectly reflect the access to, and availability of financial resources and also those that directly measure financial constraints in terms of access to critical needs for the aged.

As was done with respect to other issues, the effects of macroeconomic changes have been expressed through the cluster breakdown. The nine clusters have been grouped into two for a more meaningful assessment of change. Those that reflected socio-ethnic nuances were grouped together, and the two clusters of Agriculture and Fisheries that mirrored occupational effects as combined with sociocultural norms were considered together. They are differentiated as 'Culture-based' and 'Occupation-based'.

Indicators of Financial Capability

The elders' role as giver, especially when the gift is an income supplement is likely to enhance elder capability within the household economy. Did it also enhance their well-being? The limitations of this indicator in its failure to reflect the extent to which the elders' contributory role carried weight in providing for their own needs is explored through other indicators.

Among the sample survey of elders, 65 per cent were receivers of own income and these ranged from a low Rs 100 a month to Rs 20,000. Non-income earning and therefore non-contributing elders were 35 per cent in the sample of 270. The highest proportion of 57 per cent of non-earning and, therefore, non-contributing elders was found among the low income households, followed by 41 per cent in the middle income households. The high income households had the lowest percentage of such elders with 22 per cent. It is evident that the financially deprived households that had the least capacity to support extra members had the highest burden of supporting the aged when they had no resources of their own to supplement household income. This meant that, the elders in poorer households were most dependent on the already strained finances of the household. Elders who had contributed at different levels, from small sums to quite substantial proportions were not mere contributors but sole providers in the household economy. This indicator transforms itself into one of the dependence of children and family on the elders financially. It is recalled that in the discussion on living arrangements, the dependence of children on the elders in terms of non-cash contributions such as provision of housing was highlighted.

The majority of 35 per cent of elders had contributed between 26 per cent and 50 per cent while nearly one-fifth (17 per cent) had contributed 76 to 100 per cent, thus bearing the brunt of the household financial burden. Their contributions are as stated below:

- Contributions of 01–10 per cent of cash income by 17 per cent of elders
- Contributions of 11–25 per cent by 22 per cent of elders
- Contributions of 26–50 per cent by 35 per cent of elders
- Contributions of 51–75 per cent by 9 per cent of elders
- Contributions of 76–100 per cent by 17 per cent of elders

Cluster differences were evident in the two groups of clusters, the culture-based and the occupation-based. The culture-based group had 62 per cent elders who had contributed an average of 37 per cent of household income, ranging from a low 1 per cent to 100 per cent.

The contribution of elders, and therefore, the dependence of children was substantially higher in the occupation-based group of clusters. For instance, the low-income households were supported by an average of 85 per cent of household income derived from elder contributions, with a range of 4 to 100 per cent in the Agriculture Cluster. In the Agriculture Cluster, the average contribution was high even in the other two income groups; 54 per cent and 58 per cent in the high-income group. The Agriculture Cluster average itself was a high 65 per cent. In the Fisheries Cluster, the elders' contribution was a low average of 11 per cent while the middle income group had a much higher average contribution of 20 per cent.

The gender difference in the financial roles was highlighted, showing a majority of females who were low contributors when compared with males; nearly 60 per cent of females contributed only one quarter or less of household income, while among males, 69 per cent of them contributed 50–100 per cent. In the Agriculture Cluster 67 per cent of females and in the Fisheries Cluster 100 per cent of females contributed less than 25 per cent of household income, while among males 86 per cent of them contributed 50–100 per cent of household income. The average contributions by gender show very clearly the gender disparity, with males contributing an average of 72 per cent of household income and females only 18 per cent in the Agriculture Cluster and in the Fisheries Cluster an even greater disparity of an average of only 4 per cent by females and 38 per cent by males. The earner role of females in both the above clusters seems to be masked within a label of 'unpaid family workers' so that their contribution is not monetized. In Fisheries, net clearing and other fringe activities brought little or no cash benefits to women.

Source of Main Income for Elderly

It was apparent from the data that some incomes, even some of the high incomes were derived from uncertain sources, and could affect the stability of not only elders but also of the households whose economies they were supporting substantially. When these sources failed there was nothing to cushion their impact.

A quarter or so of elders (26 per cent) were government pensioners and were the most stable. This is a retirement benefit that accrues to retired government servants. Incomes from pensions ranged from Rs 3,000 a month to Rs 15,000. 82 per cent of pensioners received Rs 5,000 to Rs 15,000. Another 5 per cent of elders received government pensions, perhaps they were small sums and not their main source of income.

Self-employment in agriculture was the next important source with 19 per cent obtaining incomes that spanned a wide range from an average of Rs 100 a month to Rs 20,000 a month. The higher incomes were derived from leasing out paddy land for cultivation while retaining ownership. The next most important source was that of casual labour, which was the main source of income for 12 per cent; nearly half of those in casual labour were earning between Rs 1,500 and Rs 3,000 a month.

Nearly 10 per cent of elders depended solely on the government poverty allowance which amounted to Rs 100 to Rs 1,500 a month for those defined as poor. In fact, these beneficiaries formed the bulk (43 per cent) of elders who were getting low incomes; they would have been destitute otherwise. A small proportion received a charity allowance, a government allowance for the indigent aged. It was evident that over half (59 per cent) of elders obtained income from remunerative work, the majority with incomes that were uncertain.

A cluster-based analysis indicated that the government pension was the highest single source of income for both males (35 per cent) and females (23 per cent) among the culture-based elderly. For 21 per cent of females, it was a widows' benefit from the spouses' occupation in government service. It appeared that more males remained in active work for remuneration (37 per cent) when compared with females (16 per cent). Among the Agriculture Cluster, those in the age group of 70–80 years too, had reported incomes of Rs 15,000–20,000 probably from ownership of cultivated land rather than from their labour. The Fisheries Cluster had no such assets and when fishing was no longer possible they became receivers of the government poverty allowance, which ranged from Rs 100 to Rs 1,500 at most.

Financial Adequacy for Critical Needs of Elderly

A direct enquiry that encompasses all dimensions provides information on the availability of selected critical needs of special food supplements, medicine and health care. As a 'wrap-up' indicator, therefore, this provides evidence of the overall economic well-being of the aged.

It was found that elders both with and without own income had faced shortages of money for critical needs. Overall, over half of them – 59 per cent had declared they had experienced shortages of funds for critical needs. Being without regular medication for long-term chronic ailments could have grievous consequences even to the point of rendering them disabled and non-functional if not a hazard to life itself. Significantly, 56 per cent of those who had shortages were those who had their own income and nearly 20 per cent of them with incomes over Rs 5,000 a month and up to Rs 20,000. Elders with own incomes even as high as Rs 15,000–20,000 a month reported shortage of money to buy medicine, special food or access health care.

Table 1: Distribution of elders with/without income and shortages of critical needs

Critical Needs	% of elders with income				% of elders without income			
	Low	Middle	High	All	Low	Middle	High	All
Food	71	66	63	69	54	73	71	67
Health Care	50	60	53	57	68	68	71	66
Medicine	33	32	42	34	59	34	57	44

Source: Author's survey.

Table 1 presents a disturbing picture of the prevalence of deprivation among elders with serious consequences to the household as well when avoidable disabilities of an elder can compound the problems of the household. Out of the total sample of 270, 66 per cent of elderly reported chronic illnesses and of them, over half (56 per cent) reported they were often short of money for essential medicines. The proportion was relatively high among low and middle-income households with 67 per cent and 60 per cent of chronically ill elders in low and middle-income households respectively. In the high-income households too, surprisingly, 26 per cent had been without medication intermittently. The consequences of such deprivation can flow into the social and economic fabric of the country and as such have wide implications on national policy.

Elders who had their own incomes or belonged to households with high incomes being short of critical essentials could indicate their supplying the deficits in the household, most likely demands of young children or grandchildren. The other disturbing finding was the money spent on smoking, alcohol and betel chewing by some elders who were short of money for critical needs. Among them were elders who had their own money as well as those who were dependent on their children.

Financial Assets

The elder's financial assets were in the form of bank deposits; 66 per cent had bank accounts. Within income groups even the low income households had 41 per cent of elders having bank accounts. Bank accounts of low income householders were mainly deposits that were compulsory from the Samurdhi allowance, or from their membership in Savings and Thrift Cooperatives in which they could obtain membership by paying small sums each month. The savings were small but entitled them to obtain relief loans in times of special need. The two main banks for these beneficiaries were the Samurdhi Bank and the Federation of Thrift & Credit Co-operative Societies Ltd. in Sri Lanka (SANSA). The proportions with bank account were progressively higher as household income increased. Some of the elders in middle income households too could be holders of such accounts while those in the high income households or who had their own income could have personal savings deposited in commercial banks. An income related classification showed that a high proportion – 81 per cent of elders in the high income households and 67 per cent in the middle income had bank accounts. Conversely, the low and the middle income groups had the highest proportions without any savings.

The proportion of males with bank accounts was higher than that of females by about 20 per cent. Likewise, the lowest proportion of bank account holders was from the 'very old' group of elders. Female account holders were primarily beneficiaries from women's savings schemes within the two group savings schemes mentioned earlier. Nonetheless, in each of the classifications, by income, gender and age, proportions that had some financial deposit were higher than those that did not. An additional query elicited information on the elders' role in managing the bank account. Although 68 per cent of them stated that they 'managed' these accounts by themselves, another 3 per cent did so with another family member. In fact, the small savers in group savings schemes could only apply and obtain small loans. The gender disparity in the elder managing the account was 11 per cent, more males than females who were in fact managing their own accounts.

Awareness of Social Security Benefits

Meanwhile, 62 per cent of elders (over 70 per cent in the low and 67 per cent in the middle income groups and close to half in the high), were not aware of any social assistance or government welfare schemes for the aged. 71 per cent females and 56 per cent males were unaware.

Knowledge of specific concessions to elders too appeared to be low. Three such measures were cited each of which was unknown to more than half the elders.

- Reserved seats in public buses – 64 per cent were unaware
- Enhanced interest rates for savings account – 68 per cent were unaware
- Elders card – 86 per cent were unaware.

The elder's card allowed elders to avoid standing in queues and a 5 per cent discount on pharmaceuticals from government pharmacies. The latter was of limited use since travel to a government pharmacy would incur more cost and time. The hospital out-patient clinics could be a good place to introduce separate queues for elders.

Property Rights in the Context of Resource Empowerment among the Elderly

The discussion on property rights of the aged in Sri Lanka explores the aspect of empowerment of the aged through ownership of property. The aged had used it as a form of security to ensure that children would continue to care for them when they were beholden to parents for providing housing. The reason given by elders for children living with them because it was 'their house' implied authority of the elders over children, and, conversely, denoted a sense of obligation for children to care for the parents. Conversely, by implication, elders who did not own property would be highly vulnerable in their status of dependency.

Ancillary to the core issue of well-being this section describes the manner in which property came into the possession of the aged and the way in which these were disposed of. Their use and movement have definite cultural underpinnings and thus, practices related to property can differ significantly according to ethnicity. These practices could be beneficial or detrimental to elders' well-being. These issues are examined with data disaggregated by population clusters. In this section, the Fisheries Cluster was not considered since by the time this part of the research was to be undertaken all fisheries communities were adversely affected by the tsunami and all their property destroyed.

Ownership of House

A high proportion – 70 per cent of the sampled elders owned at least one house. This is not typical of the national scenario. The cluster-wise distribution too showed high prevalence of home ownership, except the Plantation Tamil Cluster whose homes were owned by the state or private owners of the plantation. A very high proportion – 92 per cent of elders were single owners; only 4 per cent owned jointly with spouse and with others. Owners were primarily males – 64 per cent. The highest proportion of owners was 58 per cent among the 'young-old', followed by the 'old-old' – 37 per cent. Among those who kept their ownership of the house were 5 per cent of the 'very old' elders. Most of them, it was found, lived with their children but kept the house in their name.

Table 2: Home ownership and source classified according to clusters

	House Ownership (%)	Inherited Property (%)	Built/Purchased Property (%)	Government Grant/Scheme (%)
Rural Hill Country Sinhalese	80	57	40	3
Rural Southern Sinhalese	84	88	12	0
Sri Lankan Tamils	94	53	47	0
Muslims	70	52	48	0
Plantation Tamils	14	0	100	0
Urban Low Income Communities	80	38	50	12
Mixed Urban	80	25	75	0
Agriculture Community	97	17	35	48
All Clusters	70	51	38	11

Source: Same as Table 1.

Elders among Plantation Tamils appear to be a specially disadvantaged group as is also highlighted in the next section on homeless elders. Home ownership itself was high within clusters, with the exception of the Plantation Tamil Cluster.

Ownership was predominantly by males with exceptions of the Low Income Urban Cluster which had 75 per cent owned by females. Female headed households were more common in these communities and when their semi-permanent housing was replaced with permanent ones within the government housing programme these females obtained title to their house. In the Muslim Cluster, the male–female difference in home ownership was small (54 per cent males and 46 per cent females). In general, ownership was high among the 'young-old' elders. Not surprisingly, ownership was highest among elders in high income households.

As evident from Table 2, the two major sources were inheritance and building or purchasing in all clusters with the exception of the Agriculture

Cluster in which government grants was uppermost. The two main sources of inheritance and built/purchased had significant culture-based inter-cluster and gender, age and income driven intra-cluster differences. However, the Agriculture Cluster differed significantly with government grants being its major source of house ownership which was given as a package which included substantial extents of agricultural land.

Inherited Homes

The major source of inheritance was seen in clusters that were basically culture driven. Prominent among these were the two Sinhalese Clusters, with their rural-based traditions, the Sri Lankan Tamil Cluster governed by traditional (the Sawalamai) inheritance property laws but left behind in their locations in the north, and Muslims in the old property owning community in which they lived.

Inheritance was from two sources, the main being parents and the other spouses (from parents, 38 per cent, from spouse, 13 per cent). Equal proportions of both males and females had inherited but a gender difference was seen in that more males (63 per cent) had inherited from parents than females (37 per cent). This could arise from gender-based gift practices discussed in a later section. Conversely, 83 per cent of females as compared with only 17 per cent of males had inherited from a deceased spouse. The latter was a more untypical phenomenon in Sri Lankan society. Females had a less direct route for owning a house. Among clusters, the exception was the Low Income Urban Cluster in which more females than males inherited from deceased husbands. In the Agriculture Cluster, the sole source of inheritance by females was from male spouses who had left the house to their widows. This pattern of male dominance was repeated in the clusters which had mainly inherited houses with the exception of the Muslim Cluster in which female ownership was higher.

Retention of inherited houses was high among the 'young-old' – 57 per cent and about one-third in the 'old-old' group. A significant feature was that even the 'very old' elders (6 per cent) had decided to retain ownership of inherited houses. This last category was high in the rural hill country cluster, in which traditional family structures were dominant.

The pattern of ownership followed the income gradations, the highest (40 per cent) in the high income group and the lowest (25 per cent) in the low income group, the middle income group falling in between (35 per cent). This pattern appeared to have no significant changes in the relevant clusters.

Built/Purchased Homes

The pattern of distribution of built/purchased houses showed some notable features in the cluster distribution. There appeared to be an inverted pattern with the more urbanized clusters owning greater proportions of built/ purchased land, as clear in the figures given above. This type differed from inherited homes in the requirement for capital investment as a precondition for ownership. The majority (79 per cent) of males had used their own resources. In contrast, females predominated (60 per cent) among those who used their spouses' resources to build or purchase a home, indicating a dependence on husbands assets after his demise. The next notable feature was that these were owned because they were purchased more by the 'young-old' (60 per cent) with much smaller proportions among the older age groups. Markedly, only half the proportion of the 'very old' owned this type of house, in contrast more of the 'old-old' and the 'very old' owned inherited houses. The middle income group had the highest proportion (45 per cent) of owners as compared with the high income group having the highest proportion of inherited home owners. This could be a result of the government imposed ceiling on house ownership which had benefited the middle class population clusters in particular. Besides these features, the patterns of distribution in other aspects were very similar to that of inherited houses.

The major beneficiaries of outright grants of housing were farmers who were given agricultural houses in colonization schemes in new irrigated land. Apart from this, 9 per cent of elders had obtained their homes through low income housing and urban housing schemes that were launched extensively by the government in the 1980s. The highest proportion of (56 per cent) was owned by the high income elders, 25 per cent by the middle income and 19 per cent by low income elders. Their ownership was preponderantly by males – 88 per cent – following government policy of recognizing males primarily as farmers, and only 12 per cent by females. The 'young-old' owned half of these (50 per cent), 44 per cent was owned by the 'old-old' and 6 per cent by the 'very old'.

Ownership of Land

The other substantial asset was land holdings. Two types of land – agriculture and homestead were included. Of all elders in the sample 28 per cent owned some type of land. Ownership by type is given below.
- Agriculture land – 57 per cent
- Homestead – 20 per cent
- Agriculture and Homestead – 23 per cent

As in housing, land as an asset was examined in terms of the manner in which it devolved to the present owner. The sources were similar to housing; land was inherited, purchased or from a government grant. Land ownership was restricted to the rural population clusters in the sample. A division was seen in the distribution of homestead and agricultural land within these clusters. The figures are given in Table 3.

Table 3: Land ownership by source according to clusters

Agricultural Land	Land Ownership (%)	Inherited (%)	Purchased (%)	Govt. Grant (%)
Rural Hill Country Sinhalese	12	83	17	0
Rural Southern Sinhalese	32	87	13	0
Sri Lankan Tamils	20	100	0	0
Plantation Tamils	2	0	100	0
Agriculture Community	50	10	34	56
All Clusters	57	46	25	29
Homestead Land				
Rural Hill Country Sinhalese	18	24	72	12
Rural Southern Sinhalese	02	0	100	0
Agriculture Community	50	0	0	100
Sri Lankan Tamils	25	83	17	0
Rural Hill Country Sinhalese	18	24	72	12
All Clusters	46	23	23	54

Only five clusters had elders owning agricultural land and four owning homestead land. Altogether, the highest source of agricultural land was inheritance (46 per cent). In the cluster breakdown, inheritance was high for three clusters – these were the more tradition-based clusters. A difference was seen in the less traditional one of Plantation Tamils who had purchased land. These were, however, not the workers themselves but officials who had the option of owning land. The government grant was the main source for the Agriculture Cluster. This was so in the case of homestead land as well as for this cluster, with inheritance and purchases taking a lower place as sources. Notably, three clusters of Muslim, Low Income Urban and Mixed Urban did not own any extra land. Income differences were not significant in the Agriculture Cluster. These were high in the other clusters of the two Sinhalese, the Sri Lankan Tamils and the Plantation Tamils.

Use of Currently Owned Assets

House

Most of the elders being single house owners occupied their houses with a spouse or children. The Sri Lankan Tamil Cluster stood out as one which had a fair proportion of two house owners with the second house being located in the north. These second houses were unoccupied being within the conflict area. Only two elders had rented their second house and they were in the up country Sinhalese Cluster and in the middle and high income groups.

Land

The majority of the agricultural land owned by elders was cultivated. All land in the Agriculture Cluster had been cultivated while over 80 per cent was under cultivation in all social clusters that had agricultural land with the exception of the Sri Lankan Tamil Cluster, in which land in the north was left uncultivated. In the case of homesteads, all were under cultivation in the Agriculture Cluster but over 90 per cent were left uncultivated in the other clusters. Some of this land may have been unsuitable for agriculture and kept as an investment for future buildings.

Gifting of Currently Owned Assets

The more critical issue in relation to asset ownership was the manner of their intended disposal. The figures below point to a son-dominance in gifting of property (Table 4).

The preference for a son was evident in intentions for disposal of both assets. This was more of a practical consideration in the case of land – mainly agricultural – with primarily males being recognized as farmers. There was no significant difference in the gender of elders in their preference for gifting the house to sons. In all age groups, the preference for sons was maintained, the 'old-old' indicated a higher proportion who preferred to gift property to sons. The preference pattern was repeated in all clusters for both house and land with the exception of a higher proportion of undecided elders in their disposal of land; especially the Sri Lankan Tamil and the Agriculture Clusters had relatively high proportions of undecided elders with respect to disposal of both house (16 per cent and 21 per cent respectively) and land (60 per cent and 37 per cent respectively).

Table 4: The intended gifting of currently owned assets by the elderly

To whom	House (%)	Land (%)
To Sons	59	49
To Daughters	25	7
To Spouse	2	2
To Children	2	7
Other	2	1
Not decided	10	34

While the general pattern was maintained without a significant disparity between male elders and female elders in their preference for sons, there were significant cluster-wise variations. In gifting the house, rural southern Sinhalese, Muslim and Low Income Urban Clusters had a majority of females over males who preferred to gift to sons. Similar differences were not evident in gifting land. The contradictions apparent in their preferences for gifting the house are evident when cross classified by the co-residence arrangements (Table 5). It appears that co-residence did not figure as a determining factor in the decision to gift the house elders were occupying currently.

Table 5: Living arrangements and intended gifting pattern among the elderly

Living With	Gifting to Sons (%)
Daughters & Spouse	14
Children & Spouse	41
Daughters	15
Children	57
Alone	100

House and Land Already Disposed of among the Elderly

The foregoing discussion was regarding disposal of property. This section proceeds to examine how property was in fact disposed of by elders who have transferred them already. It was significant that only 10 per cent had disposed of their houses and 15 per cent of their land. A consistent disparity between practice and intent was evident (Table 6). The ways in which intentions could be vitiated showed that elders with property could be victims of undue coercion to part with property. These could then become a burden with disposal fanning resentment and friction between elders and children. A house was gifted to a daughter primarily at the time of marriage (71 per cent). Other occasions were partition (14 per cent), because it was demanded by the daughter (7 per cent) and demanded by the daughter at her marriage (7 per cent). Sons were gifted a house mainly at partition (39 per cent) and when demanded (8 per cent).

Table 6: Intentions and actual disposal of house and land among the elderly

	Intentions (%)		Actual (%)	
	House	Land	House	Land
Sons	59	49	5	8
Daughters	25	7	5	7
Children	2	2		
Spouse	2	2		
Other	2	6		
Undecided	10	34		

Elders who had disposed of land had transferred it to daughters, mainly as a gift at marriage and a share during partition (44 per cent each), and as demanded (11 per cent). Whereas sons had received mainly as a share at partition (41 per cent), 23 per cent had to give it to sons because they demanded it. Land was sold by 2 per cent of elders mainly owing to unsatisfactory neighbours, but also to pay for a child's marriage and to buy land elsewhere. Meanwhile 2 per cent had mortgaged their land to pay off family debts, for funeral expenses of family members and to buy medicine for illness among elderly from low income households.

Transferring Property through a Will

A critical issue related to transfer of property was the knowledge of the right to do so through a will. Elder's awareness as well as the practice of making a will was explored. It was an encouraging finding that nearly 78 per cent of elders were aware of their right to leave a will. Conversely 23 per cent did not know of it at all. While most elders in the middle and high income households reported awareness – 71 per cent and 92 per cent respectively, a fairly high proportion – 66 per cent of elders in the low income households too had this knowledge. Yet, there were 8 per cent in the high and 29 per cent in the middle income households and 34 per cent in the low income households who were not aware. A lower proportion – 69 per cent among female elders were aware as compared to the male elders – 81 per cent. Despite high proportions in each age category being aware, over a quarter of the 'young-old', close to a third of the 'very old', and close to one-fifth of the 'old-old' were unaware.

When the number of elders who were aware of the right to make a will was distributed among the clusters, the elders in the Mixed Urban and Low Income Communities were low down on the scale with under 5 per cent of elders being aware, while the Sri Lankan Tamil and the Plantation Tamil Clusters came next with around 10 per cent who had awareness. The two Sinhalese Clusters came next with 21 per cent each followed by the Muslim Cluster – 18 per cent. Knowledge was low – 13 per cent in the Agriculture Cluster. It was noted that the highest proportions of elders who were unaware of this right were in the Plantation Tamil Cluster – 46 per cent – and the Muslim Cluster – 22 per cent. Among the Plantation Tamils, except the few who had built houses, the question does not arise since they did not own their homes.

However, awareness of the right to make a will had not been translated into practice since, only 12 elders, just 6 per cent of those who owned property had, in fact, done so. These were distributed unevenly among the income groups, among males and females and among the three age groups. The highest defaulters were the elders in the high income households – 42 per cent, followed by 37 per cent of middle income and 23 per cent of low income elders. While 66 per cent of those who had not made a will were males, 34 per cent were females. The lowest age category of 'young-old' was high (62 per cent) among those who had not made a will at the time of the study, with 33 per cent of the 'old-old' and 5 per cent of the 'very old'. Interestingly, most of those who had not made a will belonged to the high income households in which the highest proportion had reported awareness.

When individual clusters were examined, it was significant that none of the property owning elders among the Sri Lankan Tamil, Plantation Tamil, Low Income Urban Community, Mixed Urban or Agriculture Clusters had in fact made a will. A majority in each of the Muslim Cluster – 91 per cent, Hill Country Sinhalese Cluster – 75 per cent and Southern Sinhalese Cluster – 98 per cent had not made a will.

Property Transfers to Children at Marriage

The discussion on the disposal of property – houses and land cited instances of transfer to sons and daughters at their marriage. The bestowal practices of gifts to children at marriage are more explicitly pursued in an inquiry on the type of gift bestowed.

A distinction was sought on type of transfers made to females compared to males. These were transfers at or on account of marriage. Out of those elders who had daughters, 19 per cent had not given them any gifts, and a higher proportion of 64 per cent of sons had not been given gifts either. The obligation to bestow gifts at a daughter's marriage has been observed by a majority of elders, to sons by a lesser number of elders (Table 7).

Table 7: Type of gifts offered to daughters and sons among the elderly

Type of gift	Sons (%)	Daughters (%)
Land only or with other	8	7
Gold only or with other	2	77
Cash only or with other	55	15
Consumer durables only or with other	16	37

This pattern is typical of the practices that accompany marriage. The breakdown by individual clusters presents the culture mores that differentiate the types of gifts given to sons and daughters. The cluster-wise data is given in Table 8. Some features stand out as typical of the clusters. In general, all clusters displayed a practice of giving gifts to daughters more than to sons as seen in higher proportions of sons having no gifts when compared with daughters. All clusters showed a higher proportion of gifts to daughters. Most sons were not getting anything in the Plantation Tamil, the Sri Lankan Tamil and the Low Income Urban Clusters.

Traditional norms that determined the type of gift was clearly seen in the higher practice of bestowing gold and cash and some amount of consumer goods to daughters. The clusters of Agriculture and Fisheries had gifted land to sons and gold to daughters. Over half the sons had got no gifts at all. The Agriculture Cluster in particular has restrictions on gifting land to more than one child to prevent fragmentation of government granted land. Many in this cluster had reported to being undecided about property transfers. Nonetheless, elders in the Agriculture and Fisheries Clusters too had gifted gold to their daughters. A classification by income showed that high proportions of sons had been without any gifts in the low and middle income classes, while a little less than half in the high income class had not received anything. It appeared that even the low and middle income elders had provided gifts to most of their daughters.

The strength of the social obligation for gifting girls at marriage is amply evident. Also clear is the likely burden on the household in providing gifts for a daughter's marriage and the disadvantageous position of young females in their prospects for marriage. The pre-eminence of gold as the traditional requirement for females at marriage is borne out with respect to all three income groups. As related to this practice of giving gifts to children, especially girls at marriage, an inquiry on whether a dowry was requested during marriage of sons and conversely whether dowry was demanded of the parents when daughters got married, attempted to probe further on the practices relating to dowry.

Table 8: Type of gifts offered to daughters and sons among the different clusters

Clusters	Type of gift	Sons (%)	Daughters (%)
Hill country Sinhalese	Land only or with other	24	18
	Gold only or with other	14	60
	Cash only or with other	21	24
	Consumer goods only or with other		12
Sinhalese Southern	Land only or with other	3	0
	Gold only or with other	0	87
	Cash only or with other	16	66
	Consumer goods only or with other		29
Sri Lanka Tamils	Land only or with other	0	0
	Gold only or with other	0	100
	Cash only or with other	21	100
	Consumer goods only or with other		36
Muslim	Land only or with other	2	9
	Gold only or with other	0	76
	Cash only or with other	21	60
	Consumer goods only or with other		9
Plantation Tamil	Land only or with other	0	0
	Gold only or with other	0	74
	Cash only or with other	6	56
	Consumer goods only or with other		0
Low Income Urban	Land only or with other	0	0
	Gold only or with other	0	78
	Cash only or with other	28	78
	Consumer goods only or with other		14
Mixed Urban	Land only or with other	13	0
	Gold only or with other	0	100
	Cash only or with other	24	100
	Consumer goods only or with other		50
Agriculture & Fisheries	Land only or with other	17	15
	Gold only or with other	3	72
	Cash only or with other	3	34
	Consumer goods only or with other		27

Out of the elders who had sons an overwhelming majority, 85 per cent said they did not, and would not demand for their sons. This proportion was high in all three income groups, 92 per cent in the low, 87 per cent in the middle and 77 per cent in the high income group. It was significant that 23 per cent in the high income households would and did ask for dowry. The practical consideration of economic capability too appeared to have had play in the tradition of expecting and giving of dowries. While only 15 per cent of elders had requested dowries for their sons, a higher proportion, 24 per cent said dowries were demanded by prospective bridegrooms of their daughters. These findings appear to be inconsistent with the proportions even in low income households that had in fact provided gifts for their daughters and even sons.

The data showed that 80 per cent of elders had in fact 'gifted' to daughters at marriage. At the same time, 24 per cent of elders stated that dowry had been demanded at their daughter's marriage. It appears, therefore, that out of the 80 per cent who had 'gifted' 24 percent had in fact given gifts as dowry, gifts which could then belong to the husband and not to the daughter. Differences among the clusters indicate cultural differences that remain embedded in their societies.

A clear example is the high proportion, 98 per cent in the Hill Country Sinhalese Cluster that state they will not ask dowry when their sons seek brides. This is very much in keeping with tradition even today where in the common form of Diga marriage a gift of dowry is not compulsory. This could be disadvantageous to the female according to analysts. Nevertheless, the tradition of giving and receiving dowry is still evident among some more than others. The Sri Lankan Tamil Cluster was typical of such cultural mores and had 65 per cent of elders declaring that they did and will ask for dowry for their sons.

There is evidence that the high income households are more likely to be traditional in this respect, as for instance 73 per cent of high income elders in the Sri Lankan Tamil Cluster, 67 per cent in the Mixed Urban Cluster, and 30 per cent in the Southern Sinhalese Cluster adhered, or would adhere to this practice. The tradition appears to be fading away in most other clusters. Much less elders, only 24 per cent reported that dowries were in fact demanded when their daughters got married, even in the Sri Lankan Tamil Cluster (57 per cent) gifts were given to daughters in this cluster by all elders. Although this convention was adhered to in practice, an ideological shift was apparent in their intentions.

Health Status of the Elderly
Elders Perception of Health Status
In an earlier study, (Marga Institute, 1998) no elderly had described their health as 'excellent' and only 4 per cent of the rural elders had perceived their health as being 'very good'. In the current study too, 4 per cent of elders described their health as 'good' with 10 per cent of these being over the age of 80. Health was considered 'fair' by 81 per cent, 'poor' by 13 per cent and 'very poor' by 2 per cent. It is not possible from this to conclude that the health of the elderly had changed over time.

Interestingly, no significant differences were seen among the three age groups. Instead, income differentials appeared to have some significance. Of those whose health was considered poor, 50 per cent were in the low income group with only 15 per cent in the high income group while among those who said health was very poor, 50 per cent was in the middle, 33 per cent in the low and only 17 per cent in the high income group. It was also evident that poor health status was more a reality for females than for males with 67 per cent of them describing their health as 'very poor'. Conversely, in each of the categories of elders whose health was seen as 'good' and 'fair', there were higher proportions of males than females.

Table 9: Self assessment of health by the elderly in Sri Lanka

Self Assessment of Health	Gender (%)			Income Group (%)		
	All	Male	Female	Low	Middle	High
Good	4	60	40	20	30	50
Fair	81	67	33	18	47	34
Poor	13	35	65	50	35	15
Very Poor	2	33	67	33	50	17

The pattern was not significantly different among the culture-based clusters. The two occupation-based clusters, however, had differences that may have arisen from their work and rural environment. The perception of well-being in terms of health by elders in the two occupation-based clusters had added implications for their economic capability since their activities depended on their physical fitness. Among the Agriculture Cluster, 17 per cent of elders reported their health was 'poor', another 73 per cent as 'fair' in health and only 10 per cent said their health was 'good'.

Income differences had significantly affected the health of elders in these two clusters with 57 per cent of those who perceived their health as 'poor' placed in the low income group. The middle and high income households too had small proportions of elders with poor health. Health of elders in low income agricultural and fisheries households could have a significant impact on their ability to contribute the much needed labour into their farming and fishing activities.

Male elders in these two clusters perceived their health as better than female elders. Among the elders who stated their health was 'good', 67 per cent were males; among those who thought their health was 'fair', the majority, 92 per cent were males; of those whose health was seen as 'poor' nearly half, 43 per cent were females. In these clusters too, age differences were not directly related to a perception of health since the 'old-old' group of 71–80 years in fact had more elders (18 per cent) who considered themselves as being in 'good' health as compared with only 5 per cent in the 'young-old' (60–70) group.

A perception of good health by rural elders as compared to urban elders, and reaffirmed by the rural agriculture cluster in the current study could reflect no more than a lesser preoccupation with illness among those mainly engaged in physical activities, as in rural agriculture households, rather than absence of illness per se. In contrast, more elders in the Fisheries Cluster – 33 per cent considered their health status 'poor', as was rational in a community that depended on a more uncertain income even than in agriculture. The balance 67 per cent in fisheries stated their health was 'fair'. In their case too the nature of the occupation could have influenced the way they assessed capability in terms of health. More males would have felt the effects of poor health when they were unable to brave the high seas in pursuit of their occupation.

Actual Health Problems

Although 72 per cent of elders in all clusters had perceived their health as 'good', yet, not all of them were free of health problems, since in an inquiry on health problems more elders (80 per cent) stated they had one or more health problems. The health problems probed in this inquiry were primarily symptoms of general debility such as low energy, trembling of hands, weak voice, forgetfulness, sleeping problems and so on. Of the 80 per cent that had some of these symptoms, 33 per cent had one symptom while the balance 67 per cent had multiple complaints numbering from two to nine. Females appeared to have more problems than males. Males had a maximum of seven each but females had combinations of seven, eight or nine symptoms. All the elders having multiple problems – of seven or more, belonged to low income households.

Elders in Agriculture and Fisheries notably complained of one or two at most. As was evident in their assessment of health, their specific problems too would be perceived minimally, their aches and pains considered as part of their occupation and not as a disease. Among the other clusters, the Plantation Tamil Cluster stood apart with 100 per cent of elders having at least one health problem. At the other end of the spectrum the Sri Lankan Tamils and Low Income Urban Clusters reported low incidence of health problems with 35 per cent and 40 per cent respectively. A low incidence of ill health in these two clusters was reported mainly among the high and middle income groups.

Long-Term Chronic Diseases

The natural symptoms of debility and ageing are compounded by the onset of chronic long-term diseases, which although emerging in the disease pattern of the general population, acquires special significance as geriatric diseases were exacerbated with increased lifespans. Some hard core diseases that are typical of this category among the aged in Sri Lanka are diabetes, heart disease, hypertension, arthritis, cancer and asthma. As a single disease, these entail high costs to the patient, the household and health services. Health services provided by the government are largely non-fee levying. But, in combinations of two or more of these diseases, they turn into millstones that plunge households inexorably into depths of poverty and deprivation.

Although in this sample the highest proportions of elders had asthma, hypertension/stroke and diabetes, all the hard core chronic diseases including arthritis, cancer, and heart disease were found among smaller proportions of elders. Nearly 43 per cent of the sample elders had at least one of the diseases listed above which was a bad enough situation for the elder and the household and also for the ageing population in the country. But, as was the case for 16 per cent of the sampled elders, these hard core diseases were present as multiple diseases with some having a combination of three of them, and the implications are very grim for both the elder and the household. There were 43 such elders in this sample of 270 households. It was noted that while there was no significant differences by gender or by age, the higher proportions with these combinations present among of the 'young-old' (63 per cent) and the 'old-old' (33 per cent) could signify low survival beyond age 80. The hard core diseases were combined with other diseases such as respiratory ailments, dementia and renal infections, 7 per cent of the sample elders reported such a situation. The considerable proportions of elders from the low (70 per cent) and middle (76 per cent) income households and close to half (48 per cent) in the high income households who had single or multiple hard core illnesses indicate the likely cost and care burden. These diseases entailed long-term regular management practices carried out through constant monitoring at specified appropriate clinics in government or private hospitals for allopathic treatment. Considerable utilization of critical assets to procure treatment and care, even to the extent of depriving the next generation of their future has been shown to be a common enough practice in households, even the non-poor ones, in their efforts to meet the needs of management of chronic diseases of their elders (Perera, et al., 2007a, 2007b).

Both males and females were prone to these diseases, the cost and care practices were weighted in favour of males who had greater opportunities to meet the cost needs than were females. Females were seen to have been more at a disadvantage in accessing appropriate health care, in terms of travel facilities and cost (Perera, et.al, 2007a; 2007b). The higher proportions of females (73 per cent) than males (62 per cent) with chronic illnesses affirmed the greater vulnerability. The presence of hard core diseases among the Agriculture and Fisheries Clusters bears out the finding of their prevalence in rural populations. In the Agriculture Cluster 30 per cent and 50 per cent in the Fisheries Cluster of the total elders had one hard core disease while another 7 per cent and 50 per cent respectively in the two clusters had a combination of two or more hard core diseases.

Cost of Treatment for Illness
Both the public and private health care services had been utilized by 129 elders in the sample who reported illness in the previous year. The public sector alone was utilized by 70 per cent, the private services only by 17 per cent and both by 7 per cent. The costs were derived for the first two categories of public and private care users. Nearly 93 per cent had incurred direct costs of travel, consultation, treatment and tests. While government health care services were obtained largely free of charge, 56 per cent of elders who had accessed government hospitals had incurred costs for medicines and tests. It was evident that a realistic measurement of the burden of cost needs to differentiate between costs on account of 'hard core, long term chronic diseases' and the miscellaneous ailments of old age and debility. These were derived separately for both inpatient and outpatient services.

The hard core illnesses had cost more to all income classes for which they had utilized the private facilities as well whereas the elders from low income households had not used the private facilities for other illnesses but had been compelled to use them for hard core diseases. When cost ranges were examined, elders had spent a sum between Rs 60 and Rs 6,000 for government allopathic services, Rs 600 and Rs 6,000 for private services, for total treatment when they were ill in the previous year.

Elders in the agriculture sector had spent between Rs 150 and Rs 750 while those in the fisheries had spent up to Rs 2,500. There were no significant differences in spending by gender or by age. The major items included in this total were cost of consultation, medicine, other treatment such as tests and of travel. The higher costs were incurred by elders in the rest of the clusters up to Rs 6,000 by the middle and high income households, while even those in low income households spent up to Rs

5,500. These costs for consultation were incurred by 19 per cent of those who were sick the previous year in the seven clusters. Some of them had accessed the private hospitals but among them were some who had consulted government medical officers when they worked as private consultants after working hours in government hospitals. This is permitted as a concession to retain specialists within the government. The next item of medicine had cost up to Rs 6,000 for elders in both the low and middle income households among all nine clusters.

Out of the elders (129) who were ill in the previous year, 44 per cent had inpatient treatment for periods ranging from one week to two months. Nearly 70 per cent of these were for a hard core chronic disease, and the rest for a mix of other ailments. The government indoor allopathic services were used by 82 per cent and one patient or 2 per cent with paralysis had accessed both government allopathic and government ayurveda hospitals. The private allopathic hospital alone was used by 13 per cent, while a combination of public and private allopathic hospitals were used by 3 per cent of elders.

Of the clusters, the agriculture and fisheries had not used private care but had used government services exclusively. The other clusters had used private care but sparingly. The low income households had used government hospitals exclusively as well as a majority of 94 per cent of middle income households. The highest utilization of private hospitals was by high income households; this group contained 67 per cent of all users of private hospitals. However, even among the high income households over half (53 per cent) within the income group had used public hospitals for indoor treatment. In the case of inpatient care too, the costs for long-term chronic diseases were consistently higher than for other illnesses.

As of now, 45 per cent were under medical care, but 49 were on medication. The additional 4 per cent were taking medication from old prescriptions without consulting a doctor. Medication was being continued for a variety of illnesses: cancer (2 per cent), arthritis (3 per cent), asthma (28 per cent), diabetes (21 per cent), heart disease (18 per cent) and hypertension (20 per cent). Accordingly, 85 per cent of those on regular medication had one or more of the hard core diseases. These were distributed among income groups such as 24 per cent among the low income group, 52 per cent in the middle, and 23 per cent in the high income group.

They were divided equally between male and female. In an age-wise analysis, 7 per cent were 'very old', 38 per cent were 'old-old' and 55 per cent were 'young-old'. The large majority of 95 per cent were on allopathic treatment alone, 2 per cent on a combination of allopathy and ayurveda and another 2 per cent on ayurveda alone. Costs for accessing health care currently were an average of Rs 700 per month and varied from Rs 639 for low income households, Rs 532 for the middle to Rs 1,054 for the high income households. These were monthly costs for patients with chronic diseases which if neglected could lead to impairment or loss of life itself. The burden of care for families and households could be very heavy for elders with chronic ailments.

Impairment

Three major characteristics of impairment typical in the aged have been probed; they are, vision, hearing and walking. In the sample, 62 per cent had one or more of these and 38 per cent were free of such disabilities. Vision alone was deficient in 98 per cent. Vision can be more disabling and lead to mental depression than the other two functions. Both vision and hearing deficiency was reported by 12 per cent and all three together were reported by 8 per cent, while another 12 per cent had low vision and walking disabilities combined. More females than males experienced these disabilities and among the three age groups the highest proportion of disabled was found in the 'very old' age group as is to be expected.

It was found that the majority – 75 per cent of elders with these disabilities were using some aids, such as spectacles, walking and hearing aids, and wheel chairs to mitigate their disability. Nevertheless, more elders in the high and middle income households and less among the low income households could afford such aids and this is also reflected in the case of females compared to males.

The 33 per cent who needed such aids for disability but were not using aids, cited reasons such as 'do not like' and 'can manage without'. But serious note needs to be taken of the 60 per cent who had no money, and they did not know where to go for such aids. A higher proportion – 69 per cent of females were deprived owing to lack of money for them. As can be expected, the low income households contained the highest proportion of elders who had no money for aids (71 per cent), followed by 60 per cent in the middle income households and 33 per cent in the high income households. The high cost of spectacles which were needed by most of the elders would have kept elders non-functional for lack of affordability. Elders themselves and their children were the primary providers of aids (88 per cent), voluntary agents picked up only 8 per cent and the government was a minor provider for only 2 per cent of elders.

Falls being very much a hazard of ageing, the incidence of falls in the last few years was obtained. Of the total sample, 11 per cent had had falls in the last three years. Of these, 77 per cent had fallen within the premises of the home and 23 per cent outside the home and 80 per cent had fallen once mostly by slipping or tripping. Of these, 73 per cent had injured themselves but only 9 per cent had any type of fracture and 32 per cent had minor cuts and bruises while 59 per cent had only pain at the time of the fall. Medical attention was required and obtained by 60 per cent, and 83 per cent had recovered fully.

Habits and Behaviour

Continuing the inquiry on health related lifestyles, an area of increasing concern, habits of smoking, alcohol use and betel chewing was addressed. Current users in the total sample, and in three sub-clusters of Plantation Tamils, Mixed Urban Cluster and Low Income Cluster were analysed separately to probe likely differences. Each of these habits, at least one, prevailed in 58 per cent of the total sample: smoking (25 per cent), alcohol use (22 per cent) and betel chewing (44 per cent).

The majority (65 per cent) of users had a single habit but the balance (35 per cent) had two or three together. Elders who had combinations of two or three habits together were found in all three income groups; most (46 per cent) in the middle, in the high income group (26 per cent) and lowest (18 per cent) in the low. Gender-wise, half of the males had a combination of two or three habits.

Eating Habits

In a further extension of assessment of lifestyles elders' eating habits were reviewed. All elders had two or more meals a day in general. Two meals per day was a regular affair for 3 per cent of elders, while the balance 97 per cent had three meals a day. Although this was generally so, there were two male elders, one who lived with an elderly spouse and the other with elderly spouse and a child who quite often had only one meal a day and occasionally not even one meal. The reason given was lack of money for food.

Hemapala was a 69-year-old farmer from a remote village in Moneragala. His agricultural land had been distributed to his children at marriage, leaving a small plot for him, his wife and an unmarried daughter. With advancing age, he found it difficult to cultivate the land; he leased it out (ande) on a system according to which, part of the produce was given to him as the owner of the land. This produce was uncertain and even when given insufficient even for their consumption. He has no other income other than the government poverty allowance of Rs 340 per month which is about Rs 10 a day, inadequate even for a cup of tea each. They had a rice meal and a second one of bread or yams, quite often both meals comprised yams or millets.

Many – 50 per cent elders in low income households would more often have two meals only; this proportion was lower among the middle income households (37 per cent), followed by the high income households (33 per cent). Although the reason for not taking all three meals was not enquired in the questionnaire, it is likely that those in the low income households experienced shortage of money for food.

Abdul, 65 years old, lived in a rural village with his elderly wife. Their income was generated from his wife cooking in houses in the neighbourhood and from government poverty allowance. The allowance was Rs 510 per month and from cooking in houses, Rs 50 a day. When she had such work she could bring rice and curry for a meal but at other times it was a meager fare of miscellaneous food other than rice. A bare one meal a day was a common occurrence in this household.

In addition to the number of meals, the query on regularity of food intake found that 40 per cent of all elders did not eat regular meals each day. Most of these – 49 per cent were from middle income households, some (23 per cent) from low income and 28 per cent from high income households. Meanwhile, 33 per cent of elders reported they missed meals and most of these were in middle income households (49 per cent), followed by low income households (26 per cent) and high income households (25 per cent).

The most consumed type of food was non-vegetarian (71 per cent). About 27 per cent consumed special diet, 77 per cent prescribed by doctors and another 23 per cent followed a self-prescribed diet. Vitamin, iron and calcium supplements were taken by 13 per cent.

Conclusion

The discussion can be structured within a framework with three distinct scenarios that comprehensively capture the situations and needs of elders. The sociological changes that came about with modernization and the demographic transition with their impact on the status of elders are expressed through a set of indices that attempt to capture shifts in tradition and cultural mores in different population clusters.

The next set of issues capture changes in capability, vulnerabilities and deprivations of elders placed in different household environments. These are expressed through another set of indices. The indicators derived from a large volume of data gathered in the field have been rendered more succinct in these sets of indices derived to flag some of the critical issues on ageing. These were derived for two groups into which the population clusters were classified since significant differences were seen in this division. The two occupation-based ones of Agriculture and Fisheries had many similarities and were grouped together and the rest as a separate group. They are designated as culture-based and occupation-based respectively. The analysis attempts to identify the gaps in the well-being of elders and indicate measures that can enhance their quality of life.

References

Marga Institute, 'Sri Lanka's Population Future and its Implications for the Family and Elderly', Colombo, Sri Lanka, 1998.

Perera, Myrtle, Whitehead, Margaret, Molyneux, David, Weerasooriya, Mirani and Gunatilleke, Godfrey, 'Neglected Patients with a Neglected Disease? A Qualitative Study of Lymphatic Filariasis', *Neglected Tropical Diseases*, Vol. 1, No. 2, 2007a.

Perera, Myrtle, Gunatilleke, Godfrey and Bird, Philippa, 'Falling into the Medical Poverty Trap in Sri Lanka: What Can be Done?', *International Journal of Health Services*, Vol. 37, No. 2, pp.379–98, 2007b.

Ruggles, S, 'Living Arrangements of Older Persons', *Population Bulletin of the United Nations,* Special Issue Nos. 42 & 43, 2001.

Chapter 9

SOCIAL SETTING AND DEMAND FOR SENIOR HOMES IN THE NETHERLANDS AND SRI LANKA

Carla Risseeuw

Introduction

This chapter tries to compare the social settings of elders within intergenerational relationships in Colombo, Sri Lanka and urban Holland. It mainly focuses on the so-called 'private contract', while occasionally referring to the so-called 'public contract'. Finally, it refers to some preliminary results of visiting senior homes in Colombo of all religious backgrounds, while mainly focusing on the women inmates of two established Buddhist homes in Colombo (in total, data from 27 homes were collected).[1]

These terms have been taken from the comparative study of Akiko Hashimoto on elders in US and Japan (1996). With the public contract, the focus is on the elder as a citizen and forms of state or commercial provisions. With the private contract, the focus is on the relations an elder has with family, a wider circle of friends, neighbours, acquaintances and community. For me, the value of Hashimoto's approach is her perspective of viewing the two contracts as a continuum – the public contract and policymaking equally being part of the social–cultural realm.

Comparison and Intergenerational Relations

Akiko Hashimoto's comparative study on Japanese and American perspectives on ageing provides a framework within which to reflect on expectations of family relations next to expectations of governmental services, both of which are (partly) taken for granted within one sociocultural and political context. Thus, specific sociocultural settings (can) differ in certain crucial respects. For example, the expectation of need in old age is based on specific cultural meanings given to life course trajectories. Specific expectations of security depend on cultural assumptions as to what is needed in old age. Further, cultural difference is found in the sense of equity and assumed fairness between generations, while the cultural script on self-sufficiency reflects cultural notions of independence and dependence. Finally, the ideal meanings of primary bonds of affection (held by the different generations) and their expression can be expected to differ.

It is not always easy to find the right terms to express the cultural meanings of such differences. In her analysis, Hashimoto makes use of a Bourdieu inspired framework emphasizing that cultural assumptions as described above, are not always consciously and articulately held by all. These assumptions/dispositions bear a quality that Bourdieu has coined with the Latin term 'habitus' or the term 'learned ignorance', implying a matter-of-fact quality: unarticulated and often not fully consciously part of, but nevertheless effortlessly enacted cultural scripts, which shape people's actions, thoughts and emotions, as well as providing them with a cultural shared base, from which to deviate, create alternatives, etc. (Bourdieu did not explicitly mention emotions).

Hashimoto compared the trajectories of intergenerational caring in two medium-sized towns in the US and in Japan. Hashimoto terms the Japanese cultural setting, as one operating from a logic that frailty *will occur* in old age. Preparing for it is necessary. The Japanese government's policy was made to leave this to the family and city council initiative rather than developing a government based, countrywide responsibility. Elders and (preferably) their first son and his family, ideally jointly provide a place for the parent in the son's home.

If the cultural script operates from a perspective that frailty in old age *might occur*, preparations take on a fundamentally different character, more along the lines of contingency measures, as found in her research locations in the US.

In the first case, the individual is absolved of any blame of becoming frail. In the second case, one is responsible for curbing and handling one's frailty as long as one can. While in the Japanese case, the elder's security is expected to take a form of *'dependency'*, which is (ideally) received; in the (white) American case, security is provided through a substantial degree of *autonomy*, with an ideal that a younger generation has the right to claim independence. In the latter case, the (conjugal) couple is the central arena, within which a dependency can be expressed and care expected in old age. Accepted age differences as well as gendered notions of care, tend to provide husbands more security than wives in this respect. In Japan, it would be the intergenerational blood bonds which tend to form the primary life bond.

I shall now take this framework to look into the ideas on concepts as 'home', 'family', 'coupledom', 'personhood' as well attempt to understand the specific cultural ways of maintaining networks within and beyond families – in order to understand the differences in ideal cultural scripts for shaping intergenerational relationships for ageing populations.[2]

The Idea of 'The Home' and of Intergenerational Relations

Currently, Dutch social scientists describe the Netherlands as an individualized society, with an ethos of the (individualized) nuclear family (Broese and Knipscheer, 1999). The latter term refers to the practice of grown-up children to initiate and prioritize their own households and nuclear families. So an elder couple usually lives on their own, and after the death of one spouse, the other tends to live alone. In most cases, this is the widow. Care and support from the children can be expected, but it is one of what Hashimoto called 'the might need scenario'.

In this respect, social historians tend to point to a high degree of historical continuity. Anthropologist Jack Goody, well-known for his comparative research on family in Asia, Africa and Europe, described the smaller households of western Europe as having relations with elder generations marked by 'non contractual elements of a more affective or merely exchangist kind' (Goody, 2000, p.166).

The specific form of the (nuclear) family with its non-contractual relations towards (grand)parents, frequency of unmarried daughters and sons leaving the parental home before marriage to find employment, its inheritance systems, relatively and relative high prevalence of celibacy shows a remarkable historical continuity in western/northern Europe, according to historian, Alan Macfarlane (1978, 1994). In this context, urban Netherlands itself has been said to have been strikingly characterized by such homely nuclear family formations with companiable spousal relations, where husband and wife were believed to have godly sanctioned complementary tasks.

In contrast, in urban Sri Lanka, elder couples live alone, but not as a cultural ideal or norm. The living alone of elder women rarely occurs. People, young and old, complain this 'Western' way of life can come to them, with their children migrating for work and study within or outside the country. The rise and expressed need for senior homes and new forms of care for elders is indeed noticeable, although the first old age homes for elder women in Colombo were established sometime in the early twentieth century.

From the perspective of comparison, such homes of elder middle class couples and elderly single women in urban Holland and Colombo, Sri Lanka, may seem the result of similar processes, but there remains marked cultural differences in the notions of 'home' and 'family'.

Urban Sri Lankan homes are periodically (or permanently) expected to be able to absorb family members and guests coming home to stay, without a sense of privacy being curbed.[3] The availability of servants often facilitates this hospitality. Likewise, elders ideally (traditionally) can remain living in the home, slowly relinquishing their central power over the household and/or budget.

If an older mother prefers living alone, she can still periodically stay for weeks or months, in principle as long as she likes, in the homes of different sons and daughters. One quite regularly comes across these examples of 'travelling grannies', at times moving on for a new birth; for a change in climate or a need to dilute some family tension. Either permanently living in or regularly staying with, she would be part of all social gatherings in the house and would know the friends of her children quite well. It could also well happen that visiting friends of the children make a visit to a mother in the home where she then is.

This degree of 'fluidity' of the boundaries of 'the home' is not found or is highly exceptional in urban Holland, as we shall see below. Likewise, in relation to intergenerational relations, there seems to be a greater fluidity in perceived social boundaries than in urban Netherlands. In Sri Lanka, one usually knows most friends of direct family members well, meaning (grand)parents, siblings and children. Thus, an elder person seems to have more opportunities not only to form linkages with different generations of family, but also with their friends. Lastly, compared to urban middle class Holland, the 'speed' of making connections and acquaintances seems to be higher and done with more social ease. Within several social circles one can get to know people comparatively quickly and easily. Within one's own network, one can tap the contacts of many of them on request. Here the challenge can well be getting to know the right people, rather than having a very small network of friends coupled with the challenge of expanding this circle. The exception is found with those elders who become bedridden or suffer from serious impairments as lack of hearing or sight. Here, social contact starts diminishing and one often finally retains only the close family member(s) as support.

In the Netherlands, an elder person has to depend to a far larger extent on his/her own ability to maintain a network and this is done through shared activities or mutual visiting. Usually, the home is not equipped to have people to regularly stay, while it is also not customary to do so. The high number of elders living alone in Holland has stimulated research on their well-being. Certain marked differences were found as to who in the society is prone to degrees of loneliness. Considerable research has been carried out on this (Gierveld and Dykstra, 1998; Dykstra, 1995; Gierveld, 1998). As it takes a substantial amount of time to build a circle of friends and acquaintances; the friends one has in old age, to a large extent depends on the relations built up earlier in life. Older, single men proved a vulnerable category, especially recent divorcees (Gierveld and Dykstra, *Ibid.*, p.176). Widowhood was also noted as a risk factor in relation to intense loneliness among women. Single, elder women (unmarried or divorced early in life) were found having the most extensive and varied networks, next to a close circle of friends, which was explained by the fact that such women had had to build up their own social life during most parts of their life, and not only during the last phase of life (*Ibid.*, p.178; Dykstra, 1998). Further, retired working women usually had acquired a more adequate financial base from which to undertake activities in old age, than those of their female peers who had never entered the labour market.[4] These studies form a powerful indication of the working of an underlying cultural script of personally being (held) responsible for shaping one's life at all ages ('the ideal of personal autonomy').

Further differences are found in what can be termed 'sociality': the ways of keeping company. In (urban) Holland, maintaining a circle of friends, (distant) relations and sometimes neighbours is done in a culturally specific way, involving a high degree of voluntariness, given shape through the making of appointments well ahead in time and keeping them. Punctuality and reliability are part of these contexts. Once the initiative to return invitations, telephone calls, etc. is no longer taken, the size of one's network gradually becomes smaller. Only the close friendships tend to remain. In other words, the voluntary nature of remaining in contact underlies the cultural script of networking, friendships and to a certain extent family (also see, Edwards and Strathern, 2000).

In this respect, the situation of a middle class elder in urban Sri Lanka follows a different life trajectory. If one's life has not had too many mishaps, an elder middle class person can expect to enjoy company without having to make a comparable effort to maintain social linkages. This is facilitated by the practice of maintaining many links jointly as a family, even when residing in different homes.[5] People of differing generations experience a matter-of-fact dimension to this practice. For many purposes, the maintaining of networks is most relevant for all generations. I don't want to imply that all elders would be interested in their children's friends. But they would have to appear to be so, as they are expected to meet them and get to know some of them better. For many, it is done without a sense of effort, often enjoying the company. For those who refrain, one can retreat to one's rooms, provided no feelings are hurt.

Next to family networks, society also provides a wide array of associations of many kinds, for instance of retired employees, which tend to regularly organize joint outings and other social events.[6]

Finally, circles of friends and family often matter-of-factly overlap. One can well visit parents of friends and other kin and certainly call them for any special get-together, party or 'function' as it is termed in English. Likewise, one extends hospitality to a wide circle of kin as well as certain friends of one's children (with their family and/or friends).

Kin tend to have certain duties towards as well as expectations of a wider circle of elders than in the Netherlands. Reciprocity is seen as a 'natural' part of relations. This way of life also has an effect on the youngest generation. Children tend to be socialized to interact with a variety of ages within their home and family circle. They are (still) trained to welcome (family) visitors and takeover duties (with the help of servants) of absent parents. As a result, they are at home in intergenerational settings and enjoy/share the company of elders, as a part of life. This includes taking a long-term perspective of relationships, also in terms of possible, future benefits.

This is not to say that elder people in Sri Lanka do not feel lonely at times or that no changes in intergenerational family occur. But one is more likely to feel lonely in the midst of new generations and their (new) ways, while probably missing those who have died. But elders are seldom confronted with the same kind of 'self-dependence' as their Dutch counterparts, involving the single-handed running of their own homes up to a high age: domestically, financially and socially.

Before ending this section, I shall shortly mention some of my research results in Holland, on ideas on family and friendship, to further understand the nature of the differences between the two sociocultural settings. My own research on notions of family and friendship in urban Holland came up with certain results, which I later found to be paralleled by demographic research in the Netherlands.

On the issue of meeting and knowing friends of their children, many respondents indicated that they did not know them and that there was no need to know the friends of one's (grown-up) children. One had to let one's children lead their own lives, one should not interfere or be a burden to them. At times, it was even said one was not interested in their children's friends, as they had their own. (Risseeuw, 2003, 2005). Underlying this intergenerational code is the ideal of altruistic love of the parent for the child, literally expressed in the often stressed point of a child not having asked to be born. Therefore, there should be a downward flow of goods and support in generations, not involve return 'payments' back to the parent (at least not involuntarily). In the past, children were seen as gifts from god, now a person 'takes' children on the basis of their own choice. It was one's own choice and one has to take responsibility for it rather than burdening one's children.

Social research in the Netherlands has further stressed the tendency of each nuclear family member, to have their own social contacts, with mainly visits to grandparents or very close friends which could be undertaken jointly. In the latter case, children usually avoid such visits as they mature and start their own lives.[7]

Moreover, my respondents' networks of friends appeared strongly *age-bound.* Most people mainly appeared to mix with others of approximately their own age and with a similar economic and social background. A third issue was the fact that one tended to compartmentalize not only one's friends, but also friends and family. Thus, one could be friends for years without (regularly) meeting a person's other friends or family members. At most one would know the partner or the small children, much more seldom siblings and/or parents. If one does meet all these different actors at special events (weddings, examination ceremonies, birthdays, funerals), it is usually experienced positively, but is not further pursued in daily social life. Due to *this way of compartmentalizing relations,* several of my respondents had stumbled on an unexpected frailty of their social bonds.

For instance, one woman in her forties was confronted with the terminal illness of both an elder parent and a sibling, both living in her rural home area, several hours travel from her current urban home and work. During the interview she expressed the feeling that once the death of these family members occurred, she would come to know who her real friends were. Only they would be able to share her grief. But during our discussion it became clear that her friends had never joined her 'back home' and did not personally know her relations. They would only be able to mourn her loss, without their personal memory of the relatives she loved. She had never really thought of this; the compartmentalization of relations as well as the time such visits would take, had matter-of-factly just led her to experience a dissatisfaction with her partner's lack of serious involvement, but not with her friends.

Several of my respondents had thus been taken by surprise by their own unarticulated cultural script (Risseeuw, 2003, p.92).

This age-bound nature of networks in Holland, has also been noted by researchers as P Uhlenberg and J Gierveld, who have termed it 'age homophily' and which was found to strongly influence the options in social contacts of the aged (2004, p.9).

The compartmentalization of social relations of individual nuclear family members has also been partly referred to in social research on the family. It is the combination of these factors: age-centred networks and the high degree of compartmentalization of friendship, family and acquaintances, which provides the specific cultural script, in which an ageing person has to create and maintain a social circle as a couple or as someone running a single household. This way of shaping relations is part of an everyday 'sociality', which people take to be 'natural'. When questioned on its boundaries, it takes time to formulate. It belongs to what Bourdieu terms 'a culture's learned ignorance': One knows and one doesn't know it. In other words, one is not fully aware.

During the research on Holland, my Indian colleagues all noted this – they were surprised at the compartmentalization of relationships (Ganesh, 2005; Risseeuw, Palriwala and Ganesh, 2005). They had all visited Holland, and also other Euro-American societies regularly during their lives. Although differences in sociality had been experienced, the full consequences of these differing forms of relating only surfaced to all of us during the research itself. As exponents of comparable cultural settings as described for urban, middle class Sri Lanka, they were also quick to see the advantages of this Dutch way of life: If you had a conflict with a friend, no others got involved in the argument and you lost one friend at most.

In conclusion, one can say that the cultural parameters of home, hospitality, intergenerational linking and the speed of initiating, and ways of maintaining of social linkages, provide distinct differences in the social setting in which people grow old. People tend to be partially unaware of their own societal practices of inclusion and exclusion. These practices do result in different trajectories of social vulnerability in old age. In order to understand such processes further and the possibly new concepts they require to fully understand them, I shall now turn to the two sociocultural historical constructs of family in (Buddhist) Sri Lanka and urban Netherlands.

History and the Formation of (Nuclear) Families

In the Netherlands, social historians have provided an analysis of the twentieth century construction of the specific individualized family form. The Dutch language has a separate word 'gezin' for this nuclear family structure, next to the word 'familie', with which one means a wider circle of (bilateral) family. The word 'gezin' was initially firmly entrenched within the emergence of the bourgeois Christian morality in the first half of the twentieth century. The 'gezin' became a social marker for the decent, religious citizen, involving strict separate responsibilities of the breadwinner and his housewife, which slowly developed into a cultural pattern of a homely, privatized life (Risseeuw, 2005). The husband headed 'the family', but was not conceived to be 'complete' without a wife.[8] The extensive pillarization of religious life in the Netherlands is said to have played a central role in this formation (Regt, 1993b, p.222). The nuclear family model incorporated a strong mother figure, which, according to social demographers, is highlighted in twentieth century Holland, by the relatively lower pace of declining birth rates as well as the even lower speed of rising female employment figures, compared to surrounding countries in Western Europe (Risseeuw, 2005). The extensive breadwinner-based subsidies, still to a large extent part of the current welfare system, can be traced to the late nineteenth and early twentieth century formation.

Not that this (urban) family form did not undergo change. The high frequency of single mothers, rising figures of divorce, non-marital (gay) partnerships, indicate change – at least from the historical period of the pillarized society in Holland. Different values of love, understanding and more exchangeable tasks between husband and wife become a part of modern life. But this degree of change should not be overrated. While partnering lifestyles outside marriage are increasingly diverse since the 1960s, gendered division within marriage and homemaking have proved more resilient to change. Further, the taken-for-granted idea of the secludedness of the home with its substantial boundaries of privacy is retained.

Also, from the aspect of ageing parents, it is worth noting that the cultural ideal will expect mature children to extend a certain degree of support – in practice often falling on the gendered practices of a wife. But, a wife is expected to place her care for her 'own' nuclear family above the care for her parents. This script is also maintained when she has only her husband to look after. Thus, the Sinhalese notions of family, which ideally incorporates the option of a wife leaving her family to spend time with her ageing and ailing parents, would be conceived of as inappropriate (wrong sequence of priorities).

In Buddhist Sri Lanka, the extended family and its bilaterality were first challenged substantially during the British colonial rule (nineteenth and first half of the twentieth century). Nevertheless, 'family-morality' in this respect proved relatively challenging to change. In spite of British pressure to bias inheritance substantially to sons, or even the firstborn son only (primogeniture), the family idea of fairness of both sons and daughters inheriting equally was retained. Further, the equal access to education of both sexes is ideally valued, if not fully practised, but still remarkably higher numbers of women of all ages in Sri Lanka are literate compared to figures in India.

Over the course of the nineteenth and parts of the twentieth century, British policy did succeed in gendered forms of family change, for instance successfully curbing the level of security of widows, by limiting their direct access to property. Likewise, it could lay the base for the promotion of the male-centred marriage systems (the so-called '*Diga*-marriage', where the wife went to live with the husband and his (family) properties) over female-centered ones (the so-called '*Binna*-marriage', where the wife's family retained the property and the husband came to live on his wife's family land) (Risseeuw, 1990, 1996).

In more recent times, one can point to the shift in the dowry system from being the young wife's security within her new family, to a form of 'joint property' with her new husband, straight after marriage (Goonesekere, 1996). But, overall one can argue that while women lost out both during and after colonial times, the very idea of family (*Paule*) with its bilateral forms and shared responsibilities, including financial support has retained a high degree of continuity, as have the notions of family in the Netherlands.

For example, up to today no word exists in Sinhalese for the 'nuclear family' formation. The word *Paule*, or the more colloquial *Appee Katiye* implies an idea of a person's family including a person's marital partner, parents, grandparents, an in-living aunt or other family member, children and grandchildren. A sense of locality is connected to this word. Grandparents who do not live in the house wouldn't be conceived of as 'Paule', but belonging to a wider set of relations termed *Nedeyo, Neyo, Nee* or *Gnaati*.

The idea of locality is also expressed by the fact that in-living blood relatives, like the given example of the aunt, can come to be seen as *Paule*. This also depends on the developed degree of affection (*bendeema*). Blood relatives down one (blood) line are termed *paramparaawa*, while a wider circle of relations, living or dead, is referred to as *sanuharaya*. Ideas of interdependence between generations are also expressed after death. By performing yearly ceremonies/offerings (*danees*), the family aims to provide 'merit' for the departed, which should support a fortunate rebirth.

With respect to the relations with one's parents, a non-negotiable duty is the cultural ideal, based on the premise that one can never be out of debt to parents who gave one life. This ideal is expressed at many ceremonial moments during a lifetime. Due to the bilateral quality, ideally a son-in-law should actively share in taking care not only of his parents but also his wife's, while he should also understand that his wife's parental duties can involve periods away from home.

The area of change that can be mentioned in this context is the British influence on the way of life of the social layer with whom they associated, has obviously been the highest. Their descendants are also found among the middle classes of Colombo. One can question in relation to the issue of ageing and degrees of vulnerability, how family notions were transformed among them. For example, the 'habitus' of a husband could comparatively entail less sense of care and responsibility towards his in-laws, including less acceptance of his wife's absence from home.

The current high level of social mobility which certain low income groups have experienced within one/two generation(s), could initially lead to smaller housing facilities in the city, with less accommodation for the older generation. International long-term migration can lead to too few younger members of the family being available to share in housing arrangements with their elders.

Private and Public Care Arrangements

North European family systems would qualify as Hashimoto's 'might need' scenarios, embedded within an ideal of autonomy and independence for all and in relation to old age, 'for as long as it is possible'. But there are substantial variations between and within countries in this respect. For instance, in Holland, unlike a neighbouring country like Germany, no legislation currently exists to mark a degree of care-duty between family generations.

In the Netherlands, children do tend to step in when old parents require daily help (49 per cent: NIDI, 2003, p.169), but public morality seems to point towards state support for this last life phase. This is expected when the parent needs (extensive) day-to-day care. A recent large-scale survey indicated only 10 per cent respondents would prefer to keep their parents at home in such situations (SCP, 2003, Chapter 6).

Likewise, a large majority of elders indicate their strong wish not to be 'a burden' on their children: Children should be allowed to live their own lives. In this context, Kamala Ganesh in her study on urban Dutch elders and their networks, noted how this central sense of personhood involving self-dependence and a form of dignity, at times makes the elder-child relation hard to handle for both parties. For elders making 'a claim' was (often) not acceptable. For children it was not always easy to offer, as this was an indication of the parent's (coming) dependence (involving a deterioration of selfhood and dignity). It often resulted in what Ganesh describes as: 'between waiting to be asked and waiting to be offered lies an area of slippage, and some critical needs may remain un-addressed or even unnoticed' (Ganesh, 2005).

Compared to an urban setting in Sri Lanka, the inter-ageing family contract is manifestly different, as we have seen. A reciprocal script of intergenerational relations, involves more of a 'will need' scenario than in the Netherlands. Long-term reciprocity is part of a lived morality. Elders can express their dependency on their mature children and claim support, which they often do. Hence, unlike Holland, one can easily find elders refusing to suffer in silence. It can well be a world of (loudly) uttered complaints, disappointments and of demands for more care and affection. Even if a younger generation experiences discomfort at this, ideally they have to expect and deal with it. This ideally means a practice of not only looking after the elder, but also keeping him or her 'happy', making her/ him forget the complaint and rejoin home life. Further, one has the presence of domestics – although increasingly harder to get, a wider kin network and extra foreign remittances sent home. The latter involves substantial advantages in line of currency exchange.

Conclusion

My research seems to point to substantial differences in relation to networks of family, friends and acquaintances between urban middle class Holland and urban middle class Colombo. Middle class elders in Colombo are far less likely to be confronted with an old age in which one is the major actor responsibly for running one's home domestically, socially and economically.

Nevertheless, my Sri Lankan informants did point to the following: Elders who become severely handicapped in speech, hearing or maybe even eyesight, and/or are bedridden, are in the vast majority of cases confronted with a serious drop in acquaintances and even friends. Here close family only will provide support, apart from institutional care.

Further, middle class couples with little (living) family, no children, less financial resources, with one partner ill, are prone to find housing at the outskirts of Colombo, which again can have isolating effects. In such cases the personalities also play a role. If one tends to have little interest or energy left for visitors, their numbers will drop. Further, such cases would probably have less to offer in the world of being connected to the right people. But in many cases, I've seen long-standing work contacts and friendships provide small opportunities of income earning, as well as relatives coming to stay as boarders, which provides company, enhances security, but at the same time can lead to tensions.

Nevertheless, more old age homes have come up, including Day Care Centres (DCC) for elders and children. Although still having to systematically go through my interviews, I want to end with some findings out of the qualitative interviews held in several Colombo based (Buddhist) homes. My informants were mainly widowed, divorced or never married women, next to several married couples.

Some Comments on Current Research in Old Age Buddhist Homes: Middle Class Colombo

This research material needs further analysis, but a tentative overall picture emerges where the sociality and family arrangements in the majority of cases continue in roughly the same manner. Speaking of the 'breakdown of family' and a surrender to 'western ways' seems too extreme. Provided the home is a well-run establishment in this context, able to keep up a standard and the senior has adequate financial means including a reasonable pension, the 'senior's residence' can be quite comfortable, although not the traditional way to live. It is still a shame for many relatives to have a parent in a senior home.

The travel and migration of children is one of the main reasons for the selection of such a home. In many cases, married children had initially insisted their parent(s) join them in their new homes in Australia, US, etc. But in practice after trial periods, often the day to day isolation in this new home, while the children were at work as well as the social isolation, proved unsupportable. One simply missed too many ways of doing things at home. Also, the climate, the diet, the religion and – I feel, although people would seldom explicate that, the relative ease with which one could maintain one's own social life and world. Although missing the grandchildren was very painful, one thus finally chose to live 'at home'.

Research has further indicated that old age homes house a relatively high percentage of unmarried inmates. Figures of a wider research than mine came to 41 per cent of male inmates and 39 per cent of women, who had never married (CENWOR, 1995, p.75). This phenomenon is related to the Sinhalese, Buddhist marital customs. Although 'arranged' marriages are next to 'love matches', the parents often respect the will of the daughter or son on this issue. A young son or daughter can also (if strong-willed), refuse all marriage proposals and one can definitely always refuse some. Census figures over the last century, likewise, regularly reported a 5–7 per cent range of never-marrieds.

Single elders, as well as couples tend to join senior homes, at times of their own choice. They tend to join when they are physically healthy, often in their fifties and sixties. In the case of single women, they are at times even still employed. Well established homes, located centrally, at easily accessible places are most popular, while proximity to places of worship (of one's own choice) is also a high priority. Widows often come much later – in a sense at times 'too late', to have the energy to start a new life. Here the motivation is often one of not being able to 'run' a (large) house on one's own and issues of security.

Usually one has family, but the senior home facilitates keeping the right distance and connection with relatives. One is sure of not being a burden and of not being isolated in a house where inmates have gone to work for the day. One further avoids becoming too indebted in view of claims to one's inheritance, etc.

Very wealthy single women, could also come to the home to keep relatives at a distance and to gain more leeway to spend their money on themselves. It has been noticed that nephews and nieces then developed a daily routine of bringing special lunches, offering support as well as regular invitations.

Several cases reported, that single women felt a certain contentment with the secure, and relatively independent way of life they could lead. Likewise, living within the deep-seated and lifelong conflicts with family, even more so over the inheritance of parents, had at times also been too much of a strain.

In relation to this above point, it is noticeable from a Dutch perspective, how senior home management deals with 'family issues'. The logic of the management is one of 'knowing the life within extended families'. It brings security, happiness and a sense of purpose and belonging, but that same life can also cause extreme tensions which are best handled through separate living arrangements. Therefore, married women, whose husbands are alive, can easily live separately. It is the wife's choice. Likewise, the mother/daughter-in-law conflict is also taken as more than substantial reason to wish to join a home.

Often inmates had relatives to help, occasionally needing transport. They were further invited regularly to the homes of close relatives – sometimes for several weeks or months at a time. Support could also at times be extended to more tedious jobs, as obtaining the correct pension. All depended on the level of affection, closeness and at times also the level of expected inheritance.

Retired teachers, depending on their popularity and interest, could expect regular visits from former pupils and their families. On the whole, for professional women, work contacts tended to continue in various ways.

One often stayed for lengthy periods with children or relatives, in the style of the 'travelling grannies' mentioned earlier – and did not live in the institution the full year round. Also, yearly medical check-ups in other towns, were taken as an opportunity to stay with relatives, and have a short holiday.

Within the Home Itself

One home tends to have more joint activities than another – but the 'better' homes always had regular events organized, often religious engagements, meditation classes, pilgrimages (the wealthy to Bihar), specific monks coming to visit, etc. Likewise, much charity was stimulated: collecting and distributing packages of clothes, and other items after the tsunami, private teaching, assisting schools, the handicapped, etc.

Socially they brought with them the 'sociality' of their former life. Their challenge was more in keeping good terms with all, and not getting too close to anyone against one's will. Shared lunches and dinners, as well as small staff, leading the stronger, younger inmates to do small errands for the more elderly, led to much more daily forms of contact, in comparison to an urban middle class senior home in Holland. Trusted friendships took time to form, if they did.

Often financial worries were hidden from others. Relying on family members to pay for the board or even for medicines and special outings only led to insecurity. For example: the death of a major supportive family member (who paid for the home), leaving no will, perhaps due to a family conflict arising out of the will. Also, a situation where relatives paid for the home, but were unaware or disagreed with the purchase of certain medical care. It then proved very difficult to question relatives about such issues, but likewise one took great care to keep such situations secret from other inmates.

Several looked for small jobs as secretaries, one as a teacher, etc. to supplement their meager income, but also to have something to do. Once in a while, a woman would still be employed and be accepted, as she had come to live alone in her family house.

One lady hated the food, so had developed a wide knowledge of public dinners to which she subscribed: for Xmas, Christian holidays, hotel dinners of various associations etc. Once overheard a conversation between her and an inmate who told her not to go eating with the Christians all the time. She answered that there was quite a lot to say for the Christians, they sang a lot, were quite merry and gay, and not always talking about death and rebirth.

We do not in social sciences yet have enough words to clearly express how 'ways of keeping company' differ in varying social settings. The ideal and practice of the experience of 'relatedness' and the very idea of keeping company ('sociality') as well as the notion of personhood, seem difficult to grasp when applying formal kinship terms only.

The understanding of the renegotiation of intergenerational relations actors undertake, does seem to require 'developing an eye of seemingly trivial and taken for granted acts' as well as an awareness of more muted contrary themes and their forms of expression.

Interestingly enough, although these subtleties in boundaries and connectedness can matter-of-factly be acted out by those involved, many remain partially unaware of the arbitrary moment in the choices they make. It is in this arena of effortlessly enacted cultural scripts that comparison – with all its pitfalls – can make valuable contributions.

Notes

[1] Next to middle class informants, I also held interviews with the non-paying and working women inmates. These women have worked as domestics or elsewhere, and apply to become working inmates: cleaning, cooking and the like. Finally, I interviewed 45 elder women along the coastal southern belt of Sri Lanka, in the area where I have worked and kept close contacts with, since 1977.

[2] I base myself on interviews held in urban (Buddhist) Colombo and urban Netherlands (Risseeuw, 2005; Risseeuw, Palriwala, Ganesh, 2005), but also on extensive existing literature. In relation to Sri Lanka, I have undertaken research on colonial history and conditions of home-based coir workers and several other topics, periodically, over the last 30 years and have a fair speaking ability of Sinhalese.

[3] If required, a private family discussion goes on next to the entertaining of guests. If not, the visit can also form a welcome period of truce.

[4] Those with health problems as hearing, seeing and walking disability were to a far greater degree confronted with loneliness. Secondly, substantial geographical differences in support networks of older adults ware found. Older adults living in large cities formed a potential category in need, their core-networks being relatively small (compared to less urbanized and rural areas), composed of non-kin (67 per cent), relative high percentage of age-mates and with less number of children, compared to elsewhere in Holland. Their network was much wider than that of local living rural elders. (Gierveld and Fokkema, 1998).

[5] From the point of view of the younger generation this is not directly formulated as a duty, but more as 'not nice' not to do so – it can be interpreted in the wrong way. In families providing their children with more than average pocket money, often sees kids in their puberty branching out into their own youth culture and peer groups.

[6] For example a practice as 'retired teacher's day', periodically held at (the better) schools are quite common. Here the retired teachers come to meet their now professional pupils of the past. The latter on their turn assist their former teachers through their new profession : medical and legal professions, accountancy and the like.

[7] My sample consisted of 55 respondents, of all ages, with only the 20 and 30 year age group being slightly underrepresented. The majority came from urban Netherlands. Women respondents came to 60 per cent, male to 40 per cent, the majority had children, and came from middle and lower income groups. Several bi-cultural people responded and one joint living unit collectively participated in the research.

[8] A husband decided whether his wife could take up paid employment outside the home up to the second half of the 1950 ties. Likewise, a wife could not hold separate property from her husband up to this same period.

References

Adams, J, 'The Familial State: Elite Family Practices and State-Making in the Early Modern Netherlands', *Theory and Society*, Vol. 23, No. 4, 1994, pp.505–39.

Akiyama, H, Antonucci, T and Campbell, R, 'Exchange and Reciprocity among Two Generations of Japanese and American Women' in Sokolovsky, J, ed, *The Cultural Context of Aging*, Bergin and Garvey, Westport, Connecticut, London, 1997, pp.163–77.

Bijsterveld, K, Horstman K and Mesman J, 'Crying Whenever Monday Comes: Older Unmarried Women in the Netherlands and the Game of Comparison, 1955–1980' in *Journal of Family History*, Vol. 25, No. 2, April 2000, pp.221–34.

Broese van Groenou, M I and Knipscheer, C P M, 'The Onset of Physical Impairment of Independently Living Older Adults and the Support Received from Sons and Daughters in the Netherlands', *International Journal of Aging and Human Development*, Vol. 48, 1999, pp.263–78.

Broese van Groenou, M I, Van Tilburg, T G and de Jong Gierveld, J, 'Eenzaamheid bij ouderen en kenmerken van de omgeving', *Mens en Maatschappij*, Vol. 74, No. 3, pp.235–49, 1999.

Bruijnzel, Liny and Sadiraj, K, 'Oud en onverzorgd. Wanneer de AWBZ huishoudelijke hulp niet meer vergoed', *Forum for Economic Research*, Utrecht, The Netherlands.

Bulder, Elles, 'The Social Economics of Old Age: Strategies to Maintain Income in Later Life in the Netherlands, 1880–1940', PhD thesis, Rotterdam University, 1993.

Centre for Women's Research (CENWOR), *Facets of Change – Women in Sri Lanka 1986–1995*, CENWOR, Colombo, 1995.

Cox, R, 'The Development of the Dutch Welfare State: From Worker's Insurance to Universal Entitlement', University of Pittsburgh Press, Pittsburgh, London, 1993.

Dignum, K, 'Senior en Stad, de betekenis van stedelijke woonmilieus voor de sociale netwerken van minder draagkrachtige ouderen', PhD thesis, University of Amsterdam, Amsterdam Study Centre for Metropolitan Development, 1997.

Dykstra, P A and Hagestad, G O, 'A Road Less Traveled: The Implications of Childlessness for Late Life Outcomes' in Dykstra, P A and Call, V R A, eds, *Aging Without Children: a Cross-National Handbook on Parental Status in Later Life,* Greenwood, Newport: CT.

Dykstra, P A, 'The Effects of Divorce on Intergenerational Exchanges in Families', *The Netherlands Journal of Social Sciences,* Vol. 33, 1998, pp.77–93.

Edwards, J and Strathern, M, 'Including Our Own' in Carsten, J, ed, *Cultures of Relatedness,* Cambridge University Press, Cambridge, 2000, pp.149–66.

Fokkema, C M, *Residential Moving Behaviour of the Elderly: An Explanatory Analysis for the Netherlands,* Vrije Universiteit, Faculteit der Economische Wetenschappen en Econometrie, Tinbergen Institute Research Series, No. 112, Amsterdam, Thesis Publishers, 1996.

Ganesh, Kamala, '"Made to Measure". Dutch Elder Care at the Intersections of Policy and Culture' in Risseeuw, C, Palriwala, R and Ganesh, K, *Care, Culture and Citizenship.* Revisiting the Politics of the Dutch Welfare State, Spinhuis, Amsterdam, 2005.

Goody, Jack, *The European Family,* Basil Blackwell Publishers, Oxford, 2000.

Goonesekere, S, 'Gender Relations in the Family: Law and Public Policy in Post-Colonial Sri Lanka' in Palriwala and Risseeuw, ed, *Shifting Circles of Support,* Sage, 1996.

Hashimoto, Akiko, *The Gift of Generations: Japanese and American Perspectives on Aging and the Social Contract,* Cambridge University Press, Cambridge, 1996.

Higuchi, K, 'Women in an Ageing Society', *Asia Population Studies Series,* No. 141, Chapter 6, Tokyo Kasei University, pp.1–15.

Holtmaat, R, *Defective Acceleration: The Dutch Emancipation Policy. The Implementation of the UN Women's Convention in the Netherlands in 1999,* Shadow report based on the second and third government reports (November 1998 and September 2000) and prepared on behalf of the 25th session of CEDAW in New York, June/July 2001, The Hague: E-Quality, Experts on Gender and Ethnicity, 2000.

Jong Gierveld, de J, 'Intergenerationele zorg en steun kent zijn grenzen' in *Mens en Maatschappij,* Vol. 73, No. 1, 1998, pp.2–3.

Jong Gierveld, de J, 'Older adults between Kin Solidarity and Independence' in *Households, Demographic Behaviour and Changing Societies,* Louvain-la-Neuve, Academia-Bruylant/l'Harmattan, 2000.

Jong Gierveld, de J, and Dykstra, P A, 'Eenzaam of niet eenzaam? Identificatie van eenzaamheids risico-groepen onder oudere mannen en vrouwen' in Broese van Groenou, M I, Deeg, D J H, Knipscheer, C P M and Ligthart, G H, eds, *VU-visies op veroudering,* Thela-Thesis, Amsterdam, 1998, pp.173–80.

Jong Gierveld, de J and Fokkema, T, 'Geographical Differences in Support Networks of Older Adults', *Tijdschrift voor Economische en Sociale Geografie,* Vol. 89, No.3, 1998, pp.328–36.

Jong Gierveld, de J and Van Tilburg, T G, *Manual of the Loneliness Scale,* Faculty of Social Sciences, Vrije Universiteit, Amsterdam.

Jong Gierveld, de J, Van Tilburg, T G and Plomp, R, 'Feminisering van de armoede onder ouderen in Nederland', *Mens en Maatschappij,* Vol. 72, No. 3, 1997, pp.248–62.

222   Institutional Provisions and Care for the Aged

Kermer, Monique, 'Geven en claimen. Burgerschap en informele zorg' in *Europees Perspectief,* Nederlands Instituut Voor Zorg en Welzijn (NIZW), Utrecht, The Netherlands, 2000.

Knipscheer, C O M, Dykstra, P, Tilburg, van T and Jong Gierveld, de J, 'Leefvormen en sociale netwerken van ouderen' in *Tijschrift voor Gerontologie en Geriatrie,* Vol. 29, 1998, pp.110–19.

Luijn, van H and Idema, J, 'Willen Nederlandse vrouwen wel carrière maken?' in *Hollandse Taferelen,* SCP, Nieuwjaarsuitgave, 2004, pp.82–7.

Macfarlane, Alan, *The Origins of English Individualism: The Family, Property and Social Transition,* Cambridge University Press, 1978.

Macfarlane, Alan, 'The Origins of Capitalism in Japan, China and the West: The Work of Norman Jacobs', *Cambridge Anthropology,* Vol. 17, No.3, 1994, pp.43–66.

Nimwegen, van N and Esveldt, I, *Netherlands population in the year 2003,* Werkverband Periodic Reporting on Population, Report No. 65, The Hague, Netherlands Interdisciplinary Demographic Institute (NIDI), 2003.

Penninx, Kees, 'Beeldvorming over ouder worden', *Bohn Stafleu van Loghum,* NIZW, Utrecht, The Netherlands, 1995.

Regt, de Ali, 'Onderhoudsplicht en verhaal van steun 1912–1965' in *Sociologisch Tijdschrift,* Vol. 12, 1985, pp.405–45.

Regt, de Ali, 'Geld en Gezin, Financiële en emotionele relaties tussen Gezinsleden', Boom, Amsterdam, 1993a.

Regt, de Ali, 'Het ontstaan van het "moderne" gezin', 1900–1950, in Zwaan, T, ed, *Familie huwelijk en gezin in West–Europa,* Open University, Boom, Amsterdam, 1993b, pp.219–39.

Risseeuw, C, The Fish Don't Talk about the Water. Gender Transformation, Power and Resistance among Women in Sri Lanka, New Delhi, Manohar Publishers, 1991.

Risseeuw, C, 'State Formation and Transformation in Gender Relations and Kinship in Colonial Sri Lanka' in Palriwala, R and Risseeuw, C, eds, *Shifting Circles of Support: Contextualizing Gender and Kinship in South Asian and Sub-Saharan Africa,* Sage Publications, London, Delhi, 1996, pp.79–110.

Risseeuw, C, 'On Family, Friendship and the Need for "Cultural Fuss". Changing Trajectories of Family and Friendship in the Netherlands' in Sinn, Sozialersinn, Vol. 1, No. 1, pp.81–93, 2003.

Risseeuw, C, 'Changing trajectories of family and friendship in the Netherlands' in Risseeuw, Palriwala and Ganesh, eds, ibid.

Risseeuw, C, Palriwala R and Ganesh, K, eds, ibid.

Schnabel, P, 'Nationale Manterzorglezing', 6 November 2003, [www.vpro.nl/onzeouders].

Sociaal en Cultureel Planbureau, Rapportage ouderen 2001, Veranderingen in de leefsituatie, The Hague, The Netherlands.

Social and Cultural Planning Office (SCP), *The Social State of the Netherlands 2003,* The Hague, December 2003.

Stavenuiter, M, 'Last Years of Life: Changes in the Living and Working Arrangements of Elderly People in Amsterdam in the Second Half of the Nineteenth Century' in *Continuity and Change,* Vol. 11, No. 2, 1996, pp.217–42.

Stavenuiter, M, 'Younger People Are Preferred: The Self-Images of Elderly Women Represented in Their Letters to a Dutch Almshouse, 1885–1940', *Journal of Family History*, Vol. 25, No. 2, 2000, pp.211–20.

Steverink, N, 'When and Why Frail Elderly People Give Up Independent Living: The Netherlands as an Example' in *Ageing and Society*, Vol. 21, 2001, pp.45–69.

Tanner, D, 'Sustaining the Self in Later Life: Supporting Older People in the Community' in *Ageing and Society*, Vol. 21, 2001, pp.255–78.

Thomese, F and Tilburg, van T, 'Neighbouring Networks and Environmental Dependency: Differential Effects of Neighbourhood Characteristics on the Relative Size and Composition of Neighbouring Networks of Older Adults in the Netherlands' in *Ageing and Society*, Vol. 20, 2000, pp.55–78.

Tilburg, van T and Gierveld, J, 'Social Integration and Loneliness: A Comparative Study among Older Adults in the Netherlands and Tuscany, Italy' in *Journal of Social and Personal Relationships*, Vol. 15, No. 6, December 1998, pp.740–54.

Timmermans, J M, *Mantelzorg. Over de hulp van en aan mantelzorgers,* Sociaal en Cultureel Planbureau, The Hague, The Netherlands.

Uhlenberg, P and Jong Gierveld, de J, 'Age-Segregation in Later Life: An Examination of Personal Networks' in *Ageing and Society*, Vol. 24, No. 1, 2004, pp.5–28.

Van der Valk, Loes, *Van pauperzorg tot bestaanszekerheid. Armenzorg in Nederland 1912–1965,* Eburon, Delft, 1986.

Chapter 10

AGEING, HEALTH AND SOCIAL SECURITY IN THE NETHERLANDS

S Irudaya Rajan
J Retnakumar

Introduction

The European population is ageing faster than populations of the other continents. The ageing of the population is a very distinctive demographic event in the European context, considering its unique pace in demographic transition. The available estimates indicate that the elderly population (65+) is expected to increase by 40 million over the next 50 years and those who are in the working age population (15–64) are expected to decline by about 100 million. This process will lead to a decline in the worker–elderly ratio from the current 4:1 to 2:1 by the year 2050 (Economic Policy Committee, 2001). These results highlight the far-reaching transformations in the European population in general and elderly population in particular in the coming years.

This increasing elderly population has already received the attention of planners and policymakers all over the world. The European Commission has played a noteworthy attempt to highlight the issues associated with elderly population in Europe.[1] The tremendous growth of elderly population basically on account of the then post-war baby boom and the resultant child population, has now reached the retirement age. Moreover, fertility has fallen sharply and there has been a considerable increase in the life expectancy of the European population.

Demography of the Elderly

The Netherlands, one of the leading nations in the European Union (EU) is no more an exception to the greying of its population. However, the United Nations (UN) estimates indicate that the growth of the elderly in the Netherlands is expected to be slightly lower compared to other

European populations as a whole (UN, 2005). For instance, the European elderly, 60 years and above constituted 12.1 per cent in 1950. This figure has become 20.7 per cent in 2005 and is expected to reach 34.5 per cent by 2050. The Netherlands, on the other hand, had 11.5 per cent elderly in 1950. This has increased to 19.2 in 2005 and will be 31.3 per cent in 2050. (See Table 1 for details). At present, there are 3.7 million elderly above age 55 and it is expected to rise to 6.2 million by the year 2030 in the Netherlands (Social and Cultural Planning Office (SCP), 2001). Similarly, the European Commission's estimates suggest that at present, the elderly population (65+) constitute 2.3 million and is likely to arrive at 4.3 million by the year 2050 (European Commission, 2005).

Table 1: Proportion of elderly population (60+) in Europe, 1950–2050

Country	1950	2005	2025	2050
Austria	15.4	22.7	31.1	37.2
Belgium	16.0	22.4	30.1	33.3
Cyprus	9.1	16.8	23.3	29.7
Czech Republic	12.4	20.0	28.7	39.3
Denmark	13.4	21.1	27.2	28.2
Estonia	14.8	21.6	26.0	33.6
Finland	10.2	21.3	30.8	32.6
France	16.2	21.1	29.0	33.0
Germany	14.6	25.1	32.1	35.0
Greece	10.0	23.0	28.4	36.8
Hungary	11.3	20.8	27.0	36.2
Ireland	14.8	15.1	21.2	32.3
Italy	12.2	25.6	34.4	41.3
Latvia	15.6	22.5	28.0	38.3
Lithuania	13.3	20.7	27.1	37.9
Luxembourg	14.5	18.3	22.8	27.3
Malta	9.3	18.8	28.9	35.2
The Netherlands	11.5	19.2	28.6	31.3
Poland	8.2	16.8	26.6	37.9
Portugal	10.5	22.3	29.1	36.3
Slovakia	9.9	16.2	25.7	38.6
Slovenia	10.5	20.5	30.7	40.2
Spain	10.9	21.4	28.6	39.7
Sweden	14.9	23.4	28.3	30.9
United Kingdom	15.5	21.2	26.5	29.4
Europe	12.1	20.7	28.0	35.4

Source: UN, 2005.

There are different methods for assessing the impact of ageing of the population on the labour force. Among them, the most widely used method is old age dependency ratio (population aged 65 and above/population aged, 15–64). The estimates point out that the current age dependency ratio is 21 and will reach 41 by 2050. Similarly, another indicator is the potential support ratio (reciprocal of old age dependency ratio). This measures how many persons in the labour force aged 15–64 can potentially support one elderly of 65 years and above. The potential support ratio for the Netherlands has shown a considerable decline from 6.8 in 1960 to 5 in 2001 (Table 2). The trend is expected to aggravate for most of the European countries and the Netherlands in particular in the years to come.

These statistics point out the growing elderly population and the likely impact on the future demographic structure of the Netherlands. Conversely, due to demographic transition, the total population of the Netherlands will experience a decline in the coming years. For instance, the projections made by European Commission shows that the total population of the Netherlands will increase from the current level of 16.3 million to a peak level of 17.9 million by 2040 and will record a decline thereafter. The total population of the Netherlands will be about 17.7 million by 2050 (European Commission, 2005).

The population projections indicate that in all the member states of the EU, the elderly population is expected to register an increase of about 50 per cent, whereas in countries such as Ireland, Luxembourg and the Netherlands, the elderly will more than double on account of their low starting position (Economic Policy Committee, 2001). The growing elderly population and their decline in total population will have a number of socio-economic and political implications for Europe as a whole and the Netherlands in particular.

The government of the Netherlands has not stipulated any criteria for defining the elderly population. For instance, a person can become a member of a senior citizen association once he/she completes 50 years of age. Similarly, a person can avail the state sponsored pension scheme from 65 years onwards. On account of the higher life expectancy (75 years for males and 81 years for females), the real need for care and protection comes only from 75 years and above. Most of the government policies for elderly population in the Netherlands commence at age 55. Thus, a person aged 55 years and above can be considered as aged in the Netherlands.

The marital status distribution of the elderly population in the Netherlands points out that a greater proportion of male elderly remain married compared to their female counterparts in all age groups. There is

Table 2: Potential support ratio for Europe, 1960–2000

Country	1960	1970	1980	1990	2000
Austria	5.4	4.4	4.1	4.5	4.4
Belgium	5.4	4.7	4.6	4.5	3.9
Cyprus	–	–	–	–	–
Czech Republic	6.8	5.6	4.6	5.3	5.0
Denmark	6.1	5.3	4.5	4.3	4.5
Estonia[1]	6.4	5.7	5.3	5.7	4.5
Finland	8.6	7.3	5.7	5.1	4.5
France	5.3	4.9	4.5	4.7	4.1
Germany	5.9	4.7	4.2	4.6	4.2
Greece	7.0	5.8	4.9	4.9	4.2
Hungary	7.3	5.9	4.8	5.0	4.5
Ireland	5.2	5.2	5.5	5.4	6.0
Italy	7.1	6.0	4.9	4.7	3.8
Latvia[1]	6.4	5.6	5.1	5.6	4.5
Lithuania	–	6.3	5.8	6.2	4.8
Luxembourg	6.3	5.2	4.9	5.2	4.9
Malta	–	–	–	–	–
The Netherlands	6.8	6.2	5.8	5.4	5.0
Poland	10.5	7.9	6.4	6.5	5.7
Portugal	8.0	6.7	5.6	5.0	4.2
Slovakia	9.0	7.0	6.0	6.3	6.0
Slovenia	–	6.8	–	6.5	5.1
Spain	7.8	6.6	5.8	4.9	4.1
Sweden	5.6	4.8	4.0	3.6	3.7
United Kingdom[2]	5.8	4.7	4.3	4.2	4.2

Source: Bijak, J, et al., 2005.
Note: [1](figures for 1959); [2](figures for 1961 and 1971)

a significant decline in the proportion of married elderly with increasing age. For example, about 81 per cent of male elderly and 60 per cent of female elderly were married between ages 65–9. This proportion declines to 63 per cent and 18 percent respectively among elderly aged 80 and above. Among elderly aged 70 and above, a greater proportion of women belong to the unmarried category compared to men. A considerable proportion of women elderly are widowed compared to men in all the age groups, and their proportion increases alarmingly at higher ages. Among those elderly aged 80 and above, nearly three-fourth (70 per cent) of women are widowed compared to one-fourth (27 per cent) of men. The marital status distributions of the elderly population in the Netherlands and EU are presented in Table 3.

Table 3: Marital status of the elderly in the Netherlands and Europe

Marital Status	65–69		80+	
	The Netherlands	Europe	The Netherlands	Europe
% of women married	59.50	61.53	21.33	18.33
% of men married	81.39	83.48	65.20	62.55
% of women never married	5.07	7.25	7.74	8.26
% of men never married	6.67	6.13	4.01	4.04
% of women widowed	31.50	28.32	69.03	71.75
% of men widowed	6.77	7.36	26.99	31.98
% of women separated/divorced	3.93	2.91	1.91	1.87
% of men divorced/separated	5.17	3.04	3.79	1.43

Source: Lacovou, Maria, 2000.
Note: Europe includes Denmark, Netherlands, Belgium, Luxembourg, France, UK, Germany, Austria, Ireland, Italy, Spain and Portugal.

Given this demographic and other related background, the remaining part of the chapter presents an overview of labour force participation, living arrangements, livelihood issues, social security schemes and public expenditure pattern on pensions in the Netherlands.

Labour Force Participation

As of now, the working population (15–64) in the Netherlands is about 11 million. The European Commission's projection (2005) shows that the population in the working age group will reach a maximum of about 11.2 million by 2020 and start to decline thereafter. It is expected to reach 10.6 million by 2050. Fertility decline has resulted in the decline in child population and the resultant wave will lead to a lower proportion of population in the working age groups.

This decline in the working age population along with increased labour force participation could lead to a situation of increased mean working age of the Dutch population. The projections also highlight that among the total workers, the workers between 55–64 constituted about 9.9 per cent in 2003 and it is expected to increase by 15.4 per cent by 2025. The proportion is expected to decline to 13.7 per cent by 2050. The increase in labour force could be partly due to the higher labour force participation of older workers and mainly due to the effects of the baby boom generations approaching retirement age and the succeeding lower birth rate cohorts reaching working age groups (Carone, 2005). This shows that at present, one out of every ten workers is an elderly person, showing the higher proportion of elderly in the labour force. The strapping increase of the Dutch elderly aged 65 and above in the labour force will start around 2010, when the already indicated large post-war birth cohorts reach the retirement age.

Table 4 presents the employment status of elderly population in ages 60–4 in the Netherlands for the past three decades. 74 per cent of male and 12 per cent of female elderly were employed in 1971. There is a radical decline in the employment pattern of the male elderly till 1995 after which there is a slight momentum. This decline in elderly employment participation could be mainly on account of the benefits they expected to gain through various disability and pension schemes sponsored by the government once they retire from active employment. Though there is a decline in female employment after 1971, it rose significantly after 2000. It can be argued that the ageing processes have reinforced the elderly labour force participation, specifically of females since the 1990s.

It has been observed that due to the unfavourable economic conditions, lot of older people left the labour market before reaching the official retirement age resulting in the shortening of the lifetime labour careers (Liefbroer et al., 2000). They argued that males born between 1901 and 1910, on an average engaged in work about 45 years, whereas the latter cohort of males born between 1921 and 1930 engaged in work only for 40 years, before reaching 65 years. In the Netherlands, it was found that there is a growing shortage of younger people in the labour market and they may gradually be replaced by the older people (SCP, 2001).

In recent years, the government of the Netherlands is prompting the elderly work force participation, particularly in the age group of 55–65. With a view to increase the elderly employment participation, the Dutch government has set a target of employing at least half of the population in these age groups in paid employment by 2030. The recent increase in the work participation rates of the elderly can be attributed mainly to the promotional measures adopted by the government.[2] Moreover, studies have indicated that the women in the younger cohorts tend to stay in the labour market even if they get older (Liefbroer et al., 2000). The projections signify that the proportion of elderly labour force (55–65) among males constituted 13 per cent in 2005 and will be about 17 per cent by 2025. The growth of the elderly female labour force would be from 9 to 14 per cent over a similar period (Carone, 2005).

Table 4: Employment status of the elderly (60–4) in the Netherlands, 1971–2005

Year	Male	Female
1971	74	12
1975	58	7
1981	40	7
1985	29	7
1990	22	8
1995	20	8
2000	26	11
2005	32	18

Source: Ekamper, Peter, 2006.

The study indicated that most of the males in the labour force were between 30 and 39 years in 1985 and will become a part of the 35–44 years old category by 2005. The major chunk of the workers will be in the age group of 50–4 by 2025. This clearly underlines our earlier argument of growing elderly labour force participation in the Netherlands. The increasing proportions of elderly and the converse decline in young workers in the labour force of the Netherlands will have numerous implications on the labour market. The important element of this process could be the increased bargaining power of the elderly for higher benefits and other employment allowances. Also, the companies may implement policies to get rid of less older workers using unemployment benefits. It is also possible that the Pay As You Go (PAYG) system can be made more flexible which would discourage early retirement of the labour force.

In such a flexible early retirement scheme, labour will be able to withdraw from work even before their official retirement age, but at a higher cost than PAYG early retirement scheme (Van Dalen and Henkens, 2002).

The Dutch economy would have an increased demand for labourers and the current supply of labour does not match with the increasing demand for labour in various employments (SCP, 2001). This will provide an opportunity for the elderly to continue their work beyond the normal retirement age, if they are healthy and willing to work further. The labour shortage can be partially adjusted through immigration process. In this context, three migration streams are of immense importance. They are migration from other Western European countries, migration from Central and Eastern European countries and migration from rest of the world. The scope of other EU immigrants to the Netherlands is limited because of the fact that almost all the countries are passing though similar stages of demographic transition and their economic situation follow similar patterns.

However, immigration does not seem to be a final solution to tackle the problems of ageing in the country. It is because the immigrants themselves become aged or they may leave the country soon after their work contracts get over. The major concern of employing more elderly in various professions will be on the productivity frontier on account of their ill health or disability. On the other hand, their work experience and added skills will be an advantage for increasing the production.

To keep the Dutch society at the present old age dependency ratio (ratio of the population aged 65+ to the population aged 20–64) it would require an annual net migration of 150,000 immigrants (Ekamper, 2006). A similar analysis carried out by Bijak shows that the total population of the Netherlands may vary between 50–63 million by 2050 and the annual net migration would be about 1 to 1.6 million (Bijak et al., 2005). Even though a large volume of immigration occurs in the Netherlands, it partially acts as a solution to the problem of labour shortages. In the last decade, about 95,000–130,000 people immigrated to the Netherlands. But those populations who immigrated for the purpose of employment constituted 10,000–20,000 and the rest immigrated for reasons such as family formation and family reunification (Ekamper, 2006). It can be observed that more than the immigrants, the native Dutch engaged in the labour force (Table 5). More importantly, the employment rates of non-western immigrants are significantly lower than the western immigrants. This shows that though there is an inflow of immigrants to the Netherlands, they are yet to become an active part of the labour force. So the policies and programmes of the government should be directed towards attracting labour migrants to the Netherlands.

Table 5: Employment rates by sex and ethnic background characteristics for the Netherlands, 1995–2004

	Native Dutch (%)	Foreign (%)		
		All	Western	Non western
Men				
1995	74	57	67	46
2000	79	66	74	58
2004	76	63	71	55
Women				
1995	45	37	44	28
2000	54	44	51	36
2004	56	46	54	39

Source: Ekamper, Peter, 2006.

Living Arrangements for the Elderly

Living arrangements is extremely important in the context of assessing the social security and welfare position of the elderly. The increasing life expectancy and the emergence of nuclear families necessitates more housing facilities. Living arrangements of the elderly becomes a primordial concern of a person when one becomes old. Available statistics show that among the nations in the EU, the proportion of elderly living alone ranges from less than 11 per cent in Malta in 1980 to 39 per cent in Denmark in 1994 (see also Table 6). It also indicates that a higher number of female elderly tend to stay alone as compared to the male elderly. The proportion of elderly staying in the Netherlands too follows the European pattern. More than a quarter of elderly (35 per cent) stayed alone with a higher proportion of females (47.4 per cent) compared to their male counterparts (16.9 per cent) in the Netherlands in 1994.

In most of the developing countries, as parents become older, there is an inclination for the elderly to stay either with their son/daughter or other relatives. If the elderly find it difficult to adjust with such an option, they choose institutional arrangement for their care and protection. However, in most of the developed countries, there is an option of institutional arrangement for those elderly who find it tricky to manage their old age life or those who need specialized health care services (Lima et al., 2001).

The living arrangement of an elderly person in a society depends on numerous factors such as his/her sex, marital status, number of living children and siblings, etc. Few studies have attempted to assess the living arrangement of the elderly in European countries (see Lacovou, 2000; European Commission, 1997; Vogel, 1997; Grundy, 2001). Among these studies, the attempts made by Maria Lucovou was found to be the latest and most comprehensive one. This study covered 13 major European countries and noticed wide variations in living arrangements across European countries in terms of gender. The findings exemplify that among women aged 65 years and above, 39 per cent stayed with a partner, 4 per cent with a partner and a child, 3 per cent with their children and 54 per cent stayed alone. However, among male elderly, 71 per cent stayed with a partner, 8 per cent with their partner and children, 1 per cent with their children and 20 per cent lived alone. It invariably indicates that men are most likely to live with a partner, either with their children or without a child compared to women. Notably, a higher percentage of women tend to stay alone, probably they become widowed on account of their higher life expectancy compared to men.

Table 6: Proportion of the population, 60 and above, staying alone in Europe

Country	Total (%)	Male (%)	Female (%)	Year
Austria	30.7	12.9	42.0	1995
Belgium	29.3	16.2	38.9	1994
Cyprus	14.0	9.3	18.0	1992
Czech Republic	33.6	17.4	44.2	1991
Denmark	39.1	24.7	50.0	1994
Estonia	29.6	15.5	36.4	1989
Finland	35.2	21.0	45.3	2000
France	28.7	15.1	38.4	1994
Germany	33.6	15.1	45.5	1994
Greece	18.3	8.9	26.1	1994
Hungary	24.3	13.0	32.0	1990
Ireland	24.6	21.4	30.4	1994
Italy	22.6	10.0	31.9	1994
Latvia	24.0	13.2	29.3	1989
Lithuania	23.1	12.2	29.4	1989
Luxembourg	–	–	–	–
Malta	10.5	–	–	1980
The Netherlands	34.5	16.9	47.4	1994
Poland	20.7	10.4	27.5	1988
Portugal	15.8	9.2	20.6	1994
Slovakia	–	–	–	–
Slovenia	20.4	9.0	27.4	1991
Spain	14.0	7.4	19.2	1994
Sweden	37.1	24.3	47.3	1990
United Kingdom	34.7	21.5	44.7	1994

Source: UN, 2005a.

The living arrangements of the elderly change significantly as they progress towards older ages (Table 7). More than 40 per cent of elderly, aged 45 and above, stay with their partner alone. As age increases, the proportion of male elderly staying with their partner alone consistently increases in all age groups till 75–9. However, the percentage of women elderly residing with their partner alone declines after reaching 60 years. These figures underline the fact that a bulk portion of the elderly get care when they reside either with their partner or children. The number of elderly living either with their partner and children or staying alone persistently declines as age progresses, indicating the need for alternative living arrangements and care for them. The elderly residing with just children or others (other adults or relatives) forms only a negligible proportion.

Available statistics indicated that a vast majority of the elderly prefer to stay alone. About 150,000 elderly (4 per cent) population, aged 55 and above (majority 95 years of age and above) live in a care home or nursing home (Vrooman and Hof, 2004). It was also found that the inmates of the care homes belonged to the higher age group, had a low level of education, did not have a partner and had a poor social network. With the growing elderly population, there will be an increasing demand for such old age homes in the Netherlands in the coming years. In 1998, there were about 107,806 elderly residents in care homes and 65,906 living in nursing homes (Lacovou, 2000). Considering the growing demands for housing, the government of the Netherlands introduced a few new schemes especially designed to meet the needs of the elderly very recently. It includes the construction of sheltered accommodation homes, modification of the existing homes, promoting more accommodation in the existing houses, allocating funds for modification of the house, integrated neighbourhood concepts, etc.

Table 7: Age-specific living arrangements of the elderly in the Netherlands (in percentage)

Age groups	Just partner		Partner and children		Alone		Just children		Others	
	M	F	M	F	M	F	M	F	M	F
45–49	17.65	19.93	66.80	64.43	10.24	7.08	2.29	8.97	6.34	2.47
50–54	34.96	44.00	53.24	39.15	8.83	9.93	2.71	5.51	2.96	3.25
55–59	47.72	55.09	38.87	26.12	11.16	13.32	3.00	6.14	4.35	3.95
60–64	64.35	59.72	18.07	14.71	11.98	22.57	2.09	4.56	2.82	3.45
65–69	68.86	52.01	14.01	7.86	14.18	38.22	1.81	4.08	2.24	3.28
70–74	78.85	46.57	4.39	2.90	16.42	46.74	2.95	4.41	2.97	4.56
75–79	74.79	36.04	3.97	0.88	19.39	58.75	1.42	8.41	2.35	2.12
80+	59.51	19.43	4.01	1.89	32.03	75.39	4.34	9.71	3.23	3.00
Total	48.22	40.57	34.95	24.67	13.32	29.69	2.52	6.52	3.66	3.24

Source: Lacovou, Maria, 2000.
Note: Other means of living arrangement includes staying with other adults such as relatives.

Sources of Livelihood of the Elderly

Table 8 presents the sources of income of the elderly in the Netherlands. Income from public pension constituted the major source of livelihood for the elderly. This was true for the elderly who stayed alone or lived with their spouses. The income from occupational pension constituted about 29 per cent for both the categories of elderly.

As age increased, the share of public pension and the share of occupational pension slightly increased in the total income. The income from other sources constituted 4 per cent in case of those who stayed alone. Elderly couples who were aged 65–69 had a slightly higher contribution to their total income from other sources. In a nutshell, public pension scheme acts as an important tool of social security for the elderly in the Netherlands.

Table 8: Retirement income of the elderly in the Netherlands (in percentage)

	Public pensions (a)	Occupational pensions	Asset income (b)	Other income (c)
Singles				
65 years and over	49	28	19	4
65–69 years	49	28	19	4
70–74 years	48	30	18	4
75–79 years	51	27	18	4
80 years and over	50	26	20	4
Couples (d)				
65 years and over	48	29	19	4
65–69 years	44	32	16	8
70–74 years	48	29	20	3
75–79 years	49	28	19	4
80 years and over	51	24	20	5

Source: Bovenberg and Meijdam, 2001.
Notes: a) excludes other public transfers b) includes income from owner-occupied housing c) includes wages, profits and transfers d) both partners receive a public pension

Social Security Schemes in the Netherlands

There are two public pension schemes in the Netherlands for the general population aged below 65. It includes survivor's benefits (ANW Scheme) and disability benefits (WAO, WAZ and WAJOJONG schemes). All the citizens of the Netherlands irrespective of their nationality are insured. Those non-residents staying in the Netherlands and contributing income tax are also insured.

Pension Schemes for the Elderly

Due to the integration of public–private participation in providing pensions, the Dutch pension scheme of retirement is regarded as a benchmark for other continental welfare states to emulate (Riel et al., 2002). It is argued that such a system is more flexible in the context of the changing socio-economic and demographic situation and puts relatively lesser pressure on the state exchequer.

The pension scheme of the Netherlands can be broadly classified into three categories and the components constitute three pillars of the pension system (Bovenberg and Meijdam, 2001; Carey, 2002). The first component is a state sponsored retirement pension scheme meant for all the elderly citizens. It is provided under the Dutch National Old Age Pensions Act of 1957, popularly known as AOW (Algemene Ouderdom Wet). It provides a compulsory retirement pension for every living citizen in the country aged 65 and above with a fixed amount per month. In order to avail of the pension scheme, one has to be a resident of the Netherlands and between age 15 and 65. It is based on the principle of PAYG.[3] Every individual with a taxable income has to contribute a certain amount according to the specifications in the General Old Age Pension Act. The amount paid as pension depends on the statutory net minimum wage and the law determines it.

The amount an elderly receives depends upon the domestic situation and the number of years the person has been insured under the AOW scheme. Married or cohabiting retired persons who have built up their full AOW entitlement (after 50 years) receive a pension worth 50 per cent of the net minimum wage. A single pensioner receives 70 per cent of the minimum wage and a single pensioner with a child aged under 18 receives 90 per cent of the net minimum wage. The amount of pension given to an individual depends on his/her marital status as well as the other earnings of his/her partner before retirement, etc. An elderly person aged 65 and above can apply for a supplementary pension amount provided his spouse's age is below 65 years and the amount of pension is insufficient for their survival. The AOW scheme is the main source of income for about 1.7 million elderly (out of 2.2 million) aged 65 and above. Only one in five people between the ages 65 and 75 receives a supplementary pension over and above the AOW (SCP, 2001).

Secondly, there is a work related supplementary pension scheme arranged between workers and employers. The representatives of employers and trade unions manage this scheme. About 90 per cent of workers and about 50 per cent of all pensioners receive this pension scheme.

There is no statutory obligation on the part of the employer to go for pension commitments to workers. However, most employers prefer to have pension schemes. Once pension commitments have been made, they are subject to the Pensions and Savings Act, which requires that pensions must be placed outside the company.

Thirdly, individuals do arrange pension schemes for their financial support. This scheme has nothing to do either with the government or the employer. Such an insurance payment comes from either savings from their employment or income from their household properties. This form of insurance has two major compartments. The first termed as annuity, offers a fixed and periodic benefit or a unit linked product whereby the periodic benefit can fluctuate with the value of underlying investments. The second scheme covers capital insurance, linked to the financing of a home and pays out a fixed amount against the risks of death or long life.

Broadly speaking, the first pillar constitutes about 50 per cent of old-age pensions. The second and third pillar constitutes 30 per cent and 20 per cent respectively. It points out that the first two pillars have a very strong base in the pension scheme of the Netherlands.

Public Expenditure on Pensions

The countries in Europe on an average spent more than 8 per cent of their Gross Domestic Product (GDP) on public pension schemes in 2000. Austria spends the highest of 15 per cent and Ireland spends the lowest of 4.6 per cent of their GDP on pensions. The projected expenditure on pensions as a percentage of GDP for the countries among the EU is presented in Table 9.

The Netherlands' government was spending about 8.9 per cent of the GDP on public pension in 1995. It slightly declined to 7.9 per cent in 2000. The projected pension expenditure as a proportion of GDP is expected to reach 9.1 per cent in 2010 and 14.1 per cent in 2040. Between 2040 and 2050, the expenditure on public pension as a percentage of GDP is expected to decline by 13.6 per cent (14.1 per cent in 2040 to 13.6 per cent in 2050). Figure 1 presents the trend in public expenditure on pensions for the period 2000–50.

Of the public pension scheme, the old age benefits account for 85 per cent whereas the remaining 15 per cent is constituted by the disability benefits and survivor benefits (Table 10). The trends underline the importance of old age pension scheme compared to other social security schemes.

Table 9: Public pension expenditure in European Union as a percentage of GDP, 2000–50

Country	2000	2010	2020	2030	2040	2050
Austria	14.5	14.9	16.0	18.1	18.3	17.0
Belgium	10.0	9.9	11.4	13.3	13.7	13.3
Cyprus	8.0	–	–	–	–	14.8
Czech Republic	7.8	–	–	–	–	14.6
Denmark	10.5	12.5	13.8	14.5	14.0	13.3
Estonia	6.9	–	–	–	–	–
Finland	11.3	11.6	12.9	14.9	16.0	15.9
France	12.1	13.1	15.0	16.0	15.8	–
Germany	11.8	11.2	12.6	15.5	16.6	16.9
Greece	12.6	12.6	15.4	19.6	23.8	24.8
Hungary	6.0	–	–	–	–	7.2
Ireland	4.6	5.0	6.7	7.6	8.3	9.0
Italy	13.8	13.9	14.8	15.7	15.7	14.1
Latvia	9.8	–	–	–	–	–
Lithuania	5.3	–	–	6.0	–	7.0
Luxembourg	7.4	7.5	8.2	9.2	9.5	9.3
Malta	5.4	–	–	–	–	–
The Netherlands	7.9	9.1	11.1	13.1	14.1	13.6
Poland	10.8	–	–	9.6	–	9.7
Portugal	9.8	11.8	13.1	13.6	13.8	13.2
Slovakia	7.9	–	–	–	–	–
Slovenia	13.2	–	–	19.7	–	18.1
Spain	9.4	8.9	9.9	12.6	16.0	17.3
Sweden	9.0	9.6	10.7	11.4	11.4	10.7
United Kingdom	5.5	5.1	4.9	5.2	5.0	4.4
European Union	8.05	–	–	11.0	–	11.4

Source: Holzmann, Robert, 2006.

Health Status of the Elderly

The health status of any given population depends on the interaction of multifaceted factors such as the socio-economic status, genetic factors, living situation and lifestyle characteristics. Health status is generally measured in terms of what individuals subjectively perceived themselves about their health. Elderly persons tend to report a poor health status compared to persons in the younger age groups. For instance, a study conducted among

Figure 1: Trends of public expenditure on pensions as a
percentage of GDP in Netherlands, 2000–50

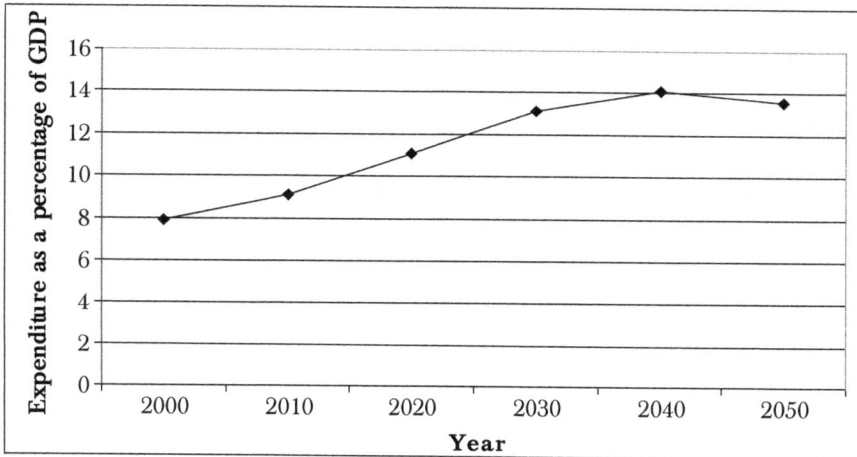

Table 10: Public expenditure on pensions as a percentage of GDP in the Netherlands, 1950–2050

	1995	2000	2010	2020	2030	2040	2050
Public Pensions	8.9	7.9	9.1	11.1	13.1	14.1	13.6
a) Old age benefits	5.0	4.8	5.4	7.0	9.0	10.2	9.7
b) Disability benefits	3.2	2.7	3.3	3.7	3.7	3.5	3.6
c) Survivor benefits	0.7	0.4	0.4	0.4	0.4	0.4	0.4

Source: NBEPA, 2000.

the elderly who stay independently found that about 14 per cent in the age group of 65–74 years reported to be of moderate or poor health status compared to 18 per cent in ages 85 and above in 1998. A greater number of elderly tend to report the feeling of being unwell from age 75 onwards. However, the elderly residents in sheltered housing or institutions assessed their health more negatively than those elderly staying independently (SCP, 2004). It was also noted that a vast number of elderly were suffering from physiological disorders. The highly prevalent disorders among the elderly of the Netherlands are anxiety, depression and cognitive disorders. Every year, about 50,000–80,000 elderly persons admitted in the hospital experience delirium (De Klerk and Timmermans, 1999). About 250,000 aged 55 years and above suffer from loneliness. Between 40 to 50 per cent of the elderly have serious sleeping disorders (Declerck, Verbeek and Neven, 1999).

The health status of the elderly is severely affected by the prevalence of various chronic diseases. More than one-third (31 per cent) in the 65–

74 age group suffer from one chronic illness compared to 28 per cent who suffer from more than two chronic diseases. Among the elderly aged 80 and above, 32 per cent suffer from more than two chronic illnesses (SCP, 2004).

Notes

[1] European Commission has premeditated a series of programmes for the elderly since 1990. This includes the commencement of a programme of action for the elderly (1990–4), setting up of a Europen observatory on ageing and older people (1991–3), decleration of 1993 as the Year of the Elderly. Notably, the Commission has taken a keen interest on studying the issues of ageing and contributed in terms of policy documents for the member counties to pursue their programmes for the elderly (European Commission, 1997).

[2] The Netherlands' government has introduced various schemes for attracting the elderly. Such schemes include, Disability Reintegration Act (REA), Sheltered Employment Act (WSW) and Unemployment Insurance Act (WW). The government also introduced certain tax rebates for employed older persons. For further discussion, see SCP, 2000.

[3] It is a pension scheme where the current contributions from the workers are used to cover the cost of current payments to pensioners.

References

Bijak, J, Kupiszewska, D, Kupiszewski, M and Saczuk, K, 'Impact of International Migration on Population Dynamics and Labour Force Resources in Europe', CEFMR Working Paper 1/2005, Central European Forum for Migration Research, Warsaw, 2005, [http://www.cefmr.pan.pl/docs/cefmr_wp2005-01.pdf].

Bovenberg, A L and Meijdam, L, 'The Dutch Pension System', in Börsch-Supan, A H and Miegel, M, eds, Pension Reform in Six Countries: What Can We Learn from Each Other?, Springer, Berlin, 2001.

Carey, D, 'Coping with Population Ageing in the Netherlands', Working Paper No. 325, Organization for Economic Co-operation and Development (OECD) Economics Department, Paris, 2002.

Carone, G, 'Long-Term Labour Force Projections for the EU 25 Member States: A Set of Data for Assessing the Economic Impact of Ageing', Economic Paper No. 235, European Commission, Brussels, 2005.

Declerck, A C, Verbeek, I, Knuistingh Neven, A, 'Intermitterend hypnotica gebruik in het huidige beleid bij slapeloosheid', Modern Medicine, Vol. 23, No. 9, 1999, pp.744–50.

De Klerk and Timmermans, 'Report on the Elderly 1998', SCP, Netherlands, 1999.

Economic Policy Committee, 'Budgetary Challenges Posed by Ageing Populations', European Commission, Brussels, ERC/ECFIN/655/01, 2001.

Ekamper, Peter, 'Ageing of the Labor Market in the Netherlands: An Overview' in Rocco, T S & Thijssen, J G L, eds, Older Workers, New Directions; Employment *and Development in an Ageing Labor Market,* Center for Labor Research and Studies, Florida International University, Miami, 2006, pp.41–54.

European Commission, 'Modernising and Improving Social Protection in the European Union', Communication from the Commission, 1997.

–, 'The Economic Impact of Ageing Populations in the EU 25 Member States', Economic Paper No. 236, Brussels, 2005.

Grundy, E, 'Living Arrangements and the Health of Older Persons in Developed Countries', *Population Bulletin of the United Nations, Special Issue, Living Arrangements of Older Persons: Critical Issues and Policy Responses,* Vol. 42/43, 2001, pp.311–29.

Holzmann, Robert, 'Toward a Reformed and Coordinated Pension System in Europe: Rationale and Potential Structure' in Holzmann, Robert and Palmer, Edward, eds, *Pension Reform: Issues and Prospects for Non-Financial Defined Contribution (NDC) Schemes,* World Bank, Washington D C, 2006.

Lacovou, Maria, 'The Living Arrangements of Elderly Europeans', Institute for Social and Economic Research, February 2000.

Liefbroer, A C and Dykstra, P A, 'Life courses in change: A Study to trends in life course of Dutch born between 1900–1970', WRR Preliminary and Background Studies, Vol. 107, SDU Publishers, The Hague, 2000.

Lima, J C and Goldscheider, 'To Independence or an Institution? The Decline in Family Living of the Non-Married Elderly: 1950–1990', Paper presented at the Population Association of America, Population and Studies Training Centre, Brown University, Washington D C, 2001.

Netherlands Bureau for Economic Policy Analysis (NBEPA), 'Ageing in the Netherlands', SDU Publishers, NBEPA, The Hague, 2000.

Riel, Bart van, Hemerijck, Anton and Visser, Jelle, 'Is There a Dutch Way to Pension Reform?', Working Paper No.202, Oxford Institute of Ageing, 2002, [http://www.ageing.ox.ac.uk].

SCP, 'What Does the Government Do for the Older People?', The Netherlands, 2001.

–, 'Report on Older People: 2004', The Netherlands, 2004.

UN, 'World Population Prospects: The 2004 Revision Population Data Base', United Nations Population Division, New York, 2005, [http://esa.un.org/unpp].

–, 'Living Arrangements of Older Persons Around the World', Department of Economic and Social Affairs, Population Division, New York, 2005a.

Van Dalen, H P and Henkens, K, 'Early Retirement Reform: Can It and Will It Work?', *Ageing and Society,* Vol. 22, 2002, pp.209–31.

Vogel, Joachim, 'Living Conditions and Inequality in the European Union', *Eurostat: Population and Social Conditions,* E/1997-3, Luxembourg, 1997.

Vrooman, C and Hof, S, 'The Poor Side of the Netherlands: Results from the Dutch Poverty Monitor, 1997–2003', SCP, The Hague, 2004.

Walkar, A, Guillemard, A M and Alber, J, 'Older People in Europe: Social and Economic Policies', European Commission, DGV, Brussels, 1993.

Chapter 11

CHANGING PUBLIC CARE FOR ELDERS IN THE NETHERLANDS

Carla Risseeuw

Introduction

Within Europe, there is a contradiction between the progressive image of the Netherlands and its local practice. The country has been portrayed as an overly generous wealthy welfare state with progressive forms of citizenship, evidenced by legislative acts concerning a number of areas such as euthanasia, gay marriages and drug use. Politically, the relatively active civil society, the long history of party coalitions and the tradition of a so-called tripartite ruling have formed an image of tolerance and mutual respect.[1] A close examination of these progressive legislations reveals a nuanced interpretation of the notion of 'citizenship' with practical consequences on gender and race relations. Whereas legislation concerning gay marriage and euthanasia bases itself on the notion of rights and duties between the individual citizen and the state, in the domain of care, the notion of rights and duties are displaced from this relationship and cited in 'citizen-to-citizen' relations.

Although north European welfare states have been undergoing similar demographic and economic changes that led to reforms[2] and care policies have acquired features of 'citizen-to-citizen' relations, the Dutch experience shows that issues of care have less political visibility and the nuclear family is particularly emphasized. For instance, in Scandinavian countries, public debates on private and unpaid caretaking activities have led to gender neutral forms of public and private care provision. By contrast, in the Netherlands, the emerging care demands are taking place in a cultural setting which has 'traditionally' taken into account neither the high numbers of women as public and private caretakers to be an issue of concern with respect to gender equality policy (also known as *emancipatie politiek*) nor the fact that quotidian care needs differs along people's lifecycles. In spite of a relatively active civil society, a care policy could seldom enter the public agenda.

The implication of this silence on care is a serious contradiction between the different goals of Dutch gender equality policy (in the labour market and at home). Furthermore, the family and traditional gender notions also find their place in migration policy, and can at times affect the citizenship of migrant women in comparison to their male counterparts. This article seeks to explain why despite the existence of different feminist political groups (female and male) and semi-political bodies which have actively lobbied within civil society and political parties for progressive citizenship, care issues have not gained a comparable level of public legitimacy as achieved in several other European countries.[3] Yet, roughly within the same time frame, lobby groups for other so-called controversial issues like 'euthanasia' and 'gay marriage' have achieved success.

Culture and Welfare: The Netherlands within Europe

Despite a large population of Jews and Muslims, social historians have argued that 'Christian Humanism' has deeply influenced the shaping of the welfare project within the European states, in which many of the key figures (male) are said to have been of the Catholic faith. (Hornsby-Smith, 1999; Papini, 1997; van Kersbergen, 1995). In the Netherlands, the Catholic population was estimated to be just over 50 per cent during much of history, and van Kersbergen argues that 'the notion of solidarity as harmony is an intrinsic component of the Christian democratic tradition and it is alternately paraphrased as "integration, compromise, accommodation and pluralism"' (1995, p.184). The Catholic tradition was further marked by a strong element of charity and social service (Coman, 1977, pp.47–59); Whyte, (1981) and van Kersbergen (1995, p.146) held explicit ideas on the dignity of an individual being firmly linked to 'labour', for which 'one' had to earn 'a just wage to maintain a family'. These premises were coupled with views on the 'proper' role of women as mothers. Parental rights in the education of children were conceived as paramount, over those of the state. These values can be traced in much of the history of Dutch politics and debate.

By contrast, the Protestant faith is historically credited for promoting issues of secularization and individualization and for laying the base of what is now termed an ungendered notion of citizenship (van Kersbergen, 1995, pp.194–5; Hornsby-Smith, 1999, p.176). These two faiths have led to markedly different 'family policies'. Broadly speaking, Catholic traditions are said to have relatively extensive policies of family support, while

Protestant or mixed (Protestant and Catholic) states have less explicit family policies. In the Catholic case, family allowances tend to be conceived of as part of the wage package, while in the Protestant case, one finds more individual taxation and the most extensive child care provisions within Europe.

Next to the dominant religious factor, the Socialists and also the Liberals added to what became known as the phenomenon of 'pillarization', which characterized Dutch society and politics. In the first half of the twentieth century, exponents of these articulate ideological divisions or pillars of Protestants, Catholics, Socialists and Liberals had their own forms of organization, including specific religious based schools, organizations, etc. Therefore, several scholars have argued that during this period, the specific character of the Dutch state was built on ideology rather than nationalism (Cox, 1993).

Within this setting, Cox points to the specific culture of political decision-making, characterized by the often unseen political ideological struggles within a consensual world of many diverse Dutch corporatist bodies involved in advising, implementing, and supervising welfare programmes (1993, p.29, p.45) – a way of governing which often excluded public accountability (*binnenskamer-politiek*).

Over time, the culture of accommodation of political interests led to the well-known Red–Roman coalition governments, rather than a political culture of articulated party opposition. Slowly, the Socialists consolidated their influence on Dutch politics. Their most famous political leader, Willem Drees (in power from 1948 to 1956) managed to pass the law on a universal old-age pension, thereby firmly extracting universal citizen rights from charity to welfare. It is relevant to realize that historically, religious forces in the Netherlands were not focused on the creation of a welfare state. They gave preference to the welfare needs of citizens being supplied by non-state organizations (Cox, 1993, p.206).

Within the often – for the public eye – unseen power struggle between religious and socialist elements in the government, the Dutch welfare state emerged later than in surrounding countries, and became full-blown in the 1960s when 'pillarization' began to fade (Social and Cultural Planning Office (SCP), 2000, Introduction). All over Western Europe, including the Netherlands, this period was marked by many forms of protest and challenge. Religions lost a substantial part of their support, while new political insights were translated into new political parties, new social movements and changing cultural lifestyles, especially of the young, leading to substantial generational conflict.

Nevertheless, the culture of consensus remained a part of Dutch politics, which continues to be ruled by coalitions. Nor have the four former ideological pillars disappeared, although the religious groupings merged and other parties gained prominence. Since 1902, the Dutch political scene only witnessed two governments (1994–8; 1998–2002), in which the Christians were forced into opposition. It is during these two governmental periods that, hesitatingly, legislation based solely on citizenship, rather than on 'a citizenship seen through the gendered matrix of the nuclear family', was proposed, and at times, passed. During the second period, legislation was passed on 'euthanasia' and 'gay-marriage'. However, it was also the period in which the first legislation was passed on something till then unknown in the Netherlands: 'care-leave'. It involved the right of a citizen to take periodic leave from work in order to look after someone very ill or dying. Here however, as will be discussed below, citizenship was not the final criterion, but remained seen through a perspective of the nuclear family.

Due to this pillarized nature of both society and politics, the Netherlands has generally come to be viewed as a hybrid welfare state, falling between the social democratic and corporate types (SCP, 2000, p.46). In the early 1990s, the Dutch system combined universal target group provisions (particularly the social insurance schemes), generous conditions and high funding costs of the social democratic model with low incentives to work, low female job-market participation and protection of achieved standards of living of the corporatist mode. The strong internal religious, societal and political divisions which ruled through negotiation and coalition provided a certain inward looking element in Dutch society, which at first glance would remain unnoticed.

In the following sections, I will look into how this chequered political background and the format of political consensus, shaped the policies on care of elders as well as the emergence of the concept of 'care-leave'.

The Shift from Public Senior Residencies to Home Care Services in the Netherlands

With the care policy on society's seniors in the 1950s and 60s, the government aimed for a citizen centred policy, devoid of the family as a direct source of care. Many institutional homes were built during this period as well as the 1970s, reflecting the usual divisions of society in various religious and income groupings. By the end of the 1960s, voices went up, however, that providing an independent serviced home would involve very high costs in the long run. Like other Western European countries, the government policy slowly changed from one claiming top priority for joint senior residences, to one which prioritized elders to remain independent in their own homes. The entry criteria were based on health and lack of family support. By this time, the high pressure on post-war housing targets was also much lessened.

The difference to this overall European development in the Netherlands was two-fold. One was the initial straight out policy involving the right for all to enter an old age home. Secondly, once policy shifted to home care services instead of joint homes, the accompanying financial scope was not expanded. Denmark, for instance, did shift its total financial budget for residential institutions to home care (Hansen, 1992). Together with Sweden, Denmark spent the highest percentage of the Gross National Product (GNP) on home care in Europe (Rostgaard and Fridberg, 1998). Other countries tried hard to cut down on home care budgets, although they were not always successful. During the 1980s, home care budgets rose in nearly all European countries (for instance, England, France and Germany), but in the Netherlands, they were reduced several times (Kremer, 2000, p.38; Tester 1996; Goewie and Keune, 1996).

Next to a decreasing budget, one sees the growing emphasis on mobilizing family care. By 1994, the governmental policy was explicit on the involvement of 'the family' in care (SCP, 2000). Most of the care needed was to be supplied by the 'direct surroundings of the patient', later known by the term 'Mantelzorg' (Kremer, 2000, p.43). Only when this help was inadequate could professional help be claimed. This shift of policy moved the Dutch state firmly away from the initial social–democratic orientation to a more corporate model of welfare. In 1994, private home care undertook four times as much care as the government home care services did. Further, commercial care services were developed at a high speed. In 1997, the commercial care services encompassed 33 per cent of all care given to those over 60 years of age. In Great Britain, a country classified as a liberal state, comparable figures during this period amounted to 21 per cent (Walker and Maltby, 1997).

This rapid switch in care policy from a social democratic to a corporate welfare state, while also developing a strong liberal or commercial component, made the Netherlands earn its classification of 'a hybrid welfare state'. As a Dutch feminist put it – 'Home care was not to be a citizenship-right in the Netherlands' (Knijn, 1999).

One consequence of this political shift has been a reduction in quality of care services (home care, hospitals and General Practicioner facilities), which continues to receive much public critique.[4] On the whole, it seems that the full contradiction of the past shift in policy towards involving 'a gendered notion of family' in care services, especially in home care-taking, alongside a labour policy of promoting women to participate in the labour market, does not seem to have been met with serious analysis. The specific Dutch policy trajectory in this respect becomes more apparent when compared to that of other European Welfare States (SCP, 2000, Introduction, pp.1–61). While in the Netherlands, 44 per cent of home care is primarily undertaken by 'family', in Denmark 44 per cent of home care is primarily undertaken by home care services (OECD, 1994; Kremer, 2000, p.45). In Holland, 75 per cent of private home carers are (older), relatively lowly educated women. (Dykstra, 1997, cited in Kremer, *Ibid.*, p.21). Sweden followed a comparable development to Denmark. The family is only involved at their own will, while the partner is tapped by government services. These two countries have the most well developed citizen rights to care in Europe. (Rostgaard and Fridberg, 1998, cited in Kremer, 2000, p.46). England, a liberal welfare state, followed another trajectory. Here, several grass-root women's organizations supporting home-carers and the right to financial support, resulted in the provision of tax cuts for home-carers and other forms of financial compensation.

Next to the right to receive care, I will now turn to the citizen's right to provide care for others.

The Development of the Provision of Care-Leave

This new provision of care-leave was passed after extensive debate during the cabinet period of 1998–2002. At the time there was only a 1998 legislation on the possibility to interrupt one's employment track, for a period of six months in relation to care or education. This leave was obtained, once the employer's consent was acquired and the leave-taker was temporarily replaced by a jobless candidate. The latter received a small financial compensation (no salary). If leave was required to take care of a terminally ill person, the replacement requirement was dropped (Smitskam and Willems, 1999).

This law partly copied a comparable Belgium law from 1985 with the same name, but which held no specific leave conditions. Employees had the right to five periods of six months leave maximum, while one period could be extended to a year. The Belgium law further dropped the condition of the employer's approval, provided not more than 1 per cent of employees took leave simultaneously. In the case of required home-care, the right of the employee was non-negotiable.

In comparison to this Belgium law, the Dutch version did not meet with much success. In 1999 for example, 205 people in the Netherlands took such leave. By contrast, in Belgium approximately 50,000 people took this leave yearly (Kremer, 2000, p.80). In both cases, the majority of leave-takers were women. This was due to the low financial compensation involved and the fact that women were second earners in most homes. Germany and the Scandinavian countries both have more elaborate provisions (see Kremer, 2000; SCP, 2000, pp.1–61). The Netherlands is literally surrounded by countries that have developed leave and care-leave facilities to a varying but great extent.

Returning to the Care Leave Act which explicitly addressed the right to care and followed the above described law, certain progress is noted – 70 per cent of the salary is refunded, which is a major shift, aiming at attracting men next to women. This leave, however, can be taken only for ten days and requires the employer's permission, although the latter needs to specify objections. Any loss of premium security payments during this period is shared by the employer and the state. But, certain problems remain. For one, a period of ten days is often too short. Further, the law stipulates that leave can only be taken for illness of family members with whom one shares a house at the moment of requesting leave. This usually means the partner and living-in children. It excludes parents or children living elsewhere or neighbours, friends and unmarried partners. Here, one sees the notion of nuclear family clashing with the right of citizenship.

As an alternative strategy, one could, for instance, not have involved the criterion of 'family' at all and proposed the option for each citizen to register two or three other citizens for whom one, should the need arise, take care-leave. Administratively, this would be simpler than the current policy, which requires inspection of actual numbers of household members.

Nevertheless, it is from an economic angle that the stipulation of 'household' over 'nuclear family' makes sense in this context. As only one-third of Dutch households currently consist of nuclear families and one-third have partners and one-third are single, the condition of 'shared household' substantially curbs potential costs. Demographers expect families to grow even smaller in future. One could call this narrow focus aiming at budget saving politically shortsighted, in relation to the high pressure on care services and the predicted future of rising numbers of single residencies. Allowing citizens to take care of each other is often cheaper than institutional facilities. One can thus say that the Dutch care policy has regularly blurred the lines of 'family' and 'citizenship', adding 'household' to the stir, when attempting to curb the costs of state care.

In spite of globalization and change, gender biases are also noted in the Dutch case. Both national and European sources confirm the same picture in this respect. While it has become commonplace to speak of two income earners per family and statistics show rapid increase in numbers of working women, these figures are deceptive, as one even counts a low number of working hours up to one hour per week as paid employment. Women's working hours are few and 'by far the shortest in Europe' (SCP, 2000, p.220; CBS report, 2002; OECD 2002). Recently, the Dutch Central Bureau of Statistics (CBS) characterized the country as having a 'breadwinner plus' model, as 85.5 per cent of the families running on more than one income, in practice relied on the income of the male partner (2002), which the OECD confirmed (2002).

Further, from a comparative perspective, the country has a relatively underdeveloped system of crèches and after-school arrangements, leaving Holland far behind France, Belgium and Scandinavia (SCP, 2000, p.61, p.224). This curbs the possibilities of women seeking work. Maybe more importantly, the taxation policies and subsidies which privilege the (male) breadwinner in the Netherlands, are estimated to involve more than 8.6 milliard Euro per year (De Bruin en Verhaar, 1999, cited in Kremer, *Ibid*, p.21). Until very recently, taxation measures made it extremely uneconomical for wives of employed husbands to seek work. In comparison, in Denmark, 76 per cent of women undertake paid work, while in the Netherlands and Austria, this figure is 65 per cent, mostly part-time and in the lowest paid jobs (OECD, 2002). The OECD explains the relatively low percentage of parents making use of child-care facilities in Holland (20 per cent), as not only due to inadequate facilities, but also due to a cultural outlook which centralizes nuclear family life and exclusive motherhood, which decreases her individual financial security. According to research, Dutch men's contribution to household tasks is shifting very slowly and forms a marked contrast to task sharing of spouses in Sweden (SCP, 2000, p.61). In this context, the Dutch national SCP points to one of the consequences of merging the political and cultural factors. Combining career and family poses specific difficulties in Holland, resulting in young Dutch women appearing to have the highest age at the birth of their first child worldwide (nearly 32 years of age: SCP, 2000, pp.60–1).

So, in spite of globalization and the formation of the European Union (EU), the traditional, nuclear family form of the male breadwinner and the motherly wife is still a reality under a thin varnish of change and is reflected in policy-thinking in more than one way. It has no doubt contributed to the perceived lack of urgency in developing a practice of a gender neutral and non-familial based citizenship, in spite of the notion of citizenship being an old and well-defended one in the Netherlands.

Before going into this (historical development of) citizenship and its accessibility to women and also outsiders, I will shortly discuss some indications of these cultural and historical factors influencing the cultural meaning of gender and family in the Netherlands.

Gender and Family in the Netherlands: A Historical Perspective

Viewed within Europe, the current picture seems to reflect the past. The Netherlands was historically marked by a relatively low female involvement in paid work. Between 1900 and 1940, the percentage of working (un)married women was 20 to 25 per cent of the total population, compared to 30 per cent in England and 35 to 40 per cent in France (Tilly and Scott, 1978, p.70; De Regt, 1984). From 1870 to the Second World War, the birth rate declined more slowly than in the neighbouring countries, while divorce figures also scored consistently lower than in the surrounding countries during this whole period (Regt, 1993b, p.222).

Historians gave several reasons for this specific gendered demographic development: the relatively high wages paid to men in the first half of the twentieth century and the strong presence of the so-called 'homely ideology', stressing the female task of creating a 'homely and nurturing environment'. Further, pillarization facilitated religious influence on gender and family norms, while the fact that the country was not involved in the First World War meant that family life was exposed to less change than in the neighbouring countries. Dutch women, for instance, did not undertake employment and factory work, after their husbands went to war.

It was in the first half of the twentieth century, that the Netherlands was marked by the formation of the so-called bourgeois, nuclear family form[5] (*gezin*). Social and especially family historians like Ali de Regt (1993a) have described the emergence of the bourgeois Christian morality with its notion of decency (*fatsoen*): the strict separate responsibilities of the breadwinner and his housewife (with a relatively strong sense of motherhood), which slowly developed into a cultural pattern of a homely, privatized family life, in connection to a tradition of religious associations and involvement in the neighbourhood 'to keep up its standards' (Regt, 1993b, p.222). De Regt describes the newly emerging society at the end of the nineteenth century as 'A Moral Nation', in which pillarization played an important role. Working class families were influenced to incorporate the bourgeois, middle class morals, implying a certain change in lifestyle involving shifts in housing, privacy, dealing with the body as well as an exclusive linking of sexuality to procreation. Sexuality outside marriage became severely condemned. Further, the so-called Morality Laws were passed in 1911, which can be seen as the culmination of the Christian morality offensive. With these laws, brothels became prohibited as Christian men should be able to 'control' themselves, followed by punishments for abortions, contraception and homosexuality in men and women. Sevenhuysen provided an insightful study on the 1870–1900 debate on fatherhood responsibilities beyond marriage (1987). At the time, the strict Christian convictions provided the feminist movement with the momentum to hold men responsible for their non-legitimate offspring. This movement was not fully successful, but the public positions taken by leading male contributors provide a fascinating insight into this historical period's 'habitus' of a non-disputed male superiority, which to its surprise had to articulate its justification. The political arena of the early twentieth century was coloured by this religious offensive, including a greater involvement of the state in family affairs.

Mainly after the 1950s ties, but slower than in the neighbouring countries, social change emerged in the Netherlands. As a large overarching theme, this change involved the demand for a greater social space and liberty for citizens to shape personal lives and relationships. This implied a renegotiation of 'family morality', in which marriage was gradually reshaped and the undisputed male headship of marriage was countered (but not overtaken) by a notion of partnership. It was only after the Second World War, in the economical wealthy period of the 1960s, that this process culminated into a period of geographical job mobility and major sociocultural change, including the so-called 'Sexual Revolution', followed by the feminist struggle for abortion rights and birth control methods (Outshoorn and Lovenduski, 1986) and the Gay Movement.

These cultural changes did not imply equality between the sexes. For instance, it was only in 1957 that women were accorded legal and independent property rights within marriage (Bergh, 1999). Only since 1985 has Dutch citizenship become independent of a woman's marriage, a right long held by their male counterparts (Everard and Aerts, 2002, p.225). Finally, the extensive financial support to the (male) breadwinner within the Dutch wage earning and taxation system is the clearest and, until very recently, completely undisputed heritage of this specific sociocultural construct.

On the surface, this seems to contrast with the Dutch's marked long history of relatively egalitarian citizenship. But, on closer scrutiny, women as well as 'strangers' have held conditional entry during this history of egalitarianism.

Citizenship in the Netherlands

Western European welfare states all incorporate a historically developed notion of citizenship. In the Netherlands, the notion of citizenship is traced to the early Middle Ages, where it signified membership of an organized political community of a town, not a (rural) landlord (Kloek and Tilmans,

2002, p.2). Many of these early citizens were businessmen, succeeding in making their living outside the rural realm of an aristocracy and its hierarchical labour relations. Historian Pleij describes the typical businessman of this early time as a clever adventurer of a 'lower' social background, who through the successful claiming of his strict individual autonomy shaped the society of his time (2002, p.4). While citizenship initially referred only to a town membership with rights and duties, in the later seventeenth century, citizenship came to imply membership to a political community of a city, republic or monarchy. During this process, certain citizens gained more control over town regulations than others, leading to a practice of emerging inequality and a growing prominence of established families with the larger business firms, who to a large extent controlled the towns. By then, 'citizenship' had acquired a legal status, which contrasted with the position of 'strangers' – newcomers to town without citizenship.

How did one acquire citizenship? Men inherited it from their fathers; women obtained it through marriage to a citizen (and could loose it because of divorce or widowhood) and it could be purchased as well. Citizenship could also be lost through 'unworthy behaviour'. This start and growth of the concept of citizenship shaped the later nineteenth century form of national citizenship. This latter citizenship emerged out of a relatively egalitarian political tradition together with an increasing prominence of morality as to how the citizen should behave. It was further characterized by a tradition of conflict solving between citizens through negotiation and (legal) arbitration, rather than through the military conquest of aristocratic leaders. This relatively inclusive form of moral citizenship prevailed over hierarchy, military power or economic means. In this specific history, violent shifts of power were absent and contributed to a form of manhood not characterized by militarism.

Historically, it was only during the 1960s – marked as it was by cultural change and lessening of religious influence – that for the first time citizenship acquired a mainstream negative evaluation involving critical judgments on its suffocating 'reasonableness', sedateness and lack of initiative and/or courage. However egalitarian in its source, Dutch citizenship from the start included forms of exclusion of women and of those who were termed 'strangers'. After substantial (feminist) struggle, Dutch women finally achieved the right to vote in 1919, which also involved a step forward in realizing their full citizenship. Before this date, the women's right to citizenship had remained ambiguous and prone to shifting interpretations (Everard and Aerts, 2002).[6] The coming up of religious and socialist organizations in the nineteenth century, likewise emphasized women's role in motherhood and homemaking (*Ibid.*, p.212).

In relation to the issue of 'strangers', Jewish and also Catholic newcomers to town, were provided registration rather than citizenship. Acquiring the latter usually involved high costs, excluded ruling powers, and was non-transferable to the offspring (*Ibid.*, p.183). In view of the current controversial issues of immigration and a multi-cultural society in the Netherlands, this start of the relation between citizenship and outsiders is worth mentioning. A well-known Somalia-born political party member, Ayaan Hirsi Ali, was one of the first to succeed in bringing a political urgency to the existing unequal citizenship between migrant husbands and wives. If divorced within three years of arrival, the husband had the right to stay, while the wife had to return to her 'home country'. From the same set of unquestioned assumptions, policy was not developed to support migrant women's entry in the job market nor to educational facilities. Domestic violence remained a secluded family affair (only in 2003 a parliamentary proposal was made to enforce change in this context). Here, the traditional Dutch values on the centrality of the family and gendered male prominence, left the migrant women in a marked unequal position vis-à-vis their men as well as access to Dutch citizenship. The dominant political view was one of respecting 'culture', 'religion' and 'family', echoing earlier formed traditional values and quite successfully blurring the fact that rights to citizenship remained secondary to migrant women. In this way, the gender neutral concept of citizenship surfaced its resilient gendered and family based practice once again.

Care Policy, Citizenship and the Continuity of the Notion of Nuclear Family

Over the recent years, the concept of 'care' as a theoretical concept has gained the attention of feminist authors. Western feminists have criticized the implications of Euro-American (state) ideologies which viewed 'care' as a private, gendered and above all an apolitical issue, undervalued next to the over-evaluation of public accomplishment and autonomy combined with a far right image of care-receivers as helpless and pitiful. For example, the work of Joan Tronto (1993) offered the first definition and discussion of 'care'.[7]

In the Netherlands, Selma Sevenhuijsen (1998) has developed the issue, while the American economist Nancy Folbre strived to 'globalize' the political component of care: If capitalism is considered global, what global social obligations are to accompany it? (2001). The yearly Human

Development Report (UNDP, 1999) has recently also for the first time taken the concept of 'care' on board in an attempt to integrate it within its development goals.

All these authors/publications point to forms of systematic misrecognition operating in the field of 'care'. Usually, the powerful do not participate in actual care-giving tasks, while their tapping of care services remains simple to realize. Tronto termed this a form of 'privileged irresponsibility', which can take the form of 'sincere' ignorance (Tronto, 1993, pp.120–2). Wealthy, privileged sections of societies and, often but not only, men are privileged in this case.

The Dutch welfare state developed substantial forms of security for citizens, based on its' relatively egalitarian notion of citizenship. Currently, several forms of universal benefits and allowances stand as proof of this inclusive heritage. But during periods of (perceived) economic downturn, historical and cultural gendered notions of family have provided the accepted morality from which to legitimize deviations from this egalitarian perspective on citizenship. For instance, as most social benefits are built up through paid employment, one finds the (traditionally male) breadwinner gaining access to extensive financial privileges and security.

Further, as was discussed, since the 1980s, state care services relatively smoothly shifted their orientation from citizen support to forms of conditional citizen support – in absence of family only. Government policy thus successfully curbed state costs in public care systems, while stimulating commercial and/or unpaid family care. In practice, 75 per cent of this family care is provided by elder, less educated women. It is relevant to realize that women as home carers are not targeted on the basis of their sex, but as (unemployed) family members.

Simultaneously, however, in an era of globalization and change, the Dutch government emphasizes the need for increased female paid labour participation. Policy reports and research regularly emphasize the (coming) care gap, which will especially affect the lower income sections of society (J Outshoorn and J Oldersma, forthcoming; Timmermans and Woittiez; SCP, 2004a). Timmermans predicts the care gap for elders to be at its peak from 2020 onwards, which is currently met with a lack of government planning, while no bilateral agreements are foreseen to facilitate the entry of international migrant care workers, as one finds in South European countries.

As described above, the social fabric of Dutch society changed enormously in the twentieth century, especially after the 1960s. During pillarization and the Christian moral offensive of the end nineteenth century, the 'nuclear family' gained central importance. During the economic expansion of the 1960s, there was a culmination of the contrary swing. It aimed at a private domain from the state in family and in 'private relationships', which could exclude marriage and official family all together. Sexual liberation became paramount, probably understandable, after the former era of tight Puritanism. Marriage also changed the undisputed male head of family in practice to a negotiated headship. Further alternatives to the traditional marriage were formed in the so-called 'couples living together' and 'couples living apart together'. Next, the gay rights activists started their assertion, creating yet another form of 'partnership' – later marriage, in the new age. Divorce and serial monogamy became more acceptable. This led the period between 1960 and 1990 to experience a remarkable shift of households: the 'modern nuclear family', which had formed a three-fourth majority of households up to the 1950s, shrank to one-third of all households by 1988 (Zwaan, 1993, p.258, Table 417). In this process of change, the ideological concept of 'nuclear family' (*gezin*) itself initially became viewed as a relic from the narrow-minded, petit bourgeois past – without relevance to the modern era (Brink, 1997).

Several decades later, from 1995 onwards, however, due to growing atheism, drug problems and crime among youth, the issue of family turned on the political agenda and societal debate (Brink, 1997). Some promoted a return to traditional family values, which was firmly contested by others. Within this debate, the concept of family proved a powerful metaphor, which due to its cultural strength was prone to be used a-historically. Authors often acclaimed the (nuclear) family to be the deeply natural form of living together, unchanged since the Stone Age. Support for this view was even found in the animal world. Its specific, resilient end nineteenth/ early twentieth century sociocultural construct of nuclear family was often overlooked. A fairly mono-cultural society tended to facilitate such a perception. Thus, long after the 1960s momentum of change, the 'natural' family was (again) seen as nuclear, monogamous and lifelong, with economically dependent wives primarily concerned with motherhood and care, and men primarily interacting with men in the public world, while offering protection to their dependent wife and children at home. Seldom to no recollection was, for instance, made of the pre-bourgeois and pre-industrial era of agriculture and shared work activities of husbands and wives or of more extended family forms, as were customary in non-urbanized parts of the country.[8]

During the 1990s, increasing work pressures, job mobility and an ageing population, made the issue of care provisions – both public and private, rise rapidly on the political horizon, but this process was not accompanied by political recognition. It is the temporarily outlawed, specific historic form of nuclear family that returned to the debate in the 1990s as a 'natural' (and universal) family form, which explains much of the Dutch government's successful appeal to a non-citizenship based model of family care, which successfully curbed state costs.[9]

Further, the lack of perceived urgency in the past and future planning is an example of the earlier mentioned and historically grown systematic misrecognition or 'privileged irresponsibility', as Tronto termed it in relation to care. The extensive feminist analyses of Dutch care policy, however perceptive, on the whole remained without serious response from mainstream politics and policymaking (for example, Outshoorn, 2002; Kremer, 2000; Knijn 1999).[10]

Research on gender and care in the Netherlands, therefore continues to be a relevant issue, manifesting more societal insights than one would initially expect. In relation to gendered care provisions and their planning, government policies have reflected a remarkable tenacity to hold on to a (reinvented) 'tradition' in which women somehow 'take care', without the domain of care further requiring much domestic and/or political reflection. If situated along the Amazon instead of the Rhine, the 'Dutch' would no doubt have been applauded for their ability to retain their way of life and outlook, while surrounded by forces of change.

And, may be indeed, this is a central question: How did they do it? Using the European Value study data collected during 1999-2000, van Luijn & Iedema (2004) found that all countries reflected (slightly) differing attitudes between men and women and their priorities to achieve within public life and/or work. Comparatively, Dutch men indicated a marked higher attraction to public achievement than Dutch women. But, overall, both sexes in the Netherlands held the lowest score of all European countries studied. Both men and women reported to prioritize their home(ly) life over career as well as a public goal, to a far greater degree than was found in countries such as England, Spain, Portugal, Belgium and the Scandinavian countries (van Luijn and Iedema, 2004). It is tempting to see this specific score as a reflection of Dutch sociocultural history as is expressed in its extensive breadwinner subsidies, and articulate views on exclusive and full-time motherhood.

Apart from care receivers/providers and related policy documents, only the policymaker himself/herself seems to have still remained unstudied. Such a research focus seems long overdue, as it could provide insights into not only blind spots in care policymaking, but also contribute to an analysis of the sociocultural setting in which such policy seems so effortlessly shaped.

Notes

[1] The government, the employers' and employees' organizational bodies, local organizations and movements, next to a wide political spectrum of political parties and media, reflecting the various religious and political groupings.

[2] For example: (i) the rapidly rising numbers of ageing citizens coupled with underdeveloped facilities of public care (ii) the increasing pressure of paid work for growing numbers of (female) citizens, which reduces the time availability for private care-taking in an environment of under-resourced care services including childcare.

[3] When comparing recent percentages of government funded 'Home-Care' to seniors in different European countries, the Dutch score (9.5 per cent) is markedly lower than Denmark (24 per cent) and Sweden (16.6 per cent), (Kremer, 2000, p.37). Likewise, its childcare arrangements still hamper women's ability to join the labour market (Bettio and Plantenga, 2004).

[4] The media regularly highlight falling standards within institutional senior care, while in a recent major survey, 90 per cent of the population indicated a fear of landing up in them (SCP, 2004, p.444).

[5] The Dutch have a specific concept for the specific nuclear family form of husband, wife and children: *het gezin*. This term is widely used and carries a different meaning from the word 'familie', which involves a larger bilateral sense of kin, in which both sets of parents are included. The latter are not part of the first construct of *gezin*, which contributes to the explanation of the research finding that Holland is marked by relatively strong family norms, while care of one's elders is at the same time conceived of as primarily the state's responsibility (see also Bettio and Plantenga, 2004). In urban Holland it already has been a practice for centuries that elders, widows live alone and separate from their offspring. (Stavenuiter, M, 1996)

[6] Women acquired citizenship through marriage and could lose it after separation or death of their spouse. Single women were accorded temporary citizenship on the basis of their employment. Women with citizenship found their status adjusted to that of their husbands. If widows retained citizenship after death of spouse on the basis of shared business, they could lose citizenship at remarriage. Only during two short historical periods (as the influence of the French Revolution in 1798) was equal citizenship for the sexes articulated without success.

[7] 'We suggest caring to be viewed as a special activity that includes everything that we do to maintain, continue and repair our "world" so that we can live in it as well as possible. That world includes our bodies, our selves and our environment, all of which we seek to interweave in a complex, life-sustaining web.' (Tronto, 1993, p.103).

[8] In relation to care, this nuclear family form excludes the day to day care for one's elders, who in their turn lived in their own nuclear family unit. Therefore, in spite of a close knit family life, the care of elders tends to be perceived as mainly an issue of state concern. This is in contrast with the close knit Southern European family forms (see also Bettio and Plantenga, 2004).

[9] Further, the political choice of leaving arrangements on childcare and care-leave to negotiations between employer and employee, coupled with the slow speed of dismantling the breadwinner advantages, culminate in a successful

strategy of weighing the new issues down, instead of pushing them forward with forceful state legislation.

[10] Currently, new legislation on care-leave is in process and it remains to be seen to what extent, next to care for children, care for one's elders will be facilitated. But progress should not be overestimated. In the same country, in order to curb their future financial flows, the major pension funds halved the pension entitlement to the remaining partner after death of the main breadwinner in 2004 (National Research Council, 25 September 2004). Interestingly enough, only the main breadwinner was informed, without the requirement of the partner co-signing, in order to make sure the latter was aware of this significant shift. Obviously, widows without independently built-up pensions – still the majority – will be the unwitting victims of such policy.

References

Bergh, v.d. G, 'Gehuwde vrouwen en (on) vermogen' in Holtmaat, Rikki, Eeuwige kwesties: honderd jaar vrouwen en recht in Nederland: jubileumuitgave van Nemesis, tijdschrift over vrouwen en recht/onder eindredactie van Rikki Holtmaat, Kluwer, Deventer, 1999.

Bettio, F and Plantenga, J, 'Comparing Care Regimes in Europe' in *Feminist Economics*, Vol. 10, No. 1, March 2004, pp.85–113.

Brink, van der, Gabriel, *Hoge Eisen, Ware Liefde, de opkomst van een nieuw gezinsideaal in Nederland*, Utrecht, Nederlands Instituut Voor Zorg en Welzijn (NIZW), 1997.

Bruijn, J and Verhaar, O, *Waar blijven de financiën voor een nieuwe zorginfrastructuur? Jaarboek Emancipatie, Wie zorgt in de 21ste eeuw?*, Elsevier, The Hague, 1999.

Central Bureau of Statistics, *Yearly Report 2002*, CBS, The Hague, 2002.

Coman, P, *Catholics and the Welfare State*, Longman, London, 1977.

Cox, Robert, *The Development of the Dutch Welfare State: From Worker's Insurance to Universal Entitlement*, University of Pittsburgh Press, Pittsburgh and London, 1993.

Davie, G, 'Unity in Diversity: Religion and Modernity in Western Europe' in Fulton, J and Gee, P, eds, *Religion in Contemporary Europe*, Edwin Mellen Press, Lampeter, 1994.

Dykstra, P, 'Employment and Caring', Working Paper 7, Netherlands Interdisciplinary Demographic Institute (NIDI), The Hague, 1997.

Everard, Myriam and Aerts, Mieke De Burgeres, 'Geschiedenis van een politiek begrip' in Kloek, Joost and Folbre, Nancy, *The Invisible Heart, Economics and Family Values*, New York Press, New York, 2001.

Goewie, R and Keune, C, 'Naar een algemeen aanvaarde standaard. Opvattingen en normen over de inzet van gezinsverzorging', Stichting Verwey-Jonker Instituut, Utrecht, The Netherlands, 1996.

Hansen, F K, *Social Services in Denmark: Consolidated Report 1990-1992*, Casa, Copenhagen, 1992.

Hornsby-Smith, Michael, 'The Catholic Church and Social Policy in Europe' in Chamberlayne, P, Cooper, A, Freeman, R and Rustin, M, eds, *Welfare and Culture in Europe: Towards a New Paradigm in Social Policy*, Jessica Kingsley Publishers, London and Philadelphia, 1999.

Kersbergen, V Kees, *Social Capitalism: A Study of Christian Democracy and the Welfare State,* Routledge, London, 1995.

Kiely, G and Richardson, V, *Family Policy: European Perspectives,* Family Studies Centre, Dublin, 1991.

Kloek, Joost and Tilmans, Karin, *Burger, een geschiedenis van het begrip 'burger' in de Nederlanden van de Middeleeuwen tot de 21ste eeuw,* Amsterdam University Press, Amsterdam, 2002.

Knijn, Trudie, 'Strijdende zorglogica's in de kinderopvang en de thuiszorg' in Brinkgreve, C and Lieshout, van P, *Geregelde gevoelens, Collective Arrangementen en de intieme leefwereld,* Maarsen, Elsevier/De Tijdstroom, 1999.

Kremer, Monique, 'Geven en Claimen, Burgerschap en informele zorg' in *Europees Perspectief,* NIZW, Utrecht, 2000.

Luijn, van H and Iedema, J, 'Willen Nederlandse vrouwen wel carrière maken?' in *Hollandse Taferelen,* SCP, 2004, pp.82–7.

Ministerie van Volksgezondheid, Welzijn en Sport, 'Gezond en Wel, Het kader van het volksgezondheidsbeleid 1995–1998', Bijlagen Handelingen Tweede Kamer 1994–1995, Tweede kamer der Staten Generaal, The Netherlands.

Nielsen, J S, *Muslims in Western Europe,* Edinburgh University Press, Edinburgh, 1992.

Oldersma, Jantine and Outshoorn, Joyce, 'The "Home Care Gap": Neoliberalism, Feminism, and the State in the Netherlands' in Haussman, Melissa and Sauer, Birgit, ed, *Gendering the State in the Age of Globalization. Women's Movements and State Feminism in Post Industrial Democracies,* Rowman and Littlefield, London, 2007, pp.209–26

Organization for Economic Co-operation and Development (OECD), *Caring for Frail Elderly People: New Directions in Care,* Vol. 14, OECD, Paris, 1994.

OECD, *Babies and Bosses,* OECD, Paris, 2002.

Outshoorn, Joyce, *De Politieke Strijd Rondom de Abortuswetgeving in Nederland 1969-1984,* Vuga, Amsterdam, 1986.

–, *The Provision of Home Carers as a Policy Problem,* forthcoming.

–, 'Gendering the "Graying of society": A discourse analysis of the Care Gap', in *Public Administration Review,* March–April 2002, Vol. 62, No. 2, pp.185–95.

Outshoorn, Joyce and Lovenduski, Joni, eds, *The New Politics of Abortion,* Sage Publications, London, 1986.

Papini, R, *The Christian Democrat International,* Rowman and Littlefield, London, 1997.

Praag, van, C S and Niphuis-Nell, M, eds, *Het Gezinsrapport, een verkennende studie naar het gezin in een veranderende samenleving,* SCP, The Hague, The Netherlands, 1997.

Regt, de, Ali, 'Arbeiders, burgers en boeren; gezinsleven in de negentiende eeuw' in Zwaan, T, ed, *Family, Huwelijk en Gezin,* Meppel, Boom, 1984, pp.193–218.

Regt, de, A, *Geld en Gezin, Financiële en Emotionele relaties tussen Gezinsleden,* Boom, Amsterdam, 1993a.

Regt, de A, 'Het Ontstaan van het "moderne gezin", 1900–1950' in Zwaan, T, ed, *Familie, huwelijk en gezin in West-Europa,* Boom/Open Universiteit, Amsterdam/Heerlen, 1993b, pp.219–39.

Rostgaard, T and Fridberg, T, *Caring for Children and Older People: A Comparison of European Policies and Practices,* The Danish National Institute of Social Research, Copenhagen, 1998.

Sevenhuijsen, Selma, *De orde van het Vaderschap, Politieke Debatten over ongehuwd moederschap, afstamming en het huwelijk in Nederland, 1870–1900*, IISG, Amsterdam, 1987.

Sevenhuijsen, Selma, *Citizenship and the Ethics of Care: Feminist considerations on Justice, Morality and Politics*, Routledge, London and New York, 1998.

Smitskam, C J and Kronenburg-Willems, E J, *Wet Financiering Loopbaanonderbreking*, Kluwer, Deventer, 1999.

SCP (2000), *The Netherlands in a European Perspective*, The Hague, The Netherlands, 2001.

Social and Cultural Report, 'In het Zicht van de Toekomst', SCP, The Hague, 2004.

Stavenuiter, Monique, 'Last Years of Life: Changes in the Living and Working Arrangements of Elderly People in Amsterdam in the Second Half of the Nineteenth Century', *Continuity and Change*, Vol. 11, No. 2, 1996, pp.218–39.

Tester, S, *Community Care for Older People: A Comparative Perspective*, Macmillan, Basingstoke, 1996.

Tilly, Louise and Scott, Joan, *Women Work and the Family*, Holt, Rhinehart and Winston, New York, 1978.

Timmermans J and Woittiez, I, *Verpleging en verzorging verklaard*, SCP, 2004.

Tronto, Joan, *Moral Boundaries, A Political Argument for an Ethic of Care*, Routledge, London, 1993.

United Nations Development Programme (UNDP), *Human Development Report*, 1999.

Walker, A and Maltby, T, *Ageing Europe*, Open University Press, Buckingham, 1997.

Whyte, J H, *Catholics in Western Democracies: A Study of Political Behaviour*, Gill and Macmillan, Dublin, 1981.

Zwaan, T, 'De verbroken viereenheid: een interpretatie van recente transities' in Zwaan, T, ed, *Familie, Huwelijk en Gezin*, Boom, Open Universiteit, Amsterdam/ Heerlen, 1993.

APPENDIX

Table 1: Percentage of aged persons owning both property and assets by sex, all India

Age	Rural			Urban		
	Male	Female	F/M	Male	Female	F/M
60–69	72.09	42.80	0.59	71.85	39.91	0.56
70–79	66.16	35.98	0.54	64.89	33.39	0.51
80–89	59.46	31.48	0.53	55.44	27.85	0.50
90–99	53.48	28.96	0.54	53.25	21.60	0.41
Total	69.03	39.89	0.58	68.28	36.75	0.54

Table 2: Percentage of widowed persons owning both property and assets by state

State	Rural			Urban		
	Male	Female	F/M	Male	Female	F/M
Andhra Pradesh	35.51	24.74	0.70	44.26	13.88	0.31
Tamil Nadu	28.97	22.95	0.79	39.64	20.37	0.51
Karnataka	60.32	29.64	0.49	43.48	19.13	0.44
Kerala	31.34	22.05	0.70	43.33	20.07	0.46
Maharashtra	63.95	29.88	0.47	56.74	33.33	0.59
Goa	27.27	13.04	0.48	22.22	25.81	1.16
Gujarat	61.54	37.50	0.61	65.91	41.10	0.62
Rajasthan	78.41	28.05	0.36	73.91	32.69	0.44
Punjab	60.00	30.23	0.50	57.14	24.79	0.43
Haryana	72.41	23.13	0.32	67.44	32.84	0.49
Uttar Pradesh	81.33	60.26	0.74	75.00	88.00	1.17
Madhya Pradesh	86.84	62.50	0.72	61.11	50.88	0.83
Bihar	71.65	37.19	0.52	70.59	41.41	0.59
Orissa	63.55	30.77	0.48	57.41	32.28	0.56
West Bengal	61.74	38.86	0.63	73.33	40.58	0.55
Assam	67.59	44.18	0.65	57.89	35.48	0.61
Jammu & Kashmir	63.39	30.79	0.49	63.16	35.32	0.56
Himachal Pradesh	56.25	44.35	0.79	71.43	31.08	0.44
North East Region	67.04	52.45	0.78	72.73	51.18	0.70
India	62.89	34.85	0.55	59.27	31.72	0.54

Table 3: Financial assets of aged persons by sex, sector and state

State	Ownership of financial assets (%)						Participation in management (%)					
	Rural			Urban			Rural			Urban		
	Male	Female	F/M	Male	Female	F/M	Male	Female	F/M	Male	Female	F/M
Andhra Pradesh	47.77	26.25	0.55	55.45	20.54	0.37	34.58	9.98	0.29	43.32	8.71	0.20
Tamil Nadu	45.97	28.85	0.63	59.57	28.86	0.48	34.25	12.11	0.35	48.75	15.11	0.31
Karnataka	67.04	33.84	0.50	64.38	27.73	0.43	34.93	10.12	0.29	41.93	8.16	0.19
Kerala	42.50	22.71	0.53	53.13	22.45	0.42	51.27	10.86	0.21	48.13	10.91	0.23
Maharashtra	67.22	35.37	0.53	68.89	34.72	0.50	54.88	17.26	0.31	57.35	14.72	0.26
Gujarat	71.54	44.17	0.62	80.66	51.89	0.64	59.18	16.96	0.29	67.90	24.24	0.36
Rajasthan	82.37	38.86	0.47	79.75	41.36	0.52	71.05	15.45	0.22	68.18	18.64	0.27
Punjab	67.88	30.31	0.45	74.23	29.07	0.39	53.77	15.03	0.28	68.85	19.77	0.29
Haryana	73.99	33.78	0.46	78.17	41.15	0.53	61.82	16.72	0.27	65.07	16.87	0.26
Uttar Pradesh	78.25	46.84	0.60	81.91	47.38	0.58	65.31	24.51	0.38	71.86	25.76	0.36
Madhya Pradesh	76.32	46.14	0.60	74.31	41.45	0.56	63.42	26.10	0.41	62.06	24.36	0.39
Bihar	77.42	50.00	0.65	81.85	56.77	0.69	65.83	22.77	0.35	66.90	23.31	0.35
Orissa	73.67	49.40	0.67	70.21	41.14	0.59	49.91	13.40	0.27	53.19	17.09	0.32
West Bengal	73.54	32.24	0.44	76.97	39.12	0.51	60.40	12.31	0.20	59.50	16.67	0.28
Assam	68.40	44.51	0.65	67.26	34.29	0.51	49.29	8.46	0.17	49.56	8.57	0.17
Jammu & Kashmir	89.57	66.67	0.74	79.43	56.25	0.71	71.59	31.54	0.44	69.50	24.11	0.35
Himachal Pradesh	90.79	66.04	0.73	90.00	82.61	0.92	81.07	49.20	0.61	86.00	69.57	0.81
North-East Region	73.42	56.17	0.59	79.76	60.38	0.76	55.89	25.60	0.46	61.43	23.63	0.38
India	70.24	41.24	0.59	71.29	38.48	0.54	56.72	18.87	0.33	58.64	17.58	0.30

Table 4: Percentage of aged people who own both property and assets by state

State	Rural			Urban		
	Male	Female	F/M	Male	Female	F/M
Andhra Pradesh	45.63	24.58	0.54	49.50	18.30	0.37
Tamil Nadu	44.69	27.09	0.61	53.91	25.81	0.48
Karnataka	65.35	33.08	0.51	60.63	25.37	0.42
Kerala	40.69	21.89	0.54	47.66	21.43	0.45
Maharashtra	66.51	34.73	0.52	66.95	33.62	0.50
Goa	54.76	13.89	0.25	45.16	23.26	0.51
Rajasthan	81.32	37.27	0.46	77.27	40.00	0.52
Punjab	66.67	29.02	0.44	73.46	27.13	0.37
Haryana	73.65	31.77	0.43	75.11	40.33	0.54
Uttar Pradesh	76.36	45.25	0.59	80.40	46.26	0.58
Madhya Pradesh	75.26	44.47	0.59	73.52	39.74	0.54
Bihar	77.12	49.11	0.64	79.00	53.01	0.67
Orissa	73.13	48.80	0.67	70.21	38.61	0.55
West Bengal	71.71	31.72	0.44	72.44	37.37	0.52
Assam	67.92	43.89	0.65	66.37	33.33	0.50
Jammu & Kashmir	88.99	65.95	0.74	78.72	55.36	0.70
Himachal Pradesh	90.54	61.23	0.68	90.00	80.43	0.89
North East Region	71.55	53.41	0.74	78.33	58.95	0.75
India	69.03	39.89	0.58	68.28	36.75	0.54

Table 5: Proportion of aged men and women who own only property by state

State	Rural			Urban		
	Male	Female	F/M	Male	Female	F/M
Andhra Pradesh	20.50	9.24	0.45	13.37	9.60	0.72
Tamil Nadu	29.67	15.42	0.52	12.65	7.81	0.62
Karnataka	10.42	6.31	0.61	5.63	5.60	1.00
Kerala	34.76	23.67	0.68	19.53	22.24	1.14
Maharashtra	12.93	7.18	0.56	7.41	6.13	0.83
Goa	7.14	8.33	1.17	0.00	9.30	
Gujarat	11.24	7.77	0.69	7.82	4.92	0.63
Rajasthan	4.21	3.86	0.92	4.13	4.07	0.98
Punjab	10.95	5.96	0.54	5.77	5.81	1.01
Haryana	6.76	4.68	0.69	5.68	2.88	0.51
Uttar Pradesh	10.64	6.19	0.58	5.03	4.93	0.98
Madhya Pradesh	3.59	3.76	1.05	2.37	1.28	0.54
Bihar	6.29	4.46	0.71	3.91	4.89	1.25
Orissa	10.97	3.40	0.31	7.80	7.59	0.97
West Bengal	16.14	9.53	0.59	7.73	3.86	0.50
Assam	20.99	7.21	0.34	14.16	12.38	0.87
Jammu & Kashmir	2.90	2.87	0.99	7.80	5.36	0.69
Himachal Pradesh	2.81	8.29	2.95	8.00	0.00	0.00
North East Region	6.75	6.45	0.96	3.81	5.25	1.37
India	12.89	8.01	0.62	8.21	6.97	0.85

Table 6: Percentage of aged people owning only assets by state

State	Rural			Urban		
	Male	Female	F/M	Male	Female	F/M
Andhra Pradesh	2.14	1.66	0.78	5.94	2.23	0.38
Tamil Nadu	1.28	1.76	1.37	5.66	3.06	0.54
Karnataka	1.69	0.76	0.45	3.75	2.36	0.63
Kerala	1.81	0.82	0.45	5.47	1.02	0.19
Maharashtra	0.71	0.64	0.91	1.94	1.10	0.57
Goa	4.76	0.00	0.00	3.23	0.00	0.00
Gujarat	1.50	1.06	0.71	2.88	1.52	0.53
Rajasthan	1.05	1.59	1.51	2.48	1.36	0.55
Punjab	1.22	1.30	1.06	0.77	1.94	2.52
Haryana	0.34	2.01	5.94	3.06	0.82	0.27
Uttar Pradesh	1.89	1.60	0.84	1.51	1.11	0.74
Madhya Pradesh	1.06	1.67	1.58	0.79	1.71	2.16
Bihar	0.30	0.89	2.98	2.85	3.76	1.32
Orissa	0.55	0.60	1.09	0.00	2.53	0.00
West Bengal	1.83	0.52	0.28	4.54	1.75	0.39
Assam	0.47	0.63	1.33	0.88	0.95	1.08
Jammu & Kashmir	0.58	0.72	1.24	0.71	0.89	1.26
North East Region	1.87	2.76	1.47	1.43	1.70	1.18
India	1.21	1.35	1.12	3.02	1.73	0.57

Table 7: Ownership and participation in management of property by widowed persons of age by sex, sector and state

State	Percentage who own property				Percentage who own and manage property			
	Rural		Urban		Rural		Urban	
	Male	Female	Male	Female	Male	Female	Male	Female
Andhra Pradesh	52.34	33.33	55.74	24.92	35.51	10.42	36.07	10.41
Tamil Nadu	51.40	39.73	50.45	28.04	33.64	14.38	29.73	14.81
Karnataka	66.67	36.43	45.65	25.65	41.27	13.21	26.09	12.61
Kerala	65.67	49.67	60.00	46.02	37.31	24.05	46.67	22.15
Maharashtra	70.75	37.82	63.12	40.16	48.98	15.89	46.81	18.27
Gujarat	64.62	45.00	68.18	47.85	50.77	20.00	38.64	25.15
Rajasthan	81.82	32.93	76.09	38.46	64.77	10.16	50.00	12.82
Punjab	66.25	36.63	61.90	32.48	40.00	15.70	54.76	17.95
Haryana	77.59	30.60	74.42	34.33	51.72	14.93	48.84	16.42
Uttar Pradesh	81.82	43.87	75.63	47.55	61.04	21.45	56.30	23.62
Madhya Pradesh	68.22	36.03	59.26	33.07	51.40	16.19	46.30	17.32
Bihar	69.13	43.86	73.33	47.10	52.61	16.36	55.56	16.67
Orissa	76.85	47.95	73.68	43.01	39.81	9.93	57.89	15.05
West Bengal	77.68	40.57	73.68	39.48	51.79	11.22	46.32	14.81
Assam	81.25	52.61	78.57	45.95	39.29	9.13	42.86	13.51
Jammu & Kashmir	88.16	64.58	61.11	54.39	59.21	36.81	50.00	22.81
Himachal Pradesh	85.33	70.74	100.00	88.00	69.33	46.29	87.50	56.00
North East Region	72.63	58.90	78.18	57.48	41.34	24.54	50.91	24.41
Total	73.57	44.00	66.06	39.80	50.49	18.02	45.98	17.92

Table 8: Widowed persons not owning property or assets by sex and state

State	Rural			Urban			Total		
	Male	Female	F/M	Male	Female	F/M	Male	Female	F/M
Andhra Pradesh	44.86	65.10	1.45	40.98	73.50	1.79	43.45	68.90	1.59
Tamil Nadu	46.73	58.56	1.25	43.24	68.78	1.59	44.95	64.33	1.43
Karnataka	33.33	62.86	1.89	45.65	72.17	1.58	38.53	67.06	1.74
Kerala	34.33	49.67	1.45	40.00	53.29	1.33	36.08	51.08	1.42
Maharashtra	29.25	61.66	2.11	34.75	59.04	1.70	31.94	60.45	1.89
Gujarat	32.31	54.38	1.68	29.55	50.31	1.70	31.19	52.32	1.68
Rajasthan	17.05	65.45	3.84	19.57	60.90	3.11	17.91	63.68	3.56
Punjab	32.50	62.21	1.91	38.10	65.81	1.73	34.43	63.67	1.85
Haryana	22.41	67.16	3.00	23.26	64.18	2.76	22.77	65.67	2.88
Uttar Pradesh	16.23	54.46	3.35	21.01	51.84	2.47	17.21	53.64	3.12
Madhya Pradesh	30.84	63.56	2.06	38.89	64.57	1.66	33.54	63.90	1.91
Bihar	30.00	55.00	1.83	24.44	49.28	2.02	29.09	53.63	1.84
Orissa	22.22	51.71	2.33	26.32	53.76	2.04	22.83	52.21	2.29
West Bengal	20.54	58.71	2.86	21.05	59.74	2.84	20.77	59.20	2.85
Assam	17.86	46.52	2.61	21.43	52.70	2.46	18.25	48.03	2.63
Jammu & Kashmir	9.21	34.72	3.77	38.89	43.86	1.13	14.89	37.31	2.51
Himachal Pradesh	13.33	24.02	1.80	0.00	12.00		12.05	22.83	1.90
North East Region	26.26	39.57	1.51	18.18	40.16	2.21	24.36	39.83	1.63
Total	25.10	54.79	2.18	30.59	58.60	1.92	26.80	56.32	2.10

Table 9: Percentage of widowed persons owning only property by state

State	Rural			Urban		
	Male	Female	F/M	Male	Female	F/M
Andhra Pradesh	16.82	8.59	0.51	11.48	11.04	0.96
Tamil Nadu	22.43	16.78	0.75	10.81	7.67	0.71
Karnataka	6.35	6.79	1.07	2.17	6.52	3.00
Kerala	34.33	27.62	0.80	16.67	25.95	1.56
Maharashtra	6.80	7.94	1.17	6.38	6.83	1.07
Goa	0.00	8.70		0.00	12.90	
Gujarat	3.08	7.50	2.44	2.27	6.75	2.97
Rajasthan	3.41	4.88	1.43	2.17	5.77	2.65
Punjab	6.25	6.40	1.02	4.76	7.69	1.62
Haryana	5.17	7.46	1.44	6.98	1.49	0.21
Himachal Pradesh	4.00	10.48	2.62	25.00	0.00	0.00
Jammu & Kashmir	1.32	2.08	1.58	0.00	3.51	
Uttar Pradesh	10.17	6.69	0.66	5.04	6.13	1.22
Madhya Pradesh	4.67	5.26	1.13	1.85	0.79	0.43
Bihar	7.39	5.00	0.68	0.00	6.52	
Orissa	9.26	3.77	0.41	15.79	7.53	0.48
West Bengal	14.29	9.79	0.68	10.53	4.16	0.39
Assam	25.00	8.26	0.33	7.14	14.86	2.08
North East Region	5.59	6.44	1.15	5.45	6.30	1.15
Total	10.68	9.15	0.86	6.79	8.08	1.19

Table 10: Percentage of widowed persons owning only assets by state

State	Rural			Urban		
	Male	Female	F/M	Male	Female	F/M
Andhra Pradesh	2.80	1.56	0.56	3.28	1.58	0.48
Tamil Nadu	1.87	1.71	0.92	6.31	3.17	0.50
Karnataka	0.00	0.71		8.70	2.17	0.25
Kerala	0.00	0.67		0.00	0.69	
Madhya Pradesh	0.00	0.52		2.13	0.80	0.38
Goa	9.09	0.00	0.00	0.00	0.00	
Gujarat	3.08	0.63	0.20	2.27	1.84	0.81
Rajasthan	1.14	1.63	1.43	4.35	0.64	0.15
Punjab	1.25	1.16	0.93	0.00	1.71	
Haryana	0.00	2.24		2.33	1.49	0.64
Himachal Pradesh	1.33	5.24	3.93	0.00	0.00	
Jammu & Kashmir	2.63	0.69	0.26	0.00	1.75	
Uttar Pradesh	1.95	1.67	0.86	3.36	0.61	0.18
Madhya Pradesh	0.93	0.40	0.43	1.85	2.36	1.28
Bihar	0.87	1.14	1.31	2.22	3.62	1.63
Orissa	0.93	0.34	0.37	0.00	3.23	
West Bengal	1.79	0.72	0.40	5.26	0.78	0.15
Assam	0.89	0.87	0.97	0.00	1.35	
North East Region	1.12	1.53	1.37	3.64	2.36	0.65
Total	1.33	1.21	0.91	3.35	1.60	0.48

Source: Estimated by the authors using the Unit Level data of the NSS 52nd round.